Bibliography of Holy Land Sites

PART II

ELEANOR K. VOGEL
and
BROOKS HOLTZCLAW
Cincinnati

In Volume XLII (1971) of the *Hebrew Union College Annual* Eleanor K. Vogel published a bibliography of material on Holy Land sites that had appeared prior to 1970. The present "Bibliography of Holy Land Sites II" supplements that earlier article with a listing of works published since 1970 — to which the author has added a few items omitted from her first bibliography. The Reverend Dr. Brooks Holtzclaw assisted Mrs. Vogel in the composition of this second bibliography.

The earlier work has been so much in demand that it was reprinted as a separatum. To the reprint, the eminent Palestinian archaeologist G. Ernest Wright wrote a preface, from which we quote: "Mrs. Vogel had been archaeological research assistant to Nelson Glueck for over three decades. . . . The monograph here published is one of several collections of information made for her own and Dr. Glueck's use over the years. It demonstrates the meticulousness of the ideal compiler of reference information. . . . We archaeologists are greatly in her debt. . . ." [Ed.]

ABBREVIATIONS

AASOR	*Annual of the American Schools of Oriental Research*, Cambridge, Mass.
ACOR	American Center of Oriental Research, Amman
ADAJ	*Annual of the Department of Antiquities of Jordan*, Amman
AIAR	William F. Albright Institute of Archaeological Research, Jerusalem
AJA	*American Journal of Archaeology*, Archaeological Institute of America, New York
Aramco	*Aramco World Magazine*, New York
Archaeology	Archaeological Institute of America, New York
Archaeology in the Levant	*Essays for Kathleen M. Kenyon*, P.R.S. Moorey, P.J. Parr, eds., Warminster: Aris & Phillips, Ltd., (1978)
ASOR	American Schools of Oriental Research, Cambridge, Mass.

ASR	*Ancient Synagogues Revealed*, L.I. Levine, ed., Jerusalem: Israel Exploration Society (1981)
'Atiqot	*Journal of the Israel Department of Antiquities and Museums*, Jerusalem
AUM	*Andrews University Monograph*
AUSS	*Andrews University Seminary Studies*, Berrien Springs, Mich.
BA	*Biblical Archeologist*, American Schools of Oriental Research, Cambridge, Mass.
BAR	*Biblical Archaeology Review*, Washington, D.C.
BASOR	*Bulletin of the American Schools of Oriental Research*, Cambridge, Mass.
Berytus	*Berytus Archaeological Studies*, The American University of Beirut
Biblica	Biblical Institute Press, Rome
BTS	*Bible et Terre Sainte* (*M d B*), Paris
CBQ	*Catholic Biblical Quarterly*, Washington, D.C.
CNI	*Christian News from Israel*, State of Israel, Jerusalem
EAEHL	*Encyclopedia of Archaeological Excavations in the Holy Land*, Vols. I–IV (1975–1978), Jerusalem: Israel Exploration Society
EI	*Eretz-Israel*, Jerusalem: Israel Exploration Society
Expedition	The University Museum, University of Pennsylvania, Philadelphia, Pa.
HBD	*Harper's Bible Dictionary*, New York: Harper & Row (1973)
HTR	*Harvard Theological Review*, Cambridge, Mass.
HUCA	*Hebrew Union College Annual*, Cincinnati, Ohio
IDB	*The Interpreter's Dictionary of the Bible* (Vols. I–IV 1962), Nashville: Abingdon Press
IDB-S	*The Interpreter's Dictionary of the Bible* Supplementary Volume (1976)
IEJ	*Israel Exploration Journal*, Jerusalem
ILN	*The Illustrated London News*, London
Iraq	British School of Archaeology in Iraq, London
ISBE	*The International Standard Bible Encyclopedia*, Grand Rapids: William B. Eerdmans Publishing Co. (4 vols.)
JBL	*Journal of Biblical Literature*, Philadelphia
JNES	*Journal of Near Eastern Studies, Chicago*
Jordan	Jordan Information Bureau, Washington, .D.C.
LA	*Liber Annuus*, Franciscan Printing Press, Jerusalem

Levant	*Journal of the British School of Archaeology, Jerusalem and the British Institute at Amman for Archaeology and History, London.*
M d B	*Le Monde de la Bible* (*BTS*), Paris
Muse	*Annual of the Museum of Art and Archaeology,* University of Missouri-Columbia
National Geographic	National Geographic Society, Washington, D.C.
Orientalia	Biblical Institute Press, Rome
OTA	*Old Testament Abstracts*, The Catholic Biblical Association, Washington, D.C.
PEQ	*Palestine Exploration Quarterly*, London
Qad.	*Qadmoniot,* Israel Exploration Society, Jerusalem
Qedem	The Hebrew University, Jerusalem
RB	*Revue Biblique*, Paris
RQ	*Revue de Qumran*, Paris
Symposia	American Schools of Oriental Research, F.M. Cross, ed., Cambridge, Mass.
Syria	*Revue d'art oriental et d'archéologie*, Paris
TA	*Tel Aviv*, Tel Aviv University
VT	*Vetus Testamentum*, Leiden
ZAW	*Zeitschrift für die alttestamentliche Wissenschaft*, Berlin
ZDPV	*Zeitschrift des deutschen Palästina-Vereins*, Wiesbaden

'Abdah, Avdat, Eboda

A.E. Marks, J. Phillips, H. Crew, R. Ferring, "Prehistoric Sites near 'En-'Avdat in the Negev," *IEJ* 21:1 (1971), pp. 13–24, figs. 1–6; A. Negev, "Nabataean Sigillata," *RB* 79:3 (1972), pp. 381–398, figs. 1–5, pls. 32–34; *id.*, "The Staircase-Tower in Nabataean Architecture," *RB* 80:3 (1973), pp. 364–383, figs. 1–10, pls. 2–6, table; R. Rosenthal, "A Nabataean Nose-Ring from 'Avdat (Oboda)," *IEJ* 24:2 (1974), pp. 95–96, pl. 16d; Z. Meshel, Y. Tsafrir, "The Nabataean Road from 'Avdat to Sha'ar-Ramon," *PEQ* 106:2 (1974), pp. 103–118, figs. 1–5, pls. 15–18; A. Negev, "Nabataean Capitals in the Negev," *IEJ* 24:3-4 (1974), pp. 153–159, pls. 27–29; Z. Meshel, Y. Tsafrir, "The Nabataean Road from 'Avdat to Sha'ar Ramon," Part II, *PEQ* 107:1 (1975) pp. 3–21, figs. 1–6, pls. 1–2; R. Rosenthal, "On 'Nabataean Dolphins'," *EI* 12 (1975), pp. 107–108, figs. 1–3, pl. 21 (Hebrew); A. Negev, "Eboda," *EAEHL* II (1976), pp. 345–355, figs.; *id.*, "Excavations at 'Avdat 1975–76," *Qad.* 10:1 (1977), pp. 27–29, fig. (Hebrew); A.E. Marks, C.R. Ferring, "Upper Palaeolithic Occupation near 'Avdat, Central Negev, Israel," *EI* 13 (1977), pp. 191–207; A. Baginski, A. Tidbar, "A Dated Silk Fragment from 'Avdat (Eboda)," *IEJ* 28:1–2 (1978), pp. 113–115, fig. 1, pl. 21c; A. Negev, "The Greek Inscriptions from 'Avdat (Oboda)," *LA* 28 (1978), pp. 87–126, pls. 7–20; R. Cohen, "Excavations at 'Avdat 1977," *Qad.* 13:1–2 (1980), pp. 44–46, figs. (Hebrew).

Abil, Tell, Beth-Maachah

J. Kaplan, "The Identification of Abel-Beth-Maachah and Janoah," *IEJ* 28:3 (1978), pp. 157–160, fig. 1.

Abila, Tell

W.H. Mare, "1980 Survey of Abila of the Decapolis," *BA* 44:3 (1981), pp. 179–180, figs.

Abu Ghosh, Qaryat el 'Anab

M. Lechevallier, "Abou Gosh," *RB* 78:3 (1971), pp. 406–407, pl. 12a; *id.* "Abu Gosh," *IEJ* 21:4 (1971), pp. 226–227; *id.*, "Abou Gosh," *RB* 79:3 (1972), pp. 399–400, pl. 35; J. Perrot, "Abu Ghosh Prehistoric Remains," *EAEHL* I (1975), pp. 3–5, figs.; M. Avi-Yonah, "Abu Ghosh: Later Remains: Area East and South of the Benedictine Monastery," *EAEHL* I (1975), pp. 6–8, figs.

Abu Ḥabil, Tell

H. de Contenson, "Jordan Valley," *EAEHL* III (1977), pp. 656–658, fig.

Abu Hawam, Tell, Salmonah

A. Harif, "A Mycenaean Building at Tell Abu-Hawam in Palestine," *PEQ* 106:1 (1974), pp. 83–90, figs. 1–7; E. Anati, "Abu Hawam, Tell," *EAEHL* I (1975), pp. 9–12, figs.; J.M. Weinstein, "Was Tell Abu Hawam a 19th-Century Egyptian Naval Base?" *BASOR* 238 (1980), pp. 43–46.

Abu Matar, Tell

C. Elliott, "The Religious Beliefs of the Ghassulians ca. 4000–3100 B.C., *PEQ* 109:1 (1977), pp. 3–25, figs. 1–6, 2 tables.

Abu Twain, Khirbet

A. Mazar, "Khirbet Abu Twain," *IEJ* 24:3–4 (1974), p. 276, pl. 60c; *id.*, "Khirbet Abu Twain," *RB* 82:2 (1975), pp. 266–268.

Abu Usba, see Carmel, Mount, Caves

Acco, Accho, Acre, Akka, Akko, Tell, Fukhar, Tell el-,el-Makr, Ptolemais, St. Jean D'Acre

Excavated by M. Dothan 1973–1979, for the Israel Dept. of Antiquities and Museums, the Hebrew University, the Universities of Haifa, Marburg and Copenhagen.

G. Edelstein, "Tombs of Merchant-Warriors near Acco," *Qad.* 5:1 (1972), pp. 19–21, figs. (Hebrew); W.F. Anderson, "Accho," *HBD* (1973) p. 5; M. Dothan, "Accho," *IEJ* 23:4 (1973), pp. 257–258; M.G. Edelstein, "Acre," *RB* 80:4 (1973), pp. 570–572, pl. 25; Z. Goldmann, "Saint Jean d'Acre," *BTS* 160 (1974), pp. 8–18, figs., M. Dothan, "A sign of Tanit from Tel 'Akko," *IEJ* 24:1 (1974), pp. 44–49, fig. 1, pl. 9a; A. Kindler, "Silver Coins Bearing the Name of Judea from the Early Hellenistic Period," *IEJ* 24:2 (1974), pp. 73–76, pl. 11; B. Bar-Kochva, "Notes on the Fortresses of Josephus in Galilee," *IEJ* 24:2 (1974), pp. 108–116, fig. 1; J. Prawer, "A Crusader Tomb of 1290 from Acre and the Last Archbishops of Nazareth,"

IEJ 24:3–4 (1974), pp. 241–251, figs. 1–3, pl. 54; M. Dothan, "'Akko," *IEJ* 24:3–4 (1974), pp. 276–279, pl. 60d; M. Dothan, "Tel Akko," *RB* 82:1 (1975), pp. 84–86, pl. 3b; *id.*, "'Akko 1975," *IEJ* 25:2–3 (1975), pp. 163–166; *id.*, "Acre," *RB* 82:4 (1975), pp. 566–571, pl. 46; Z. Goldmann, "Accho," *EAEHL* I (1975), pp. 14–23, figs.; M.W. Prausnitz, "Acco," *IDB-S* (1976), pp. 4–5; M. Dothan, "Akko," *RB* 83:2 (1976), pp. 274–278; *id.*, "The Fortifications of Ptolemais," *Qad.* 9:2–3 (1976), pp. 71–74, figs.; (Hebrew); *id.*, "'Akko 1976," *IEJ* 26:4 (1976), pp. 207–208; *id.*, "'Akko 1977," *IEJ* 27:4 (1977), pp. 241–242; *id.*, "Akko: Interim Excavation Report, First Season 1973/4," *BASOR* 224 (1976), pp. 1–48, figs. 1–48; *id.*, "Akko 1976–1977," *RB* 85:1 (1978), pp. 92–94, pls. 5 b, 6; *id.*, "A Red-Figured Krater from the Excavations at Akko," *Qad.* 11:1 (1978), pp. 24–26, figs. (Hebrew); M. Dothan, D. Conrad, "'Akko 1978," *IEJ* 28:4 (1978), pp. 264–266, pl. 52 b; A. Kindler, "Akko, a City of Many Names," *BASOR* 231 (1978), pp. 51–55; H. Porter, "Acco," *ISBE* I (1979), pp. 23–24, figs.; M. Dothan, D. Conrad, "Akko 1978," *RB* 86:3 (1979), pp. 441–444, fig. 3; M. Dothan, "An Attic Red-Figured Bell-Krater from Tel 'Akko," *IEJ* 29:3–4 (1979), pp. 148–151, pl. 18; M. Dothan, D. Conrad, "'Akko 1979," *IEJ* 29:3–4 (1979), pp. 227–228; B.S.J. Isserlin, Review of S. Ben-Arieh, G. Edelstein, *Akko: Tombs near the Persian Garden, 'Atiqot* 12 (1977), *PEQ* 112:1 (1980), p. 63; M. Dothan, A. Raban, "The Sea Gate of Ancient Akko," *BA* 43:1 (1980), pp. 35–39, figs.; R. Frankel, "Three Crusader Boundary Stones from Kibbutz Shomrat," *IEJ* 30:3–4 (1980), pp. 199–201, fig. 1, pl. 21 c-d; M. Prausnitz, "Accho, Plain of," *EAEHL* I (1975), pp. 19, 23–25, 71, figs.

Accho, see Acco

Achzib

W. Culican, "Phoenician Oil Bottles and Tripod Bowls," *Berytus* 19 (1970), pp. 5–18, figs. 1–3, pls. 1–2; E. Neufeld, "Hygiene," *BA* 34:2 (1971), Achzib bowl, fig. 1, pp. 41, 52; S.V. Chapman, "A Catalogue of Iron Age Pottery," (from S. Lebanon), *Berytus* 21 (1972), pp. 55–194, figs. 1–32, pls. 1–2; M. Prausnitz, "Akhziv and Avdon: On the Planning of a Port and a Fortress City in the Plain of Acre," *EI* 11 (1973), pp. 219–223, figs.; *id.*, "The Planning of the Middle Bronze Age Town at Achzib and its Defences," *IEJ* 25:4 (1975), pp. 202–210, figs. 1–3, pl. 24; E.D. Oren, "The Pottery from the Achzib Defence System, Area D: 1963 and 1964 Seasons," *IEJ* 25:4 (1975), pp. 211–225, figs. 1–4, table; M. Prausnitz, "Achzib," *EAEHL* I (1975), 26–30, figs.; E. Stern, "Phoenician Masks and Pendants," *PEQ* 108:2 (1976), pp. 109–118, figs. 1–12, pls. 9–11; M.W. Prausnitz, "Achzib (in Galilee)," *IDB-S* (1976), p. 6; W. Culican, "A Terracotta Shrine from Achzib," *ZDPV* 92:1 (1976), pp. 47–53, pls. 1 b-6; W.S. LaSor, "Achzib," *ISBE* I (1979), p. 31.

Acre, see Acco

Ader

M. Kochavi, "Ader," *EAEHL* I (1975), pp. 31–32.

'Affûlah

M. Dothan, "Afula," *EAEHL* I (1975), pp. 32–36, figs.

'Ai, et-Tell

Excavations were continued in 1970–1972 by J.A. Callaway for the American Schools of Oriental Research, Harvard Semitic Museum, Perkins School of Theology, Smithsonian Institution, Southern Baptist Theological Seminary, et al.

J.A. Callaway, *The Early Bronze Age Sanctuary at 'Ai (et-Tell)*, (1972); J.A. Callaway, K. Schoonover, "The Early Bronze Age Citadel at 'Ai (et-Tell), *BASOR* 207 (1972), pp. 41–53, figs. 1–8; R. Amiran, "Reflections on the Identification of the Deity at the EB II and EB III Temples at Ai," *BASOR* 208 (1972), pp. 9–13, figs. 1–2; A. Ben-Tor, "An Ivory Bull's Head from 'Ay," *BASOR* 208 (1972), pp. 24–29, figs. 1–3; N.E. Wagner, "Early Bronze Age Houses at 'Ai (et-Tell)," *PEQ* 104:1 (1972), pp. 5–25, figs. 1–18; J. Briend, "Les fouilles de Ai," *BTS* 151 (1973), pp. 6–15, figs.; A. Ben-Tor, E. Netzer, "The Principal Architectural Remains of the Early Bronze Age at 'Ai," *EI* 11 (1973), pp. 1–7, 3 figs.; J.A. Callaway, N.E. Wagner, "A Re-examination of the Lower City at Ai (et-Tell) in 1971, 1972," *PEQ* 106:2 (1974), pp. 147–155, pls. 23–29; J.A. Callaway, "A Second Ivory Bull's Head from Ai," *BASOR* 213 (1974), pp. 57–61, figs. 1–2; J.A. Callaway, "'Ai," *EAEHL* I (1975), pp. 36–52, figs.; S.W. Helms, "Posterns in Early Bronze Age Fortifications in Palestine," *PEQ* 107:2 (1975), pp. 133–150, figs. 1–7; J.A. Callaway, "Excavating at Ai (et-Tell) 1964–1972," *BA* 39:1 (1976), pp. 18–30, figs. 1–13; *id.* "Ai," *IDB-S* (1976), pp. 14–16, figs. 1–2; R. Amiran, A. Kempinski, Review of J.A. Callaway, *The Early Bronze Age Sanctuary at Ai (et-Tell)*, 1972, *IEJ* 27:1 (1977), pp. 57–58; J.A. Callaway, J.M. Weinstein, "Radiocarbon Dating of Palestine in the Early Bronze Age," *BASOR* 225 (1977), pp. 1–16, tables 1–4; K. Yassine, "Pre-Second Millennium Dwellings in Palestine," *ADAJ* 22 (1977–78), pp. 14–19, fig. 1; A. Ben-Tor, *Cylinder Seals of Third Millennium Palestine, BASOR Suppl.* 22 (1978), pp. 12, 102, 103, fig.; J.A. Callaway, "New Perspectives on Early Bronze III in Canaan," *Archaeology in the Levant* (1978), pp. 46–58; Y. Shiloh, "Elements in the Development of Town Planning in the Israelite City," *IEJ* 28:1–2 (1978), pp. 36–51, figs. 1–10, pls. 13, 14, 15 a; R.K. Harrison, "Ai," *ISBE* I (1979), pp. 81–84, 3 figs.; J.A. Callaway, *The Early Bronze Age Citadel and Lower City at Ai (et-Tell)* 2 (1980).

'Ain Duq, see Na'aran

'Ain el-Jarba

K. Kaplan, "Ein el-Jarba," *EAEHL* II (1976), pp. 355–356, fig.

'Ain el-Qudeirat, see Qudeirat

'Ain es-Sâmiyeh, see Sâmiyeh, Dhahr Mirzbâneh

'Ain eṭ-Ṭabgha, see Ṭabgha, 'Ain eṭ

'Ain Feshkha

R. de Vaux, "'Ein Feshkha," *EAEHL* IV (1978), pp. 984-985.

'Aitun, Tell

D. Ussishkin, "Tombs from the Israelite Period at Tel 'Eton," *TA* 1:3 (1974), pp. 109–127, figs. 1–11, pls. 21–24.

'Ajjul, Tell el-

M. Negbi, "Crescent or Legume-shaped Ear-Rings?" *IEJ* 21:4 (1971), p. 219, pl. 48; K.N. Yassine, "City Planning of Tell el'Ajjul, Reconstructed Plan," *ADAJ 19 (1974), pp. 129*–133, fig. 1; A. Kempinski, "Tell el'Ajjul-Beth-Aglayim or Sharuḥen?" *IEJ* 24:3–4 (1974), pp. 145–152; J.M. Weinstein, "Egyptian Relations with Palestine in the Middle Kingdom,"

BASOR 217 (1975), pp. 1–16, figs. 1–3; M. Artzy, F. Asaro, I. Perlman," The Tel Nagila Bichrome Krater as a Cypriote Products," *IEJ* 25:2–3 (1975), pp. 129–134, figs. 1–2, table; O. Tufnell, "el-'Ajjul, Tell," *EAEHL* I (1975), pp. 52–61, figs.; *id.*, Review of J.R. Stewart, *Tell el-'Ajjul, The Middle Bronze Age Remains*, 1974, *PEQ* 108:2 (1976), p. 136; H.A. Liebowitz, "Bone and Ivory Inlay from Syria and Palestine," *IEJ* 27:2–3 (1977), pp. 89–97, figs. 1–2.

Ajlun

Excavated by B. Van Elderen for the Jordan Dept. of Antiquities.

B. Van Elderen, "An Early Byzantine Inscription Found near Ajlun," *ADAJ* 17 (1972), pp. 73–75, pl. 1; *id.*, "Excavations of Byzantine Churches and Mosaics in 1973," *ADAJ 18 (1973), pp. 83*–84, pls. 51–54.

Akka, see Acre

Akko, see Acre

'Ali, see 'Eli, Tell

'Amal, Tell

S. Levy, G. Edelstein, "Cinq années de fouilles à Tel 'Amal, (Nir David)," *RB* 79:3 (1972), pp. 325–367, figs. 1–18, pls. 18–28; A. Lemaire, "A propos d'une inscription de Tel 'Amal," *RB* 80:4 (1973), p. 559.

'Ammân, Rabbath Ammon, Philadelphia

A. Hadidi, "The Pottery from the Roman Forum at Amman," *ADAJ* 15 (1970) pp. 11–15, pls. 1–6; S.F. Dana, "Luweibdeh Roman Tomb," *ADAJ* 15 (1970), p. 37, 5 pls.; R.S. Boraas, "A Preliminary Sounding of Rujm el-Malfuf 1969," *ADAJ* 16 (1971), pp. 31–45, figs. 1–41; V. Fritz, "Erwägungen zu dem spätbronzezeitlichen Quadratbau bei Amman," *ZDPV* 87:2 (1971), pp. 140–152, figs. 1–2; G. Bisheh, "A Cave Burial Tomb from Jabal Jofeh el-Sharqi in Amman," *ADAJ* 17 (1972), pp. 81–83, pls. 1–6; S.H. Horn, "A Seal from Amman," *BASOR* 205 (1972), pp. 43–45, fig.; R. Kutscher, "A New Inscription from 'Amman," *Qad.* 5:1 (1972), pp. 27–28, figs. (Hebrew); F. Zayadine, "Recent Excavations on the Citadel of Amman," *ADAJ* 18 (1973), pp. 17–35, figs. 1–5, pls. 11–26; P. Bordreuil, "Inscriptions des Têtes à Double Face," *ADAJ* 18 (1973), pp. 37–39, figs. 1–2; H.O. Thompson, "Rujm al-Malfuf South," *ADAJ* 18 (1973), pp. 47–50, fig. 1, pls. 28–30; A. Hadidi, "Some Bronze Coins from Amman," *ADAJ* 18 (1973), pp. 51–53, pls. 31–33; *id.*, "A Greek Inscribed Altar from Amman," *ADAJ* 18 (1973), pp. 61–62, pl. 35:2; E. Puech, A. Rofé, "L'inscription de la citadelle d'Amman," *RB* 80:4 (1973), pp. 531–546, 1 fig., pl. 20; R. H. Smith, "An Early Roman Sarcophagus of Palestine and its School," *PEQ* 105:1 (1973), pp. 71–82, figs. 1–8, pls. 1–3; B. Bagatti, "Le antiche chiese di Filadelfia-'Amman (Transjordania)," *LA* 23 (1973), pp. 261–285, figs. 1–16; H. O. Thompson, F. Zayadine, "The Works of Amminadab," *BA* 37:1 (1974), pp. 13–18, figs. 6–7; A. Hadidi, "The Excavation of the Roman Forum at Amman (Philadelphia), 1964–1967," *ADAJ* 19 (1974), pp. 71–91, figs. 1–9, pls. 24–28; F. Zayadine, "Note sur l' inscription de la Statue d'Amman," *Syria* 51 (1974), pp. 129–136, figs., pls. 3–4; V. Hankey, "A Late Bronze Age Temple at Amman," *Levant* 6 (1974), I. "The Aegean Pottery," pp. 131–159, figs. 1–10, tables 1–12, pls. 29–31; II. "Vases and Objects Made of Stone," pp. 160–178, figs. 1–3, 2 tables, pls. 32–34; A. Hadidi, "The Excavation of the Roman Forum at Amman (Philadelphia), 1964–1967, *ADAJ* 19 (1974), pp. 71–91, figs. 1–9, pls. 24–30; *id.*, "Umayyad Bronze Coins from Amman," *ADAJ* 20 (1975), pp. 9–14, figs. 1–2, 2 pls.(Arabic).

Excavations were conducted in 1976 at the Amman Airport by L. G. Herr and L. T. Geraty for the Jordan Dept. of Antiquities. The Upper Citadel of 'Amman was excavated by F. Zayadine 1975, 1977, for the Jordan Dept. of Antiquities. Excavations at the Citadel were directed by C.-M. Bennett 1975–1979 for the British School of Archaeology and the Jordan Dept. of Antiquities.

K. N. Yassine, "Anthropoid Coffins from Raghdan Palace Tomb in Amman," *ADAJ* 20 (1975), pp. 57–68, figs. 1–7, pls. 21–24; C.-M. Bennett, "Excavations at the Citadel, Amman 1975," *ADAJ* 20 (1975), pp. 131–142, figs. 1–4, pls. 48–56; K. Stemmer, "Ein Asklepios-Kopf in Amman," *ADAJ* 21 (1976), pp. 33–39, pls. 1–6; "The Amman Airport Excavations 1976," *ADAJ* 21 (1976), pp. 109–111; E. Puech, "Deux nouveaux sceaux Ammonites," *RB* 83:1 (1976), pp. 59–62, pl. 2; S. H. Horn, "Ammon, Ammonites," *IDB-S* (1976), p. 20; G. M. Landes, "Rabbah," *IDB-S* (1976), p. 724; H. Gaube, "'Amman, Ḥorane und Qasṭal," *ZDPV* 93:1 (1977), pp. 52–86, figs. 1–8, pls. 1–4, plans 1–2; A. Northedge, "A Survey of Islamic Buildings at Amman," *ADAJ* 22 (1977–78), pp. 5–13, fig. 1, pls. 1–5; F. Zayadine, "Excavations on the Upper Citadel of Amman — Area A, 1975–1977," *ADAJ* 22 (1977–78), pp. 20–56, figs. 1–27, pls. 6–25; C.-M. Bennett, A. E. Northedge, "Excavations at the Citadel, Amman 1976," *ADAJ* 22 (1977–78), pp. 172–179, figs. 1–2, pls. 96–101; M. Piccirillo, "Una tomba del Bronze Medio ad Amman?" *LA* 28 (1978), pp. 73–86, pls. 1–6; M. Avi-Yonah, E. Stern, "Rabbath-Ammon," *EAEHL* IV (1978), pp. 987–993, figs.

D. F. Graf, "The Saracens and the Defense of the Arabian Frontier," *BASOR* 229 (1978), pp. 1–26, 2 maps; W. J. Fulco, "The 'Amman Citadel Inscription: a New Collation," *BASOR* 230 (1978), pp. 39–43, fig. 1; C.-M. Bennett, "Excavations at the Citadel (el-Qal'ah), Amman, Jordan," *Levant* 10 (1978), pp. 1–9, figs. 1–7, pls. 1–5; F. Zayadine, "An EB-MB Bilobate Tomb at Amman," *Archaeology in the Levant* (1978), pp. 59–66, figs. 1–4, pls. 8–10; A. Hadidi, "The Roman Town-Plan of Amman," *Archaeology in the Levant* (1978), pp. 210–222, figs. 1–5, pls. 31–35.

W. H. Shea, "Milkom as the Architect of Rabbath-Ammon's Natural Defences in the Amman Citadel Inscription," *PEQ* 111:1 (1979), pp. 17–25, fig. 1, pl. 1; E. Olavarri, "Citadelle d'Amman 1975–1978," *RB* 86:1 (1979), pp. 119–120, pl. 8; F. Zayadine, "Citadelle d'Amman 1975–78," *RB* 86:1 (1979), pp. 120–122, fig. 3, pl. 9; W. J. Fulco, "The Amman Theater Inscription," *JNES* 38:1 (1979), pp. 37–38, figs. 1–2; V. Sasson, "The 'Amman Citadel Inscription as an Oracle Promising Divine Protection: Philological and Literary Comments," *PEQ* 111:2 (1979), pp. 117–125; C.-M. Bennett, "Early Islamic Amman," *Levant* 11 (1979), pp. 1–8, figs. 1–3, pls. 1–6; M. C. A. Macdonald, "Safaitic Inscriptions in the Amman Museum and other Collections, I," *ADAJ* 23 (1979), pp. 101–119, pls. 35–44; C.-M. Bennett, "Excavations at the Citadel (al Qal'a) Amman 1977," *ADAJ* 23 (1979), pp. 151–159, figs. 1–3, pls. 61–68; *id.*, "Excavations on the Citadel (al Qal'a) Amman, 1978 Fourth Preliminary Report," *ADAJ* 23 (1979), pp. 161–170, figs. 1–7, pls. 69–75; J. A. Thompson, "Ammon," *ISBE* I (1979), pp. 111–112, 2 figs.; A. Northedge, "Survey of the Terrace Area at Amman Citadel," *Levant* 12 (1980), pp. 135–154, figs. 1–9, pls. 20–24; N. I. Khairy, "Al-Quweismeh Family Tomb," *PEQ* 112:1 (1980), pp. 51–61, figs. 1–7, pl. 3.

'Amman, see Meqabelein

'Ammudim, Umm el 'Amed

F. G. Hüttenmeister, "The Aramaic Inscription from the Synagogue at Ḥ. 'Ammudim," *IEJ* 28:1–2 (1978), pp. 109–112; M. Avi-Yonah, "Synagogues," *EAEHL* IV (1978), pp. 1129–1138, figs., esp. pp. 1131, 1137, figs.; L. I. Levine, "Excavations at Ḥurvat 'Ammudim," *Qad.* 13:3–4 (1980), pp. 107–110, figs., L. I. Levine, "Excavations at Ḥurvat ha-'Amudim," *ASR* (1981), pp. 78–81, figs.

'Amra, Qasr, Qeseir

F. Zayadine, "The Umayyad Frescoes of Quseir 'Amra," *Archaeology* 31:3 (1978), pp. 19–29, figs.; P. Baker, "The Frescoes of 'Amra," *Aramco* 31:4 (1980), pp. 22–25, pls.

Anafa, Tell

Excavated by S. S. Weinberg for the Museum of Art and Archaeology, University of Missouri-Columbia, 1970–1973.

S. S. Weinberg, "Excavations at Tel Anafa," *Qad.* 3:4 (1970), pp. 135–138, figs. (Hebrew); *id.*, "Tel Anafa: The Hellenistic Town," *IEJ* 21:2–3 (1971), pp. 86–109, figs. 1–9, pls. 11–20; *id.*, "Tel Anafa: The Third Season, *MUSE* 5 (1971), pp. 8–16, figs.; *id.*, "Tel Anafa," *RB* 78:3 (1971), pp. 412–415, pls. 13–14 a; *id.*, "Tel Anafa: The Fourth Season 1972," *MUSE* 6 (1972), pp. 8–18, figs.; *id.*, "Tel Anafa," *IEJ* 23:2 (1973), pp. 113–117, pls. 29 b, 30 a–d; *id.*, "Excavations at Tel Anafa 1973," *MUSE* 8 (1974), pp. 14–28, figs.; *id.* "Anafa, Tel," *EAEHL* I (1975), pp. 65–69, figs.

Excavated by S. C. Herbert 1978–1980, for the Kelsey Museum of Archaeology, University of Michigan, and the Museum of Art and Archaeology, University of Missouri-Columbia.

S. C. Herbert, "New Campaign at Tel Anafa 1978," *MUSE* 12(1978), pp. 21–29, figs.; *id.*, "Tel Anafa 1978," *IEJ* 28:4 (1978), pp. 271–274, pl. 54; *id.*, "Tel Anafa 1979," *MUSE* 13 (1979), pp. 16–21, figs.; *id.*, "Tel Anafa 1978: Preliminary Report," *BASOR* 234 (1979), pp. 67–83, figs. 1–21; *id.*, "Tel Anafa 1980," *MUSE* 14 (1980), pp. 24–30, figs. 1–6, plan; *id.*, "The Joint University of Michigan/University of Missouri Excavations at Tel Anafa 1980," *AJA* 85:2 (1981), pp. 197–198.

Antipatris, see Aphek

Aphek, Antipatris, Râs el- 'Ain, Tell, Rosh ha-'Ayin

Excavated by M. Kochavi et al. for Tel Aviv University, Baylor University, Texas, New Orleans Baptist Theological Seminary 1972–1980.

M. Kochavi, "Tel Aphek (Râs el-'Ain)," *IEJ* 22:4 (1972), pp. 238–239; *id.*, "Tel Aphek," *IEJ* 23:4 (1973), pp. 245–246, pl. 67; *id.*, "Tel Aphek (Râs el-'Ain)," *RB* 81:1 (1974), pp. 85–87, pl. 7; *id.*, "Tel Aphek," *IEJ* 24:3–4 (1974), pp. 261–262; *id.*, "The First Two Seasons of Excavations at Aphek-Antipatris," *TA* 2:1 (1975), pp. 17–42, figs. 1–13, pls. 2–8; A. Eitan, "Aphek (Sharon)" *EAEHL* I (1975), pp. 70–73, figs.; P. Beck, "The Pottery of the Middle Bronze Age IIA at Tel Aphek," *TA* 2:2 (1975), pp. 45–85, figs. 1–16, pls. 9–13; A. F. Rainey, "Two Cuneiform Fragments from Tel Aphek," *TA* 2:3 (1975), pp. 125–129, pl. 24; M. Dothan, "Aphek in the Israel-Aram Border," *EI* 12 (1975), pp. 63–65, map (Hebrew); J. M. Weinstein, "Egyptian Relations with Palestine in the Middle Kingdom," *BASOR* 217 (1975), pp. 1–16, figs. 1–3.

M. Kochavi, "Tel Aphek 1975," *IEJ* 26:1 (1976), pp. 51–52, pl. 11; M. Avi-Yonah, "Antipatris," *Gazetteer of Roman Palestine, Qedem* 5 (1976), p. 29; M. Kochavi, "Tel Aphek (Râs el-'ain)," *RB* 83:1 (1976), pp. 80–87, pls. 11–13 a; A. F. Rainey, "A Tri-Lingual Cuneiform Fragment from Tel Aphek," *TA* 3:4 (1976), pp. 137–140, pls. 9–10:1–2; M. W. Prausnitz, "Aphek (in the Sharon)," *IDB-S* (1976), p. 27; M. Kochavi, "Tel Aphek 1976," *IEJ* 27:1 (1977), pp. 54–55, pl. 7; *id.*, "The Canaanite Palace at Aphek and its Inscriptions," *Qad.* 10:2–3 (1977), pp. 62–68, figs. (Hebrew); I. Singer, "A Hittite Hieroglyphic Seal Impression from Tel Aphek," *TA* 4:3–4 (1977), pp. 178–190, fig. 1, pl. 19:1–2; Y. Yadin, "The Nature of Settlement in the Middle Bronze II A and the Problem of the Apheq Fortifications," *EI* 13 (1977), pp. 91–105, pl. 12 (Hebrew); *id.*, "The Nature of the Settlements during Middle Bronze II A Period in Israel and the Problem of the Aphek Fortifications," *ZDPV* 94:1 (1978), pp. 1–23, figs. 1–9, pl. 1; M. Kochavi, A. Demsky, "An Israelite Village from the Days of the Judges," *BAR* 4:3 (1978), pp. 18–21, figs.; R. Giveon, "Two Unique Egyptian Inscriptions from Tel Aphek," *TA* 5:3–4 (1978), pp. 188–191, pl. 52:2; M. Kochavi, "Canaanite Aphek," *Expedition* 20:4 (1978), pp. 12–17, figs.; M. Kochavi, R. Gophna, "Aphek-Antipatris, Tēl Polēg, Tēl Zeror and Tēl Burgā: Four Fortified Sites of the Middle Bronze Age IIA in the Sharon Plain," *ZDPV* 95:2 (1979), pp. 121–165, figs. 1–18, pls. 8–9 a; J. F. Prewitt, "Aphek," *ISBE* I (1979), p. 150, fig.; M. Kochavi, "The History and Archeology of Aphek-Antipatris," *BA* 44:2 (1981), pp. 75–86, figs.

Apollonia, Arsuf

E. H. and B. Kaplan, "The Diversity of Late Byzantine Oil Lamps at Apollonia (=Arsuf)," *Levant* 7 (1975), pp. 150–156, figs. 1–2, table; R. Gophna, "Archaeological Survey of the Central Coastal Plain, 1977," *TA* 5:3–4 (1978), pp. 136–147, figs. 1–7, pl. 40:1.

'Arad, Tell, (Lower Mound, Early)

Excavated 1971–1977 by R. Amiran for the Israel Exploration Society and Department of Antiquities and Museums.

M. Hopf, G. Zachariae, "Determination of Botanical and Zoological Remains from Ramat Maṭred and Arad." *IEJ* 21:1 (1971), pp. 60–64, figs. 1–3, pls. 5 b–c, 6; R. Amiran, "Arad," *IEJ* 21:4 (1971) pp. 228–229; *id.*, "A Cult Stele from Arad," *IEJ* 22:2–3 (1972), pp. 86–88, figs. 1–2, pls. 14–16; *id.*, "Arad," *IEJ* 22:4 (1972), pp. 237–238; *id.*, "Tel Arad," *RB* 79:4 (1972), pp. 588–589, pl. 53 b; N. Liphschitz, Y. Waisel, "Dendroarchaeological Investigations in Israel: Tel Beersheba and Arad in the Northern and Eastern Negev," *IEJ* 23:1 (1973), pp. 31–36, 2 tables, pls. 6–9; R. Amiran, Y. Beit-Arieh, J. Glass, "The Interrelationship between Arad and Sites in Southern Sinai in the Early Bronze Age II," *IEJ* 23:4 (1973), pp. 193–197, pls. 49–51; R. Amiran, "Arad," *IEJ* 23:4 (1973), pp. 241–242, pl. 65; *id.*, "An Egyptian Jar Fragment with the Name of Narmer from Arad," *IEJ* 24:1 (1974), pp. 4–12, figs. 1–2, pl. 1; *id.*, "Tel Arad," *IEJ* 24:3–4 (1974), pp. 257–258, fig. 1; *id.*, "The Painted Pottery Style of the Early Bronze II Period in Palestine," *Levant* 6 (1974), pp. 65–68, pls. 24–28; *id.*, "Arad," *RB* 82:2 (1975), pp. 247–251, fig. 2, pl. 21 a; *id.*, "Arad — Lower City," *EAEHL* I (1975), pp. 75–81, figs.; R. Gophna "Egyptian Immigration into Southern Canaan during the First Dynasty?" *TA* 3:1 (1976), pp. 31–37, figs. 1–3; R. Amiran, "The Narmer Jar Fragment from Arad: An Addendum," *IEJ* 26:1 (1976), pp. 45–46, fig. 1, pl. 9 a–b; Y. Aharoni, "Arad," *IDB-S* (1976), pp. 38–39; R. Amiran, C. Cohen, "Arad 1976–1977," *IEJ* 27:4 (1977), pp. 238–241, pl. 36; K. Yassine, "Pre-Second Millennium Dwellings in Palestine," *ADAJ* 22 (1977–78), pp. 14–19, fig. 1; R. Amiran, "The Date of the End of the EB II City of Arad," *IEJ* 28:3 (1978), pp. 182–184, fig., 2 tables; R. Amiran, et al., *Early Arad: The Chalcolithic Settlement and Early Bronze City, First-Fifth Seasons 1962–1966,* (1978); A. Ben Tor, *Cylinder Seals of Third Millennium Palestine, BASOR Suppl.* 22 (1978); pp. 4, 102, 103, fig; R. Amiran, J. Glass, "An Archaeological-Petrographical Study of 15 W-Ware Pots in the Ashmolean Museum," *TA* 6:1–2 (1979) pp. 54–59, figs. 1–2, pls. 12, 13 a; R. Amiran, C. Arnon, D. Alon, R. Goethert, P. Louppen, "The Early Canaanite City of Arad," *Qad.* 13:1–2 (1980), pp. 2–19, figs. (Hebrew); R. Amiran, D. Alon, C. Arnon, R. Goethert, "Archaeology and Survey," D. Gavish, D. H. K. Amiran, "Geography and Air-photography," *Levant* 12 (1980), pp. 22–29, figs. 1–2, pl. 6.

'Arad, Tell, Upper Mound (Later)

Y. Yadin, "Four Epigraphical Queries," *IEJ* 24:1 (1974), pp. 30–36, figs. 1–2; Y. Aharoni, "Le Neguev," *BTS* 174 (1975), pp. 4–15, figs.; Y. Aharoni et al., *Arad Inscriptions* (1975) (Hebrew); Y. Aharoni, "Arad- Upper Mound," *EAEHL* I (1975), pp. 74–75, 82–89, figs.; *id.*, "The 'Nehemiah' Ostracon from Arad," *EI* 12 (1975), pp. 72–76, figs. 1–2, pl. 15, (Hebrew);

Y. Yadin, "The Historical Significance of Inscription 88 from Arad: A Suggestion," *IEJ* 26:1 (1976), pp. 9–14; Y. Aharoni, "Arad," *IDB-S* (1976), pp. 38–39; *id.*, "Nothing Early and Nothing Late: Rewriting Israel's Conquest," *BA* 39:2 (1976), pp. 55–76, figs. 1–22; M. and Y. Aharoni, "The Stratification of Judahite Sites in the 8th and 7th Centuries B.C.E." *BASOR* 224 (1976), pp. 73–90, figs.; J. Campbell, "The Renascence of Iron Age Arad," *BA* 40:1 (1977), pp. 34–37, figs. 1–5; A. F. Rainey, "Three Additional Hebrew Ostraca from Tel Arad," *TA* 4:3–4 (1977), pp. 97–102, figs. 1–3, pls. 5–6; M. Aharoni, "The Jar Bearing Arad Text 110," *TA* 4:3–4 (1977), pp. 103–104, fig. 4; H. Parunak, "The Orthography of the Arad Ostraca," *BASOR* 230 (1978), pp. 25–31, figs. 1–5; Z. Herzog, "Israelite City Planning, Seen in the Light of the Beer-sheba and Arad Excavations," *Expedition* 20:4 (1978), pp. 38–43, figs.; F. M. Cross, "Two Offering Dishes with Phoenician Inscriptions from the Sanctuary of 'Arad," *BASOR* 235 (1979), pp. 75–78, figs. 1–2; Y. Aharoni, "Arad," *ISBE* I (1979), pp. 227–229, figs.; H. Shanks, "Letter from a Hebrew King?" *BAR* 6:1 (1980), pp. 52–56, figs.; Z. Herzog, "A Functional Interpretation of the Broadroom and Longroom House Types," *TA* 7:1–2 (1980), pp. 82–89, figs. 1–4; M. Aharoni, "A Silver Hoard from Arad," *Qad.* 13:1–2 (1980), pp. 39–40, figs. (Hebrew).

'Arâ 'ir, Khirbet (Jordan)

W. G. Dever, "The EB IV-MB I Horizon in Transjordan and Southern Palestine," *BASOR* 210 (1973), pp. 37–63, figs.; K. Prag, "The Intermediate Early Bronze — Middle Bronze Age: An Interpretation of the Evidence from Transjordan, Syria and Lebanon," *Levant* 6 (1974), pp. 69–116, figs. 1–9; E. Olávarri, "Aroer," *EAEHL* I (1975), pp. 98–100, figs.; W. G. Dever, "Aroer," *IDB-S* (1976), p. 55; C.-M. Bennett, "Some Reflections on Neo-Assyrian Influences in Transjordan," *Archaeology in the Levant* (1978), pp. 164–171, figs. 1–4; F. E. Young, "Aroer," *ISBE* I (1979), p. 298.

'Arâq el-Emîr, Qasr el-'Abd

Excavated by E. Will 1976–1980 for l'Institut français d'archéologie du Proche Orient and the Jordan Dept. of Antiquities.

P. W. Lapp, *The Tale of the Tell*, N. L. Lapp, ed. (1975), pp. 59–65, 121, pls. 1–5; *id.* 'Iraq el-Emir," *EAEHL* II (1976), pp. 527–531, figs.; J. M. Dentzer, "Recherches archéologiques à 'Araq el-Emir: Fouilles de la porte monumentale," *ADAJ* 22 (1977–78), pp. 102–107, figs. 1–2, pls. 63–64; E. Will, "Araq al-Amir 1976–1978," *RB* 86:1 (1979), pp. 117–119, fig. 2, pl. 7; J. A. Sauer, "New French Work at 'Arâq el-Emîr," *BA* 42:3 (1979), p. 135; N. L. Lapp, "The Hellenistic Pottery from the 1961 and 1962 Excavations at 'Iraq el-Emir," *ADAJ* 23 (1979), pp. 5–15, figs. 1–2, pls. 1–2; R. M. Brown, "Excavations at 'Iraq el-Emir," *ADAJ* 23 (1979), pp. 17–30; figs. 1–3; E. Will, "Recherches au Qasr el-'Abd à 'Iraq al Amir," *ADAJ* 23 (1979), pp. 139–149, figs. 1–4, pls. 59–60.

Arbel

M. Avi-Yonah, "Synagogues," *EAEHL* IV (1978), pp. 1129–1138, figs.

'Areini, Tell esh-Sheikh Ahmed el-, 'Erani

S. Yeivin, "el 'Areini," *EAEHL* I (1975), pp. 89–97, figs; R. Gophna, "Egyptian Immigration into Southern Canaan during the First Dynasty?" *TA* 3:1 (1976), pp. 31–37, figs. 1–3.

'Arish, el-, Sinai

E. D. Oren, "The Overland Route between Egypt and Canaan in the Early Bronze Age," *IEJ* 23:4 (1973), pp. 198–205, figs. 1–2, pls. 52–54; J. Naveh, E. Stern, "A Stone Vessel with a Thamudic Inscription," *IEJ* 24:2 (1974), pp. 79–83, fig. 1, pls. 12–13.

Arjoune, Syria

L. Marfoe, L. Copeland, P. J. Parr, "Arjoune 1978: Preliminary Investigation of a Prehistoric Site in the Homs Basin, Syria," *Levant* 13 (1981), pp. 1–27, figs. 1–12.

Arôer, Khirbet Ar'arah, Negev

Excavated in 1976–1978 by A. Biran, R. Cohen for the Nelson Glueck School of Biblical Archaeology, HUC, and the Israel Dept. of Antiquities and Museums.

A. Biran, R. Cohen, "Aroer," *IEJ* 25:2–3 (1975), p. 171, pl. 19 a–d; A. Biran, "Aroer," *RB* 83:2 (1976), pp. 256–257, pls. 26–27; A. Biran, R. Cohen, "Aroer 1976," *IEJ* 26:2–3 (1976), pp. 139–140, pl. 28 b–c; A. Biran, R. Cohen, "Aroër (Negev)," *RB* 84:2 (1977), pp. 273–275, pl. 9 d; A. Biran, R. Cohen, "Aroer 1977," *IEJ* 27:4 (1977). pp. 250–251, pl. 38; A. Biran, R. Cohen, "Aroer in the Negev," *Qad.* 11:1 (1978), pp. 20–24, figs. (Hebrew); A. Biran, R. Cohen, "Aroer 1978," *IEJ* 28:3 (1978), pp. 197–199, pl. 32 c–d; A. Biran, R. Cohen, "Aroër (Negev) 1977," *RB* 85:3 (1978), pp. 425–427, fig. 14, pl. 28; A. Biran, "Aroër (1978)," *RB* 86:3 (1979), pp. 465–466.

Arôer, see 'Arâ'ir (Jordan)

'Arrub, 'Ain

Excavated in 1968 by Y. Meshorer for the Israel Dept. of Antiquities and Museums.

E. Stern, "A Burial of the Persian Period near Hebron," *IEJ* 21:1 (1971), pp. 25–30, figs. 1–3, pls. 2–3; Y. Tsafrir, "A Cave of the Bar Kokhba Period near 'Ain 'Arrub," *Qad.* 8:1 (1975), pp. 24–27, figs. (Hebrew).

Asawir, Tell el-, Arubboth

M. Dothan, "el-Asawir, Tell," *EAEHL* I (1975), pp. 100–102, figs.

Ascalon, Ashkelon

V. Tsaferis, "Byzantine Churches and Inscriptions in Israel," *EI* 10 (1971), pp. 241–244, pls. 69–70; G. S. Merker, "A Hellenistic Muse in Jerusalem," *IEJ* 23:3 (1973), pp. 178–180, pl. 47; T. Noy, A. Berman, "Prehistoric Site near Ashkelon," *IEJ* 24:2 (1974), p. 132, pl. 22 a; M. Avi-Yonah, "Two Sarcophagi from Ashkelon," *Qad.* 7:3–4 (1974), pp. 106–110, figs. (Hebrew), M. Avi-Yonah, Y. Eph'al, "Ashkelon," *EAEHL* I (1975), pp. 121–130, figs.; B. Z. Kedar, W. G. Mook, "Radiocarbon Dating of Mortar from the City Wall of Ascalon," *IEJ* 28:3 (1978), pp. 173–176, fig. 1, pl. 26 d; Y. Tsafrir, "Or ha-Ner," *EAEHL* IV (1978), pp. 937–938, figs.; J. F. Prewitt, "Ashkelon," *ISBE* 1 (1979), pp. 318–319, fig.; A. Ovadiah, C. Gomez de Silva, "Supplementum to the Corpus of the Byzantine Churches in the Holy Land (Part I)," *Levant* 13 (1981), pp. 200–261, esp. 205–206; J. Naveh, "Ancient Synagogue Inscriptions," *ASR* (1981), p. 133, fig.

'Ashan, Khirbet, Bir Abu Jekheidim

Excavated in 1976 by R. Cohen for the Israel Dept. of Antiquities and Museums.

R. Cohen, "Ḥ. 'Ashan," *IEJ* 27:2–3 (1977), pp. 163–164.

Ashdod, Tell Mor

Excavated by M. Dothan, D. N. Freedman, J. L. Swauger 1970–1972, for the Israel Dept. of Antiquities and Museums, Pittsburgh Theological Seminary and Carnegie Museum.

M. Dothan et al., *Ashdod II, III, The Second and Third Seasons of Excavations*, Text, Plates, *'Atiqot* 9–10 (1971); M. Dothan, "Tell Ashdod," *IEJ* 21:2–3 (1971), p. 175; *id.*, Tel Ashdod," *RB* 78:3 (1971), pp. 430–432, pls. b–21 a; *id.*, "Seven Seasons of Excavation," *Qad.* 5:1 (1972), pp. 2–13, figs. (Hebrew); *id.*, "Tel Ashdod," IEJ 22:2–3 (1972), pp. 166–167; *id.*, "Tell Ashdod," *RB* 79:3 (1972), pp. 419–421; *id.*, "Tell Ashdod," *IEJ* 22:4 (1972), pp. 243–244, pl. 56; *id.*, "The Foundation of Tel Mor and of Ashdod," *IEJ* 23:1 (1973), pp. 1–17, figs. 1–7, pls. 1–3; *id.*, "The End of the Late Bronze Age at Tel Mor and Ashdod," *EI* 11 (1973), pp. 122–133, figs., pls. (Hebrew); *id.*, "Ashdod," *EAEHL* I (1975), pp. 103–119, figs., D. N. Freedman, "Ashdod," *IDB-S* (1976), pp. 71–72, figs.; M. Dothan, "The Musicians of Ashdod," *BA* 40:1 (1977), pp. 38–39, 6 figs.; A. Harif, "Coastal Buildings of Foreign Origin in Second Millennium B. C. Palestine," *PEQ* 110:2 (1978), pp. 101–106, figs. 1–2; H. Porter, "Ashdod, Azotus, *ISBE* I (1979), p. 314, fig.; D. N. Freedman, "Ashdod," *ISBE* I (1979), pp. 314–316, figs.; M. Dothan, "Ashdod at the End of the Late Bronze Age and the Beginning of the Iron Age," *Symposia* F. M. Cross, ed., (1979), pp. 125–134, figs. 1–4; T. Watkins, "Levantine Bronzes from the Collection of the Rev. William Greenwell, now in the British Museum," *Levant* 13 (1981), pp. 119–155, figs. 1–12.

'Askar, Khirbet

E. Damati, "'Askar," *IEJ* 22:2–3 (1972), p. 174, pls. 35 b, 36; Z. Yeivin, "Kh. Askar," *RB* 81:1 (1974), pp. 97–98, pls. 12–13.

'Athlit

C. N. Johns, "'Atlit," *EAEHL* I (1975), pp. 130–140, figs.

'Auja el-Ḥafir, see Nessana

Avdat, see 'Abdah

Ayyelet ha-Shaḥar, see Hazor

Azekah, Tell ez-Zakariya

E. Stern, "Azekah," *EAEHL* I (1975), pp. 141–143, figs.

Azraq

A. N. Garrard, N. P. S. Price, "A Survey of Prehistoric Sites in the Azraq Desert National Park, in Eastern Jordan," *ADAJ* 20 (1975), pp. 83–90, 3 figs.

Azor

A. Ben-Tor, "Azor," *RB* 79:3 (1972), pp. 418–419; *id.*, "Excavation of Two Burial Caves at Azor," *Qad.* 6:2 (1973), pp. 48–50, figs. (Hebrew); J. Perrot, M. Dothan, A. Ben-Tor, "Azor," *EAEHL* I (1975), pp. 144–148, figs.; A. Ben-Tor, "Two Burial Caves of the Proto-Urban Period at Azor 1971," *Qedem* 1 (1975); C. Epstein, "Aspects of Symbolism in Chalcolithic Palestine," *Archaeology in the Levant* (1978), pp. 22–35, figs. 1–2, pls. 3–7; K. Prag, "Silver in the Levant in the Fourth Millennium B. C.," *Archaeology in the Levant* (1978), pp. 36–45.

Bâb edh-Dhrâ'

Excavated in 1975 by W.E. Rast and R.T. Schaub for the American Center of Oriental Research, Amman. Necropolis excavated in 1977 by D. McCreary for the Jordan Dept. of Antiquities and ACOR.

E.M. Meyers, "Secondary Burials in Palestine," *BA* 33:1 (1970), pp. 1–29, figs. 1–14; R.T. Schaub, "An Early Bronze IV Tomb from Bâb edh–Dhrâ'," *BASOR* 210 (1973), pp. 2–19, figs. 1–8; W.G. Dever, "The EB IV–MB I Horizon in Transjordan and Southern Palestine," *BASOR* 210 (1973), pp. 37–63, figs. 1–6; W.E. Rast, R.T. Schaub, "Survey of the Southeastern Plain of the Dead Sea 1973," *ADAJ* 19 (1974), pp. 5–53, figs. 1–12, pls. 1–11; A. Ben-Tor, "Bab edh-Dhra'," *EAEHL* I (1975), pp. 149–151, figs.; M.W. Several, "An Early Bronze Basalt Bowl in the Skirball Museum," *Levant* 7 (1975), pp. 139–141, fig. 1, pl. 22 b; S.W. Helms, "Posterns in Early Bronze Age Fortifications of Palestine," *PEQ* 107:2 (1975), pp. 133–150, figs. 1–7; P.W. Lapp, *The Tale of the Tell*, N.L. Lapp, ed., (1975), pp. 104–110; W.E. Rast, R.T. Schaub et al., "Bâb edh–Dhrâ' 1975," *AASOR* 43 (1978), pp. 1–60, figs., pls.; S.H. Horn, *Biblical Archaeology After 30 Years, 1948–1978* (1978), pp. 23–24; V.A. Clark, "Investigations in a Prehistoric Necropolis near Bâb edh–Dhrâ'," *ADAJ* 23 (1979), pp. 57–77, figs. 1–10, pls. 32–34; H. Shanks, "Have Sodom and Gomorrah Been Found?" *BAR* 6:5 (1980), pp. 26–36, figs.; J.R. Kautz, "Tracking the Ancient Moabites," *BA* 44:1 (1981), pp. 27–35, figs.; W.C. van Hattem, "Once Again: Sodom and Gomorrah," *BA* 44:2 (1981), pp. 87–92.

Bâb edh–Dhrâ', see Dhrâ'

Balâṭah, see Shechem.

Bālû 'ah

N. Glueck, *The Other Side of the Jordan* (1970), pp. 142, 153, 158, 159, 163, 187, 188, figs.; J.M. Miller, "Archaeological Survey South of Wadi Mujib: Glueck's Sites Revisited," *ADAJ* 23 (1979), pp. 81–82; J.R. Kautz, "Tracking the Ancient Moabites," *BA* 44:1 (1981), pp. 27–35, figs.

Banias, see Caesarea Philippi

Bardala Church

Excavated by Z. Yeivin and E. Damati in 1972.

A. Ovadiah, C.G. de Silva, "Supplementum to the Corpus of the Byzantine Churches in the Holy Land," *Levant* 13 (1981), pp. 200–261, figs., esp. 206–207.

Bashan

D. Urman, Z. Ilan, G. Barkai, A. Mazar, A. Kloner, "Archaeological Remains in Northern Bashan," *Qad.* 6:3–4 (1973), pp. 85–90, figs.; G. Barkay, Z. Ilan, A. Kloner, A. Mazar, D. Urman, "Archaeological Survey in Northern Bashan," *IEJ* 24:3–4 (1974), pp. 173–184, figs. 1–8, pls. 33–37; M. Ben-Dov, "A Lintel from the Bashan Depicting Three Deities," *IEJ* 24:3–4 (1974), pp. 185–186, pl. 38; A. Ovadiah, "Greek Inscriptions from the Northern Bashan," *LA* 26 (1976), pp. 170–212, fig. 1, pls. 17–24; W.S. LaSor, "Bashan," *ISBE* (1979), pp. 436–437, fig.

Bassah Cave, Jordan

Z. Safar, "Excavation at Bassah Cave," *ADAJ* 19 (1974), pp. 5–10 (Arabic).

Basul, Tell

N. Tsori, "A Greek Inscription from Tell Basul," *IEJ* 24:3–4 (1974), p. 227, pl. 32 c.

Batash, Tell

Excavated by G.L. Kelm 1977–79, 1981 for the New Orleans Baptist Theological Seminary, Mississippi College, the Hebrew University.

G.L. Kelm, A. Mazar, "Tel Batash 1977," *IEJ* 27:2–3 (1977), pp. 167–168, pl. 24 a; J. Kaplan, "Tuleilat el-Batashi," *EAEHL* IV (1978), p. 1204, fig.; G.L. Kelm, A. Mazar, "Tell Batash 1977," *RB* 85:1 (1978), pp. 94–96; G.L. Kelm, A. Mazar, "Tel Batash (Timnah) 1978," *IEJ* 28:3 (1978), pp. 195–196, pl. 32 a–b; G.L. Kelm, A. Mazar, "Tel Batash (Timnah) 1979," *IEJ* 29:3–4 (1979), pp. 241–243, pl. 30 a–b; A. Mazar, G.L. Kelm, "Canaanites, Philistines and Israelites at Timna/Tel Batash," *Qad.* 13:3–4 (1980), pp. 89–97, figs.

Beersheba

Excavated during 1970–1974 by Y. Aharoni for Tel Aviv University, and in 1976 by Z. Herzog for Brigham Young and Tel Aviv Universities.

Y. Aharoni, "Tel Beersheva," *RB* 78:3 (1971), pp. 433–435, pl. 22; *id.* "Tel Beersheba," *IEJ* 21:4 (1971), pp. 230–232; *id.* "Beersheba," *BTS* 141 (1972), pp. 8–16, figs.; *id.*, "Tel Beersheba," IEJ 22:2–3 (1972), pp. 169–170, pls. 32–33; *id.*, "Tel Beersheba," *RB* 79:4 (1972), pp. 589–593, pls. 55–56; *id.*, "Excavations at Tel Beer-sheba," *BA* 35:4 (1972), pp. 111–127, figs. 8–19; N. Liphschitz, Y. Waisel, "Dendroarchaeological Investigations in Israel: Tel Beersheba and Arad in the Northern and Eastern Negev," *IEJ* 23:1 (1973), pp. 31–36, 2 tables, pls. 6–9; Y. Aharoni, "Tel Beersheva," *RB* 80:3 (1973), pp. 405–408, pls. 12–13; *id.*, "Tel Beer-sheva," *Qad.* 6:3–4 (1973), pp. 75–84, figs. (Hebrew); *id.*, "Tel Beersheba," *IEJ* 23:4 (1973), pp. 254–256, pl. 71. Y. Aharoni, ed., *Excavations at Tel Beer-Sheba, I, (1973), II, (1974)*; Y. Aharoni, "Excavations at Tel Beer-Sheba 1972, *TA* 1:1 (1974), pp. 34–42, figs. 1–3, pls. 5–8; *id.* "The Horned Altar of Beer-sheba," *BA* 37:1 (1974), pp. 1–6, figs. 1–3; A.F. Rainey, "Dust and Ashes," *TA* 1:2 (1974), pp. 77–83, pl. 16; Y. Aharoni, "Tel Beersheba," *IEJ* 24:3–4 (1974), pp. 270–272, pl. 59.

E. Stern, "A Deposit of Votive Figurines from the Beersheba Region" *EI* 12 (1975), pp. 91–94, pls. 18–20, map (Hebrew); Y. Aharoni, "Tel Beer-Sheva," *RB* 82:1 (1975), pp. 92–95, pls. 6–7 a, 9 b; J.M. Matthers, Review of Y. Aharoni, ed., *Beer-Sheba* I (1973), *PEQ* 107:2 (1975), pp. 159–160; Y. Aharoni, "Tel Beer-Sheba 1975," *IEJ* 25:2–3 (1975), pp. 169–171, pl. 17; Y. Aharoni et al., "Excavations at Tel Beersheba, 1973–74," *TA* 2:4 (1975), pp. 146–168, figs. 1–8, pls. 28–36; J. Perrot, "Beersheba: Prehistoric Settlements," *EAEHL* I (1975), pp. 152–158, figs.; R. Gophna, "Beersheba: Iron Age," *EAEHL* I (1975), pp. 158–159; Y. Aharoni, "Tel Beersheba," *EAEHL* I (1975), pp. 160–168, figs.; K.M. Kenyon, "The Date of the Destruction of Iron Age Beer-Sheba," *PEQ* 108:1 (1976), pp. 63–64; M. Homsky, S. Moshkovitz, "The Distribution of Different Wood Species of the Iron Age II at Tel Beer-sheba," *TA* 3:1 (1976), pp. 42–48, figs. 1–2, 1 table; B. Boyd, "Beersheba," *IDB-S* (1976), pp. 93–95, fig.; Y. Aharoni, "Tel Beer-sheba," *RB* 83:1 (1976), pp. 72–78, pls. 6–9; Y. Yadin, "Beer-sheba: The High Place Destroyed by King Josiah," *BASOR* 222 (1976), pp. 5–17, figs. 1–9; Y. Aharoni, "Nothing Early and Nothing Late: Rewriting Israel's Conquest," *BA* 39:2 (1976), pp. 55–76, figs. 1–22; R. Amiran, "More About the Chalcolithic Culture of Palestine and Tepe Yahya," *IEJ* 26:4 (1976), pp. 157–162, figs. 1–2, pl. 29; M. and Y. Aharoni, "The Stratification of Judahite Sites in the 8th and 7th Centuries B.C.E., *BASOR* 224 (1976), pp. 73–90, figs.; M. Homsky, S. Moshkovitz, "Cypress Wood in Excavations in Eretz-Israel," *TA* 4:1–2 (1977), pp. 71–78, fig. 1; J.S. Holladay, Jr., Review of Y. Aharoni, ed., *Beer-Sheva* I (1973), *JBL* 96:2 (1977), pp. 281–284; Z. Herzog, "Tel Beer-sheba 1976," *IEJ* 27:2–3 (1977), pp. 168–170, pl. 23; Z. Herzog, A.F. Rainey, S. Moshkovitz, "The Stratigraphy at Beer-sheba and the Location of the Sanctuary," *BASOR* 225 (1977), pp.

49–58, figs. 1–4; M. Aharoni, "Some Observations on the Recent Article by Y. Yadin in BASOR 222 (1976)," *BASOR* 225 (1977), pp. 67–68, figs. 1–2; Y. Yadin, "Beer-sheba — The High Place Destroyed by King Josiah," *EI* 14 (1978), pp. 78–85, pls. 1–2 (Hebrew); Z. Herzog, "Israelite City Planning, seen in the Light of the Beer-sheba and Arad Excavations," *Expedition* 20:4 (1978), pp. 38–43, figs.; J. Naveh, "The Aramaic Ostraca from Tel Beersheba 1971–1976," *TA* 6:3–4 (1979), pp. 182–198, pls. 24–31; A.F. Rainey, "Beer-sheba," *ISBE* I (1979), pp. 448–451, fig.; M. Kochavi, "Rescue in the Biblical Negev," *BAR* 6:1 (1980), pp. 24–27, figs.; M. Tadmor, R. Amiran, "A Female Cult Statuette from Chalcolithic Beer-sheba," *IEJ* 30:3–4 (1980), pp. 137–139, pl. 17 a–d; D. Alon, T.E. Levy, "Preliminary Note on the Distribution of Chalcolithic Sites on the Wadi Beer-sheba — Lower Wadi Besor Drainage System," *IEJ* 30:3–4 (1980), pp. 140–147, figs. 1–3, table; Z. Herzog, "Beer-Sheba of the Patriarchs," *BAR* 6:6 (1980), pp. 12–28, figs.; A. Ovadiah, C.G. de Silva, "Supplementum to the Corpus of the Byzantine Churches in the Holy Land," *Levant* 13 (1981), pp. 200–261, figs., esp. 207–208.

Beidha, Wâdī, Seyl Aqlat

D. Gilead, "Beidha, Wâdī," *EAEHL* I (1975), pp. 168–170, figs.; F. Zayadine, "A Nabataean Inscription from Beidha," *ADAJ* 21 (1976), pp. 139–142, figs. 1–4; L. Copeland, C. Vita-Finzi, "Archaeological Dating of Geological Deposits in Jordan," *Levant* 10 (1978), pp. 10–25, figs. 1–5, pl. 6 a.

Beisamoun

Excavated in 1972 by J. Perrot and M. Lechevallier for the French Archaeological Mission.

M. Lechevallier, J. Perrot, "Eynan and Beisamoun," *IEJ* 23:2 (1973), pp. 107–108, pls. 23–24; M. Lechevallier, J. Perrot, "Beisamoun," *RB* 80:3 (1973), pp. 400–401, pls. 9–10 a; J. Perrot, "Beisamoun in the Hula Valley," *Qad.* 8:4 (1975), pp. 114–117, figs. (Hebrew).

Beit Jibrin, see Sandahannah

Beit Mirsim, see Tell Beit Mirsim

Beit Sahur, see Bethlehem

Beit Zar 'a, Jordan

M.M.A. Khadija, "Beit Zar'a Tombs 1974," *ADAJ* 19 (1974), pp. 157–163, figs. 1–3, pls. 76–80.

Belvoir, Kaukab el-Howa

M. Ben-Dov, "Belvoir," *EAEHL* I (1975), pp. 179–184, figs.; *id.*, "Crusader Castles in Israel," *CNI* 25;4 (1976), pp. 210–218, figs.; *id.*, "Synagogue Remains at Kokhav-Hayarden," *ASR* (1981), pp. 95–97, figs.

Bene-Beraq

J. Kaplan, "Bene-Berak and Vicinity," *EAEHL* I (1975), pp. 184–186, figs.; *id.*, "Benei Barak 1977," *RB* 85:3 (1978), pp. 416–417.

Berachot, see Bureikut

Besor, 'En

Excavated by R. Gophna 1976 for the Israel Dept. of Antiquities and Museums and Tel Aviv University.

R. Gophna, "A First Dynasty Egyptian Site near 'En-ha-Besor," *Qad.* 5:1 (1972), pp. 14–15, figs. (Hebrew); *id.*, "Egyptian Immigration into Southern Canaan during the First Dynasty?" *TA* 3:1 (1976), pp. 31–37, figs. 1–3; *id.*, "Besor Bridge (Site H)," *IEJ* 26:4 (1976), p. 199; *id.*, " 'En-Besor: An Egyptian First Dynasty Staging Post in the Northern Negev," *Expedition* 20:4 (1978), pp. 5–7, figs.

Beth Alpha

G. Foerster, "Les Synagogues de Galilée," *BTS* 130 (1971), pp. 8–15; N. Avigad, "Beth Alpha," *EAEHL* I (1975), pp. 187–190, figs.

Bethany

S. Loffreda, "La tomba n. 3 presso le Suore della Nigrizia a Betania," *LA* 24 (1974), pp. 142–169, figs. 1–9, pls. 1–6.

Bethel

Y. Yadin, "An Inscribed South Arabian Clay Stamp from Bethel?" *EI* 10 (1971), pp. 146–149, figs. 1–2, pl. 56; R.L. Cleveland, "More on the South Arabian Clay Stamp Found at Beitin," *BASOR* 209 (1973), pp. 33–36; J.L. Kelso, "Bethel," *EAEHL* I (1975), pp. 190–193, figs.; W. Ewing, R.K. Harrison, "Bethel," *ISBE* I (1979), pp. 465–467, fig.

Beth Guvrin, see Sandahannah

Beth Ha 'Emeq

P. Beck, "The Cylinder Seal Impressions from Beth Ha 'Emeq," *TA* 3:3 (1976), pp. 120–126, figs. 1–2, pl. 6.

Bethlehem, Beit Sahur

V. Tsaferis excavated the holy place at Beit Sahur for the Greek Orthodox Patriarchate at Jerusalem, 1972.

S. Saller, "The Byzantine Chapel found at Bethlehem in 1962," *LA* 22 (1972), pp. 153–167, figs. 1–9; V. Tsaferis, "Shepherds' Field (Beit Sahur)," *IEJ* 23:2 (1973), pp. 118–119, pl. 32; V. Tsaferis, "Beit Sahur," *RB* 80:3 (1973) pp. 421–422, pl. 19; *id.*, "Excavations at Shepherds' Field, Bethlehem," *Qad.* 6:3–4 (1973), pp. 120–122, figs. (Hebrew); M. Stekelis, "Prehistory," *EAEHL* I (1975), p. 198, fig.; M. Avi-Yonah, "Bethlehem," *EAEHL* I (1975), pp. 198–206, 208, figs.; V. Tsaferis, "The Archaeological Excavation at Shepherds' Field," *LA* 25 (1975), pp. 5–52, pls. 1–25; C. Katsimbinis, "La grotta dei Pastori-Betlemme," *LA* 25 (1975), p. 53, pls. 26–28; D. Chen, "The Church of the Nativity at Bethlehem: The Design of Justinian's Plan," *LA* 29 (1979), pp. 270–275, pls. 33–36; A. Ovadiah, C.G. de Silva, "Supplementum to the Corpus of the Byzantine Churches in the Holy Land," *Levant* 13 (1981), pp. 200–261, figs., esp. 208–209.

Bethlehem, Galilee

Excavated in 1975 by R. Rosenthal for the Israel Dept. of Antiquities and Museums.

R. Rosenthal, "Bethlehem in Galilee," *IEJ* 25:2–3 (1975), p. 176.

Beth-Maachah, see Abil, Tell

Beth-shan, Tell-Ḥusn, Beisan, Scythopolis

D. Bahat et al., excavated a synagogue in 1970–1972 for the Israel Dept. of Antiquities and Museums.

D. Bahat, A. Druks, "Beth Shean: Ancienne Synagogue," *RB* 78:4 (1971), pp. 585–586, pl. 27 b; E.D. Oren, "A Middle Bronze I Warrior Tomb at Beth-shan," *ZDPV* 87:2 (1971), pp. 109–139, figs. 1–5, pls. 8–9; D. Bahat, "The Syngogue at Beth-Shean," *Qad.* 5:2 (1972), pp. 55–58, figs. (Hebrew); E.D. Oren, *The Northern Cemetery of Beth-shan* (1973); N. Tzori, "The House of Kyrios Leontis at Beth-Shean," *EI* 11 (1973), pp. 229–247, figs.; E.D. Oren, "The Early Bronze IV Period in Northern Palestine and its Cultural and Chronological Setting," *BASOR* 210 (1973), pp. 20–37, figs. 1–3; B. Bar Kochva, "Notes on the Fortresses of Josephus in Galilee," *IEJ* 24:2 (1974), pp. 108–116, fig. 1; O. Negbi, "The Continuity of the Canaanite Bronze Work of the Late Bronze Age into the Early Iron Age." *TA* 1:4 (1974), pp. 159–172, 1 table, pls. 30 b–32; A. Ovadiah, "Greek Cults in Beth-Shean/Scythopolis in the Hellenistic and Roman Periods," *EI* 12 (1975), pp. 116–124, pl. 26 (Hebrew); J.M. Weinstein, "Egyptian Relations with Palestine in the Middle Kingdom," *BASOR* 217 (1975), pp. 1–16, figs. 1–3; F. James, A. Kempinski, D. Bahat, N. Tsori, "Beth-Shean," *EAEHL* I (1975), pp. 207, 209–229, figs.; T. Dothan, "Forked Bronze Butts from Palestine and Egypt," *IEJ* 26:1 (1976), pp. 20–34, figs. 1–6, pls. 4–6; C.M. Dauphin, "A Note on the Method of Laying Early Byzantine Mosaic Pavements in the Light of the Inhabited Scroll," *Levant* 8 (1976), pp. 155–158, figs. 1–3, pl. 19 b; M.W. Prausnitz, "Beth-Shan," *IDB-S* (1976), pp. 97–98; N. Tsori, "A Contribution to the Problem of the Persian Period at Beth-Shan," *PEQ* 109:2 (1977), pp. 103–105, figs. 1–2, pl. 7; *id.*, "Bet Shean in the Chalcolithic Period," *EI* 13 (1977), pp. 76–81 (Hebrew); *id.*, "Roman Stamped Amphora Handles from Beth-Shean," *IEJ* 27:2–3 (1977), pp. 125–126, pl. 20 a–d; R. Hachlili, "The Zodiac in Ancient Jewish Art: Representation and Significance," *BASOR* 228 (1977), pp. 61–77, figs. 1–18; F. James, "Chariot Fittings from Late Bronze Age Beth Shan," *Archaeology in the Levant* (1978), pp. 102–115, figs. 1–4, pls. 11–17; I. Skupinska-Løvset, "Une Figurine Supposée Scythe de Beth-Shean," *RB* 85:1 (1978), pp. 62–65, pls. 1–2; A. Ben-Tor, *Cylinder Seals of Third Millennium Palestine, BASOR Suppl.* 22 (1978), pp. 9, 102, 103; S. Geva, "A Reassessment of the Chronology of Beth Shean Strata V and IV," *IEJ* 29:1 (1979), pp. 6–10; A.F. Rainey, "Beth-Shean," *ISBE* I (1979), pp. 475–478, figs.; D. Bahat, "A Synagogue at Beth-Shean," *ASR* (1981), pp. 82–85, figs.

Beth-shan, see Isṭabah, Tell

Beth-She 'arim, Sheikh Abreiq

E.M. Meyers, "Secondary Burials in Palestine," *BA* 33:1 (1970), pp. 1–29, figs. 1–14; N. Avigad, *Beth She 'arim* III, *The Archaeological Excavations during 1953–1958. The Catacombs 12–23* (1971), (Hebrew); C. Gensburger, "Les Objets du Culte Synagogal," *BTS* 130, April (1971), fig. p.4; B. Mazar, *Beth She 'arim, Report on the Excavations During 1936–40*, I, (1973); F. Vitto, "Qiryat Tiv'on," *IEJ* 24:3–4 (1974), p. 279, pl. 61 a; N. Avigad, B. Mazar, "Beth-She'arim," *EAEHL* I (1975), pp. 229–247, figs.; J. Kaplan, "I, Justus, Lie Here'," *BA* 40:4 (1977), pp. 167–171, figs.

Beth-shemesh, 'Ain Shems, Rumeileh

Excavated 1971–1973, 1975 by D. Bahat, C. Epstein, for the Israel Dept. of Antiquities and Museums.

C. Epstein, "Beth-shemesh," *IEJ* 22:2–3 (1972), p. 157, pl. 26; *id.*, "Beth Shemesh," *RB* 79:4 (1972), pp. 583–584, pl. 54; D. Bahat, "Beth Shemesh," *IEJ* 23:4 (1973), pp. 246–247; V. Tsafrir, "The Levitic City of Beth-shemesh: In Juda or in Naphtali?" *EI* 12 (1975), pp. 44–45 (Hebrew); G.E. Wright, "Beth-Shemesh," *EAEHL* I (1975), pp. 248–253, figs.; D.

Bahat, "Excavations at Giv'at Sharett near Beth-Shemesh," *Qad.* 8:2–3 (1975), pp. 64–67, figs. (Hebrew); *id.*, "Did the Patriarchs Live at Givat Sharett?" *BAR* 4:3 (1978), pp. 8–11, figs.; W.S. La Sor, "Beth Shemesh," *ISBE* I (1979), pp. 478–479.

Beth-Yeraḥ, Khirbet el-Kerak, Philoteria, aṣ-Ṣinnabra

P. Bar-Adon, "Rare Cylinder-Seal Impressions from Beth-yerah," *EI* 11 (1973), pp. 99–100, figs. (Hebrew); B. Mazar, R. Amiran, N. Haas, "An Early Bronze Age II Tomb at Beth-Yerah (Kinneret)," *EI* 11 (1973), pp. 176–193, figs., pl. (Hebrew); R. Hestrin, "Beth-Yeraḥ," *EAEHL* I (1975), pp. 253–262, figs.; A. Ben-Tor, *Cylinder Seals of Third Millennium Palestine, BASOR Suppl.* 22 (1978), pp. 3–8, 10, 11, 12, 102, 103, 107, 109. V. Sussman, "A Relief of a Bull from the Early Bronze Age," *BASOR* 238 (1980), pp. 75–77, figs. 1–3.

Beth-zur, Khirbet et-Tubeiqeh

R.W. Funk, "Beth-Zur," *EAEHL* I (1975), pp. 263–267, figs.; A. van Selms, "Beth-Zur," *ISBE* I (1979), p. 480.

Bira, Tell, Tell Bir el-Gharbi

Excavated by M.W. Prausnitz 1978, 1980 for the Israel Dept. of Antiquities and Museums.

M.W. Prausnitz, "Tel Bira 1978, 1980," *IEJ* 30:3–4 (1980), pp. 206–207, pl. 25 b–c.

Bir'am, Kfar, Bar'am

N. Avigad, "Kefar Bir'am," *EAEHL* III (1977), pp. 704–707, figs.

Bir el 'Abd, north Sinai

E. Oren, "Bir el'Abd (Sinai Nord)," *RB* 81:1 (1974), pp. 87–89; *id.*, "Bir el'Abd (Northern Sinai), *IEJ* 23:2 (1973), pp. 112–113, pls. 28–29 a.

Bir el-Gharbi, Tell, see Bira, Tell

Bodeda, Khirbet

Z. Meshel, B. Sass, "Ḥurvat Bodeda," *IEJ* 24:3–4 (1974), pp. 284–285, pl. 55 f.

Boqeq, 'En, Qasr Umm Baghgheq

Excavated by M. Gichon for Tel Aviv University intermittently 1967–1972.

M. Gichon, "'En Boqeq," *EAEHL* II (1976), pp. 365–370, figs.

Boqeq, 'En-, see 'En Boqeq

Boqer, Naḥal

T. Noy, "Nahal Boqer," *IEJ* 26:1 (1976), pp. 48–49.

Buqê 'ah, el-Buqei'a

L.E. Stager, "El-Bouqei'ah," *RB* 81:1 (1974), pp. 94–96, pls. 10–11 a; F.M. Cross, "El-Buqei'a," *EAEHL* I (1975), pp. 267–270, figs.; L.E. Stager, "Farming in the Judean Desert during the Iron Age," *BASOR* 221 (1976), pp. 145–158, figs. 1–11.

Buqê'ah, see Qumran, 'Ain Feshkha

Bureikut, Khirbet, Berachot

Excavated by Y. Tsafrir 1976 for the Hebrew University.

Y. Tsafrir, Y. Hirschfeld, "Khirbet Bureikut," *IEJ* 26:4 (1976), pp. 206–207, pl. 36 d–e; Y. Tsafrir, Y. Hirschfeld, "Ḥ. Berachot (Khirbet Bureikut)," *RB* 84:3 (1977), pp. 426–428, pls. 28 b — 30; Y. Tsafrir, Y. Hirschfeld, "A Church of the Byzantine Period at Ḥorvat Berachot," *Qad.* 11:4 (1978), pp. 120–128, figs. (Hebrew).

Burga, Tell

M. Kochavi, R. Gophna, "Tel Burga," *RB* 79:4 (1972), pp. 576–577; M. Kochavi, P. Beck, R. Gophna, "Aphek-Antipatris, Tēl Polēg, Tēl Zerōr and Tēl Burgā: Four Fortified Sites of the Middle Bronze IIA in the Sharon Plain," *ZDPV* 95:2 (1979), pp. 121–165, figs. 1–18, pls. 8–9 a.

Burqa', Qasr

H. Gaube, "An Examination of the Ruins of Qasr Burqu'," *ADAJ* 19 (1974), pp. 93–100, figs. 1–4, pls. 31–38; A.M.H. Shboul, "On the Later Arabic Inscription in Qasr Burqu'," *ADAJ* 20 (1975), pp. 95–98; M.C.A. Macdonald, G.L. Harding, "More Safaitic Texts from Jordan," *ADAJ* 21 (1976), pp. 119–133, 3 pls.

Buseirah, Bozrah in Jordan

Excavated 1971–1974 by C.-M. Bennett for the British School of Archaeology in Jerusalem, British Academy, Palestine Exploration Fund, Jordan Dept. of Antiquities.

C.-M. Bennett, "Buseirah," *RB* 79:3 (1972), pp. 426–430, fig. 1, pls. 43 b — 44; *id.* "Buseirah," *PEQ* 104:1 (1972), pp. 3–4; *id.*, "The Third Season of Excavations at Buseirah," *ADAJ* 18 (1973), p. 85; *id.*, "Excavations at Buseirah, Southern Jordan, 1971: A Preliminary Report," *Levant* 5 (1973), pp. 1–11, figs. 1–5, pls. 1–8; *id.*, "Buseirah," *The Archaeological Heritage of Jordan*, I (1973), p. 22; *id.*, "Buseirah," *RB* 81:1 (1974), pp. 73–76, pls. 2–4; *id.*, "Excavations at Buseirah," *Levant* 6 (1974), pp. 1–24, figs. 1–16, pls. 1–6; C-M. Bennett, et al., "Excavations at Buseirah, Southern Jordan 1973," *Levant* 7 (1975), pp. 1–19, figs. 1–9, pls. 1–7; C.-M. Bennett, "Buseirah (Transjordanie)," *RB* 83:1 (1976), pp. 63–67, figs. 1–2, pls. 3–4; J.B. Hennessy, "Bozrah (in Edom)," *IDB-S* (1976), p. 119; C-M. Bennett, "Excavations at Buseirah 1974," *Levant* 9 (1977), pp. 110, figs. 1–5, pls. 1–6; E. Puech, "Documents Epigraphiques de Buseirah," *Levant* 9 (1977), pp. 11–20, figs. 1–8; E. Stern, "New Types of Phoenician Style Decorated Pottery Vases from Palestine," *PEQ* 110:1 (1978), pp. 11–21, figs. 1–11, pls. 1–4; C.-M. Bennett, "Some Reflections on Neo-Assyrian Influence in Transjordan," *Archaeology in the Levant* (1978), pp. 164–171, figs. 1–4; J.R. Kautz, "Tracking the Ancient Moabites," *BA* 44:1 (1981), pp. 27–35, figs.

Caesarea Maritima

M. W. Prausnitz excavated in 1970 for the Israel Dept. of Antiquities and Museums.
From 1971–1980 R. J. Bull directed the joint expedition for the American Schools of Oriental Research et al.

M. Avi-Yonah, "The Caesarea Porphyry Statue," *EI* 10 (1971), pp. 50–52, pls. 43–46; T. D. Newman, "Mosaic Floors at Caesarea: An Archaeological Training Ground," *BA* 34:3 (1971), pp. 88–91, figs. 6–7; M. W. Prausnitz, "The Caesarea Coastal Dunes," *IEJ* 21:4 (1971), p. 227; R. P. Simon, E. Smith, "Césarée," *RB* 78:4 (1971), pp. 591–593, pl. 29; A. Negev, "A New Inscription from the High Level Aqueduct at Caesarea," *IEJ* 22:1 (1972), pp.

2–53, pl. 8 c–d; L. Levine, "Some Observations on the Coins of Caesarea Maritima," *IEJ* 2:2–3 (1972), pp. 131–140; R. J. Bull, L. E. Toombs, "Caesarea," *IEJ* 22:2–3 (1972), pp. 78–180, pl. 40; P. R. Diplock, "Further Comment on 'An Identification of the Caesarea Statues'," *PEQ* 105:2 (1973), pp. 165–166, pls. 17–20; R. J. Bull, "Caesarea," *IEJ* 23:4 (1973), pp. 260–262; R. J. Bull, L. E. Toombs, "Césarée Maritime," *RB* 80:4 (1973), pp. 582–585, pls. 32–33; J. H. Humphrey, "Prolegomena to the Study of the Hippodrome at Caesarea Maritima," *BASOR* 213 (1974), pp. 2–45, figs. 1–21; L. I. Levine, "The Hasmonean Conquest of Strato's Tower," *IEJ* 24:1 (1974), pp. 62–69; Y. Olami, Y. Ringel, "Two New Inscriptions of the Tenth Legion in the Caesarea Aqueduct," *Qad.* 7:1–2 (1974), pp. 44–45, figs. (Hebrew); L. Y. Rahmani, "A Lead Coffin from the Ḥefer Valley," *IEJ* 24:2 (1974), pp. 124–127, pls. 20–21; R. J. Bull, "A Mithraic Medallion from Caesarea," *IEJ* 24:3–4 (1974), pp. 187–190, pl. 30 c; A. Siegelman, "A Mosaic Floor at Caesarea Maritima," *IEJ* 24:3–4 (1974), pp. 216–221, figs. 1–2, pls. 47–48; R. J. Bull, "Caesarea," *IEJ* 24:3–4 (1974), pp. 280–282, pl. 61 e; J. Ringel, "Deux nouvelles inscriptions de l'aqueduc de Césarée maritime," *RB* 81:4 (1974), pp. 597–600, pl. 24.

G. Lease, L. M. Hopfe, L. Moore, "The Caesarea Mithraeum: A Preliminary Announcement," *BA* 38:1 (1975), pp. 1–10, figs. 1–4; R. J. Bull, "Césarée Maritime," *RB* 82:2 (1975), pp. 278–280, pls. 31–32; Y. Olami, Y. Ringel, "New Inscriptions of the Tenth Legion Fretensis from the High Level Aqueduct of Caesarea," *IEJ* 25:2–3 (1975), pp. 148–150, fig. 1, pl. 13 b; Y. Olami, Y. Peleg, "The Aqueducts of Caesarea," *Qad.* 8:2–3 (1975), pp. 83–86, figs. (Hebrew); A. Siegelman, "A Mosaic Pavement and Inscription of the Byzantine Period at Caesarea," *Qad.* 8:2–3 (1975), pp. 87–89, figs. (Hebrew); Y. Porat, "The Gardens of Caesarea," *Qad.* 8:2–3 (1975), pp. 90–93, figs. (Hebrew); J. H. Humphrey, "Summary of the 1974 Excavations in the Caesarea Hippodrome," *BASOR* 218 (1975), pp. 1–24, figs. 1–17; J. A. Riley, "The Pottery from the First Session of Excavation in the Caesarea Hippodrome," *BASOR* 218 (1975), pp. 25–63, 5 figs., 11 pls., 9 tables; L. I. Levine, "Roman Caesarea: An Archaeological-Topographical Study," *Qedem* 2 (1975); C. T. Fritsch, ed., *Joint Expedition to Caesarea Maritima*, I, *BASOR Suppl.* 19 (1975); A. Frova, M. Avi-Yonah, A. Negev, "Caesarea," *EAEHL* I (1975), pp. 270–275, 277–285, figs.; R. J. Bull, "Caesarea," *IDB-S* (1976), p. 120, fig.; H. W. Attridge, Review of L. I. Levine, *Caesarea under Roman Rule*, 1975, *JBL* 95:2 (1976), pp. 317–321; A. Flinder, "A Piscina at Caesarea," *IEJ* 26:2–3 (1976), pp. 77–80, fig., pl. 17.

Y. Olami, Y. Peleg, "The Water Supply System of Caesarea Maritima," *IEJ* 27:2–3 (1977), pp. 127–137, figs. 1–7, pls. 16–17; L. I. Levine, Review of R. J. Bull, L. Holland, C. T. Fritsch, eds., *The Joint Expedition to Caesarea Maritima*, I, *BASOR Suppl.* 19, 1975, *IEJ* 27:4 (1977), pp. 262–264; L. I. Levine, E. Netzer, "New Light on Caesarea," *Qad.* 11:2–3 (1978), pp. 70–75, figs. (Hebrew); L. E. Toombs, "The Stratigraphy of Caesarea Maritima," *Archaeology in the Levant* (1978), pp. 223–232, figs. 1–4, pl. 36; D. E. Groh, "North Syrian Mortaria Excavated at Caesarea Maritima," *Levant* 10 (1978), pp. 165–169, 1 fig., pl. 26; L. Y. Rahmani, "Un autel funéraire romain à Césarée maritime," *RB* 85:2 (1978), pp. 268–276, figs. 1–2, pls. 17–20; A. Raban, "Césarée Maritime 1976," *RB* 85:3 (1978), pp. 412–415, figs. 6–8; W. Ewing, R. K. Harrison, "Caesarea," *ISBE* I (1979), pp. 567–569, figs.; D. W. Roller, "Hellenistic Pottery from Caesarea Maritima: A Preliminary Study," *BASOR* 238 (1980), pp. 35–42, figs. 1–2; A. Raban, R. L. Hohlfelder, "The Ancient Harbors of Caesarea Maritima," *Archaeology* 34:2 (1981), pp. 56–60, figs.; M. Spiro, "Recent Mosaic Discoveries at Caesarea Maritima: Winter and Spring," *AJA* 85:2 (1981), p. 219; R. J. Bull, "The Ninth Season of Excavation at Caesarea Maritima," *AJA* 85:2 (1981), p. 188.

Caesarea Philippi, Banias, Neronias, Paneas

M. Ben-Dov, "Banias — A Medieval Fortress-Town," *Qad.* 11:1 (1978), pp. 29–33, figs. (Hebrew); W. Ewing, R. K. Harrison, "Caesarea Philippi," *ISBE* I (1979), p. 569, fig.

Capernaum, Tell Hum, Kfar Naḥum

Excavated by V. Corbo, S. Loffreda for the Franciscan Custody of the Holy Land 1970–1975.

V. Corbo, "Nuovi scavi archeologici nella sinagoga di Cafarnao," *LA* 20 (1970), pp. 7–52, figs. 1–25; S. Loffreda, "La ceramico della sinagoga Cafarnao," *LA* 20 (1970), pp. 53–105, figs. 1–12, plan; A. Spijkerman, "Moneta della Sinagoga di Cafarnao," *LA* 20 (1970), pp. 106–117; V. Corbo, "Aspetti urbanistici di Cafarnao," *LA* 21 (1971), pp. 263–285, figs. 1–10; S. Loffreda, "Stampi su terre sigillate di Cafarnao," *LA* 21 (1971), pp. 286–315, figs. 1–6; V. Corbo, "Capharnaüm," *RB* 78:4 (1971) pp. 588–591; G. Foerster, "Notes on Recent Excavations at Capernaum," *IEJ* 21:4 (1971) pp. 207–211; S. Loffreda, "The Synagogue of Capharnaum," *LA* 22 (1972), pp. 5–29.

V. Corbo, "La sinagoga di Cafarnao dopo gli scavi del 1972," *LA* 22 (1972), pp. 204–235, figs. 1–22; S. Loffreda, "The Late Chronology of the Synagogue of Capernaum," *IEJ* 23:1 (1973), pp. 37–42, fig. 1 (Reply by M. Avi-Yonah, pp. 43–45); S. Loffreda, "A Reply to the Editor," *IEJ* 23:3 (1973), p. 184; A. Negev, Review of S. Loffreda, *Cafarnao II, La Ceramica* 1974, *IEJ* 25:2–3 (1975), pp. 187–188; V. Corbo, S. Loffreda, "Capernaum 1975," *IEJ* 25:4 (1975), pp. 261–262; N. Avigad, "Capernaum," *EAEHL* I (1975), pp. 286–290, figs.; J. F. Strange, "Capernaum," *IDB-S* (1976), pp. 140–141; V. Corbo, S. Loffreda, "Sarcofago e pietra miliare di Cafarnao," *LA* 26 (1976), pp. 272–276, pls. 45–46; P. Benoit, Review of V. Corbo, *Cafarnao* I (1975), II, S. Loffreda (1964), III, A. Spijkerman (1975), IV, E. Testa (1972), *RB* 84:3 (1977), pp. 438–445; R. North, "Discoveries at Capernaum," (Critique of 4 vols. on Capernaum), *Biblica* 58:3 (1977), pp. 424–431; V. Corbo, "Il Mausoleo di Cafarnao," *LA* 27 (1977), pp. 145–155, figs. 1–4, pls. 1–4; *id.*, "Sotto la Sinagoga di Carfarnao un'insula della città," *LA* 27 (1977), pp. 156–172, figs. 1–9, pls. 1–7.

J. F. Strange, "The Capernaum and Herodium Publications," *BASOR* 226 (1977), pp. 65–73; D. Chen, "The Design of the Ancient Synagogues in Galilee," *LA* 28 (1978), pp. 193–202, pls. 47–50; J. F. Strange, "The Capernaum and Herodium Publications, Part 2," *BASOR* 233 (1979), pp. 63–69; S. Loffreda, "Potsherds from a Sealed Level of the Synagogue at Capharnaum," *LA* 29 (1979), pp. 215–220, pls. 19–20; R. H. Mounce, "Capernaum," *ISBE* I (1979), pp. 609–610, figs.; E. M. Meyers, "Ancient Synagogues in Galilee: Their Religious and Cultural Setting," *BA* 43:2 (1980), pp. 97–108, figs.; J. Wilkinson, "Architectural Procedures in Byzantine Palestine," *Levant* 13 (1981), pp. 156–172, figs. 1–11; A. Ovadiah, C. G. de Silva, "Supplementum to the Corpus of the Byzantine Churches in the Holy Land," Part I, *Levant* 13 (1981), pp. 200–261, figs.; N. Avigad, "The 'Galilean' Synagogue and its Predecessors," *ASR* (1981), pp. 42–44, figs.; S. Loffreda, "The Late Chronology of the Synagogue of Capernaum," *ASR* (1981), pp. 52–56, fig.; G. Foerster, "Notes on Recent Excavations at Capernaum," *ASR* (1981), pp. 57–59, figs.; M. Avi-Yonah, "Some Comments on the Capernaum Excavations," *ASR* (1981), pp. 60–62.

Carmel, Mount

E. Wreschner, "Prehistoric Rock-Engravings in Nahal ha-Mea'rot, Mount Carmel," *IEJ* 21:4 (1971), pp. 217–218, fig. 1, pls. 46–47; T. Noy, E. Higgs, "Raqefet Cave," *IEJ* 21:4 (1971), pp. 225–226; A. Ronen, "Tirat-Carmel," *IEJ* 21:4 (1971), p. 226; A. Ronen, D. Gil'ad, "The Tannur Cave on Mount Carmel," *Qad.* 8:1 (1975), pp. 18–20, figs. (Hebrew); O. Bar-Yosef, "Abu Uṣba Cave," *EAEHL* I (1975), pp. 13–14, figs.; T. Noy, E. Wreschner, "Carmel Caves," *EAEHL* I (1975), pp. 290–298, figs.; M. Stekelis, "Kebara Cave," *EAEHL* III (1977), pp. 699–702, figs.; A. J. Jelinek, "A Preliminary Study of Flakes from the Tabun Cave, Mount Carmel," *EI* 13 (1977), pp. 87–96; T. Schick, M. Stekelis, "Mousterian Assemblages in Kebara Cave, Mount Carmel," *EI* 13 (1977), pp. 97–149, pls. 7–8; S. Davis, "The Ungulate Remains from Kebara Cave," *EI* 13 (1977), pp. 150–163; P. Smith, B. Arensburg, "A Mousterian Skeleton from Kebara Cave," *EI* 13 (1977), pp. 164–176; E. E. Wreschner, "Newe Yam — A Submerged Late-Neolithic Settlement near Mount Carmel,"

EI 13 (1977), pp. 259–270; M. W. Prausnitz, "The Pottery at Newe Yam," *EI* 13 (1977), pp. 271–275, pl. 18; O. Bar-Yosef, "Sefunim Caves," *EAEHL* IV (1978), pp. 1050–1051; *id.*, "Shuqba Cave," *EAEHL* IV (1978), pp. 1109–110.

Chorazin, Korazin, Kerazeh

C. Gensburger, "Les Objets du Culte Synagogal," *BTS* 130 (1971), p. 4, fig.; G. Foerster, "Les Synagogues de Galilée," *BTS* 130, April (1971), pp. 8–9, 11, 12, figs.; Z. Yeivin, "Excavations at Khorazin 1962–1964," *EI* 11 (1971), pp. 144–157, figs., pl. (Hebrew); Y. Meshorer, "Coins from the Excavations at Khorazin," *EI* 11 (1973), pp. 158–162 (Hebrew); N. Avigad, Z. Yeivin, "Chorazin," *EAEHL* I (1975), pp. 299–303, figs.; J. Naveh, "Ancient Synagogue Inscriptions," *ASR* (1981), pp. 133–139; Z. Yeivin, "Two Lintels with Menorah Reliefs from Chorazin," *ASR* (1981), pp. 162–163, figs.

Choziba Monastery, see Qelt

Dabbura, Golan

D. Urman, "Jewish Inscriptions from Dabbura in the Golan," *IEJ* 22:1 (1972), pp. 16–23, figs. 1–3, pls. 4–7; V. Corbo, "Scavo della chiesa 'Nemini dixeritis' a Dabburiya," *LA* 28 (1978), pp. 247–251, pls. 77–80; D. Urman, "Jewish Inscriptions from the Village of Dabbura in the Golan," *ASR* (1981), pp. 154–156.

Dalhamiya, Tell, Jordan

H. de Contenson, "Jordan Valley," *EAEHL* III (1977), pp. 656–658, fig.; R. Amiran, "Pottery from the Chalcolithic Site near Tell Delhamiya and Some Notes on the Character of the Chalcolithic Early Bronze I Transition," *EI* 13 (1977), pp. 48–56, Pls. 6–7 (Hebrew).

Dalit, Tell

Excavated by B. Cresson, R. Gophna, 1978–79 for Baylor and Tel Aviv Universities.

B. Cresson, R. Gophna, "Tel Dalit 1978–79," *IEJ* 29:2 (1979), pp. 122–123, pl. 16 a; R. Gophna, B. Cresson, "Tel Dalit, 1978–79," *RB* 86:3 (1979), pp. 459–460, fig. 9, pl. 26 a.

Dâliyah, Wâdî edh-

P. W. and N. L. Lapp, eds., *Discoveries in the Wâdī ed-Dâliyeh, AASOR* 41, (1974), figs., 102 pls.; P. W. Lapp, *The Tale of the Tell*, N. L. Lapp, ed., (1975), pp. 66–76, pls.; R. T. Schaub, Review of P. W. and N. L. Lapp, eds., *Discoveries in the Wâdī ed-Dâliyeh, AASOR* 41, 1974, *BASOR* 226 (1977), p. 75–77; P. W. Lapp, "Bedouin Find Papyri Three Centuries Older than Dead Sea Scrolls," *BAR* 4:1 (1978), pp. 16–24, figs.; F. M. Cross, "The Historical Importance of the Samaria Papyri," *BAR* 4:1 (1978), pp. 25–27, figs., M. Avi-Yonah, "Shinjeh Cave," *EAEHL* IV (1978), p. 1111, fig. on p. 1110.

Damiya

J. Undeland, "A Cultic Slab at Damiya," *ADAJ* 18 (1973), pp. 55–59, figs. 1–3, pls. 34–35:1.

Dan, Laish

Excavated 1975–1980 by A. Biran for the Nelson Glueck School of Biblical Archaeology HUC, Israel Dept. of Antiquities and Museums, Harvard Semitic Museum.

A. Malamat, "Laish," *IEJ* 21:1 (1971), pp. 35–36; A. Biran, "Tel Dan," *RB* 78:3 (1971), pp. 415–418, pls. 14 b–15; *id.*, "Tel Dan," *IEJ* 22:2–3 (1972), pp. 164–166, fig. 1; *id.*, "Tel Dan," *IEJ* 23:2 (1973), pp. 110–112, pl. 27; *id.*, "Tel Dan," *RB* 80:4 (1973), pp. 563–566, pl. 23 a; *id.*, "Tel Dan," *BA* 37:2 (1974), pp. 25–51, figs. 1–24; *id.*, "An Israelite Horned Altar at Dan," *BA* 37:4 (1974), pp. 106–107, fig. 15; *id.*, "Tel Dan," *IEJ* 24:3–4 (1974), pp. 262–264, pl. 56; *id.*, "Tel Dan," *RB* 82:4 (1975), pp. 562–566, pls. 44–45.

A. Biran, "Dan, Tel," *EAEHL* I (1975), pp. 276, 313–321, figs.; *id.*, "Tell Dan 1975," *IEJ* 26:1 (1976), pp. 54–55, pl. 12; *id.*, "Tel Dan," *RB* 83:2 (1976), pp. 278–281, pl. 37; *id.*, "Tel Dan 1976," *IEJ* 26:4 (1976), pp. 202–206, fig. 1, pl. 35; *id.*, "Dan," *IDB-S* (1976), p. 205; *id.*, "Tel Dan 1977," *IEJ* 27:4 (1977), pp. 242–246, pl. 37 a–d; *id.*, "Tel Dan," *RB* 84:2 (1977), pp. 256–263, pls. 5–7 a; P. Wapnish, B. Hesse, A. Ogilvy, "The 1974 Collection of Faunal Remains from Tell Dan," *BASOR* 227 (1977), pp. 35–62, figs. 1–42; A. Biran, V. Tsaferis, "A Bilingual Dedicatory Inscription from Tel Dan," *Qad.* 10:4 (1977), pp. 114–115, figs. (Hebrew); A. Biran, "Tel Dan 1977," *RB* 85:3 (1978), pp. 402, 404–408, figs. 2–3, pl. 21 a; *id.*, "Tel Dan 1978," *IEJ* 28:4 (1978), pp. 268–271, pl. 53; A. Ben-Tor, *Cylinder Seals of Third Millennium Palestine, BASOR Suppl.* 22 (1978), pp. 5–8, 10, 11, 102, 103, 106; A. Biran, "Tel Dan 1978," *RB* 86:1 (1979), pp. 107–109; A. Biran, "Two Discoveries at Tel Dan," *IEJ* 30:1–2 (1980), pp. 89–98, figs. 1–8, pls. 5–8; *id.*, "Tell Dan," *BA* 43:3 (1980), pp. 168–182, figs.; *id.*, "The Discovery of the Middle Bronze Age Gate at Dan," *BA* 44:3 (1981), pp. 139–144, figs.

J. C. H. Laughlin, "The Remarkable Discoveries at Tel Dan," *BAR* 7:5 (1981), pp. 20–37, figs.

Dananir, Khirbet Umm ad-

P. McGovern, "Baq'ah Valley Project 1980," *BA* 44:2 (1981), pp. 126–128, figs.

Dardara, Golan

D. Urman, "Dardara," *EAEHL* II (1976), p. 466.

David, Naḥal

N. Avigad, "Judean Desert Caves, Naḥal David," *EAEHL* III (1977), pp. 666–668, 670, fig.

Dead Sea Scrolls, see Qumran

Debir, see Tell Beit Mirsim; see Rabud, Khirbet

Degania

M. Kochavi, "A Built Shaft-Tomb of the Middle Bronze Age I at Degania A," *Qad.* 6:2 (1973), pp. 50–52, figs. (Hebrew).

Deir 'Alla, Tell

Excavated 1976–1978 by H. J. Franken, M. M. Ibrahim, 1979 by M. M. Ibrahim, G. van der Kooij for the Jordan Dept. of Antiquities, and University of Leiden.

H. J. Franken, "Deir 'Alla, Tell," *EAEHL* I (1975), pp. 321–324, figs.; J. A. Sauer, "Pottery Techniques at Tell Deir 'Allā," Review of H. J. Franken, J. Kalsbeek, *Potters of a Medieval village in the Jordan Valley* 1975, *BASOR* 224 (1976), pp. 91–94; J. Hoftijzer, "The Prophet Balaam in a 6th Century Aramaic Inscription," *BA* 39:1 (1976), pp. 11–17, fig.; H. J.

Franken, M. M. Ibrahim, "Two Seasons of Excavations at Tell Deir 'Alla 1976–78," *ADAJ* 22 (1977–78), pp. 57–80, figs. 1–14, pls. 26–42; J. B. Segal, Review of J. Hoftijzer, G. van der Kooij, eds., *Aramaic Texts from Deir 'Alla* 1976, *PEQ* 110:1 (1978), p. 69; J. Naveh, Review of J. Hoftijzer, G. van der Kooij, eds., *Aramaic Texts from Deir 'Alla* 1976, *IEJ* 29:2 (1979), pp. 133–136; S. Abbadi, "Ein neues ammonitisches Siegel," *ZDPV* 95:1 (1979), pp. 36–38, fig. 1, pl. 4; G. van der Kooij, M. M. Ibrahim, "Excavations at Tell Deir 'Alla, Season 1979," *ADAJ* 23 (1979), pp. 41–50, figs. 1–3, pls. 10–31; M. Dahood, Review of J. Hoftijzer, G. van der Kooij, eds., *Aramic Texts from Deir 'Alla* 1976, *Biblica* 62:1 (1981), pp. 124–127.

Deir 'Aziz

D. Urman, "Deir 'Aziz," *EAEHL* II (1976), p. 466, fig.

Deir el-Balaḥ, near Gaza

Excavated by T. Dothan 1972, 1977–78, 1981 for the Hebrew University.

T. Dothan, "Anthropoid Clay Coffins from a Late Bronze Age Cemetery near Deir el-Balaḥ (Preliminary Report 1)," *IEJ* 22:2–3 (1972), pp. 65–72, figs. 1–2, pls. 9–13; *id.* "The Cemetery near Deir el-Balah and Burial in Anthropoid Sarcophagi in Eretz-Israel," *Qad.* 5:1 (1972), pp. 21–25, figs. (Hebrew); T. Dothan, Y. Beit-Arieh, "Rescue Excavations at Deir el-Balah," *Qad.* 5:1 (1972), p. 26, figs. (Hebrew); T. Dothan, "Anthropoid Clay Coffins from a Late Bronze Age Cemetery near Deir el-Balaḥ, (Preliminary Report 2)," *IEJ* 23:3 (1973), pp. 129–146, fig. 1, pls. 33–45; I. Perlman, F. Asaro, T. Dothan, "Provenance of the Deir el-Balaḥ Coffins," *IEJ* 23:3 (1973), pp. 147–151; T. Dothan, "Deir el-Balaḥ," *EAEHL* I (1975), pp. 324–328, figs.; R. Giveon, "Egyptian Finger Rings and Seals from South of Gaza," *TA* 4:1–2 (1977), pp. 66–70, fig. 1, pls. 3–4; T. Dothan, "Deir el-Balaḥ 1977–1978," *IEJ* 28:4 (1978), pp. 266–267; *id.*, *Excavations at the Cemetery of Deir el-Balaḥ, Qedem* 10 (1979).

Deir Wâdî el-Qelt Monastery, see Qelt

Dhahrat el-Humraiya

J. M. Weinstein, "Egyptian Relations with Palestine in the Middle Kingdom," *BASOR* 217 (1975), pp. 1–16, figs. 1–3.

Dhahr Mirzbâneh

E. M. Meyers, "Secondary Burials in Palestine," *BA* 33:1 (1970), pp. 1–29, figs. 1–14; W. G. Dever, "Middle Bronze Age I Cemeteries at Mirzbâneh and 'Ain-Sâmiya," *IEJ* 22:2–3 (1972), pp. 95–112, figs. 1–7; P. W. Lapp, *The Tale of the Tell*, N. L. Lapp, ed., (1975), pp. 77–82, pls.; Z. Yeivin, "Ein Samiya and Dhahr Mirzbaneh," *EAEHL* II (1976), pp. 357–358, figs.

Dhahr Mirzbâneh, see Sâmiyeh, 'Ain es-

Dhobai, Wâdî

E. Yeivin, "Dhobai, Wâdî," *EAEHL* I (1975), p. 329.

Dhra'

C.-M. Bennett, "Soundings at Dhra' Jordan," *Levant* 12 (1980), pp. 30–39, figs. 1–8, pl. 7; T. D. Raikes, "Notes on Some Neolithic and Later Sites in Wadi Araba and the Dead Sea Valley," *Levant* 12 (1980), pp. 40–60, figs. 1–16.

Dibôn, Dhībân

S. Ahituv, "Did Ramesses II Conquer Dibon?" *IEJ* 22:2–3 (1972), pp. 141–142; A. D. Tushingham, *The Excavations at Dibon (Dhībân) in Moab, The Third Campaign 1952–53, AASOR* 40 (1972); J. M. Miller, "The Moabite Stone as a Memorial Stela," *PEQ* 106:1 (1974), pp. 9–18; J. A. Sauer, Review of *The Excavations at Dibon (Dhiban) in Moab* 1972, *ADAJ* 20 (1975), pp. 103–109; E. Stern, Review of A. D. Tushingham, *The Excavations at Dibon (Dhibân) in Moab, The Third Campaign 1952–53, AASOR* 40 (1972), *IEJ* 25:1–3 (1975), pp. 179–181; A. D. Tushingham, "Dibon," *EAEHL* I (1975), pp. 330–333; C.-M. Bennett, "Some Reflections on Neo-Assyrian Influence in Transjordan," *Archaeology in the Levant* (1978), pp. 164–171, figs. 1–4.

Dikkeh, el-

M. Avi-Yonah, "Synagogues," *EAEHL* IV (1978), pp. 1129–1138, figs.

Dor, Khirbet, Jordan

M. Weippert, "Nabatäisch-römische Keramik aus Hirbet Dor im südlichen Jordanien," *ZDPV* 95:1 (1979), pp. 87–110, figs. 1–5.

Dor, Tanturah

Excavated 1980 by E. Stern for the Hebrew University and Israel Exploration Society.

G. Foerster, "Dor," *EAEHL* I (1975), pp. 334–337, figs.; N. Avigad, "The Priest of Dor," *IEJ* 25:2–3 (1975), pp. 101–105, pl. 10 c–d; M. Haran, "A Temple at Dor?" *IEJ* 27:1 (1977), pp. 12–15; A. Raban, "Dor 1977," *RB* 85:3 (1978), pp. 410–412, figs. 4–5; S. Wachsmann, K. Raveh, "Underwater Investigations by the Department of Antiquities and Museums," *IEJ* 28:4 (1978), pp. 281–283, pl. 56; C. M. Dauphin, "Dor Byzantine Church," *IEJ* 29:3–4 (1979), pp. 235–236, pl. 29; E. Stern, "Tel Dor 1980," *IEJ* 30:3–4 (1980), pp. 209–213, figs. 1–2, pl. 26; H. P. Goldfried, "The 1980 Excavations," *AJA* 85:2 (1981), p. 195.

Dothan, Tell

D. Ussishkin, "Dothan," *EAEHL* I (1975), pp. 337–339, figs.; S. W. Helms, "Early Bronze Age Fortifications at Tell Dothan," *Levant* 9 (1977), pp. 101–114, figs. 1–7, pl. 11; J. P. Free, "Dothan," *ISBE* I (1979), pp. 985–986, fig.

Durusiya, Khirbet, see Midras

Duweir, Tell ed-

J. R. Bartlett, "The Seal of *ḤNH* from the Neighbourhood of Tell ed-Duweir," *PEQ* 108:1 (1976), pp. 59–61, pl. 8.

Duweir, Tell ed- , see Lachish

Eboda, see 'Abdah

'Edriya

D. Urman, "'Edriya," *EAEHL* II (1976), p. 466, fig.

Eglon, See Ḥesi, Tell el-

'Einan, see Mallaḥa

Eleutheropolis, see Sandahannah, Tell

'Eli, Tell, 'Ali, Alumoth, Khirbet esh-Sheikh 'Ali

M. W. Prausnitz, "Tell 'Ali," *EAEHL* I (1975), pp. 61–65, figs.

Elusa, see Khalasa

'Emeq, Bet ha-

R. Frankel, A. Kempinski, "Bet ha-'Emeq," *IEJ* 23:4 (1973), pp. 242–243, pl. 66 a.

Emmaus, 'Amwās, Nicopolis

Excavated in 1977 by M. Gichon for Tel Aviv University.

M. Avi-Yonah, "Emmaus," *EAEHL* II (1976), pp. 362–364, figs.; Y. Hirschfeld, "The Roman Byzantine Network of Aqueducts at Emmaus," *Qad.* 9:2–3 (1976), pp. 85–88, figs. (Hebrew); *id.*, "A Hydraulic Installation in the Water-Supply System of Emmaus-Nicopolis," *IEJ* 28:1–2 (1978), pp. 86–92, figs. 1–4, pls. 19–20, 21 a; M. Gichon, "The Roman Bath at Emmaus Excavations in 1977," *IEJ* 29:2 (1979), pp. 101–110, figs. 1–3, pls. 12–13; M. Gichon, "Thermes d'Emmaus 1977–78," *RB* 86:1 (1979), pp. 125–126, pl. 11.

'En Boqeq, Qasr Umm Baghgheq

Excavated by M. Gichon for Tel Aviv University intermittently 1967–1972.

M. Gichon, "Fine Byzantine Wares from the South of Israel," *PEQ* 106:2 (1974), pp. 119–139, figs. 1–11, pls. 19–22; *id.*, "'En Boqeq," *EAEHL* II (1976), pp. 365–370, figs.

'En-Gedi, Tell el-Jurn

Excavated 1971–72 by D. Ussishkin for the Hebrew University and Israel Exploration Society.

A. Kempinski, "The Sin Temple at Khafaje and the En-Gedi Temple," *IEJ* 22:1 (1972), pp. 10–15, fig. 1; D. Barag, Y. Porat, "The Second Season of Excavations in the Synagogue at En-Gedi," *Qad.*, 5:2 (1972), pp. 52–54, figs. (Hebrew); D. Barag, Y. Porat, E. Netzer, "En-Gedi," *RB* 79:4 (1972), pp. 581–583, pls. 50 b–52 a, 53 a; D. Barag, Y. Porat, "En-Gedi," *RB* 81:1 (1974), pp. 96–97, pl. 11 b; B. Mazar, "Engaddi," *BTS* 162 (1974), pp. 8–17, figs.; P. Bar-Adon, "An Early Hebrew Graffito in a Judean Desert Cave," *EI* 12 (1975), pp. 77–80, figs. 1–2, pls. 15–17 (Hebrew); *ibid. IEJ* 25:4 (1975), pp. 226–232, figs. 1–2, pl. 25; Y. Rak, B. Arensburg, H. Nathan, "Evidence of Violence on Human Bones in Israel, First and Third Centuries C. E.," *PEQ* 108:1 (1976), pp. 55–58, pls. 6–7; D. Barag, "En-Gedi," *EAEHL* II (1976), pp. 370–380, 396, 448, figs.; D. Ussishkin, "The Ghassulian Shrine at En-gedi," *TA* 7:1 (1980), pp. 1–41, 43–44, figs. 1–13, pls. 1–14; D. Barag, Y. Porat, E. Netzer, "The Synagogue at 'En-Gedi," *ASR* (1981), pp. 116–119, figs.; L. I. Levine, "The Inscription in the 'En-Gedi Synagogue," *ASR* (1981), pp. 140–145, fig.; A. F. Rainey, "En-Gedi," *ISBE* II (1982).

‘En-Gev

Excavated 1978 by G. Martin for the Centre de Recherches Préhistoriques Français de Jérusalem and the Hebrew University.

B. Mazar, "‘En Gev," *EAEHL* II (1976), pp. 381–385, figs.; G. Martin, "‘En Gev III 1978," *IEJ* 28:4 (1978), pp. 262–263; *id.*, "En Gev III (1978)", *RB* 86:1 (1979), pp. 109–110.

‘En ha-Naṣiv

Excavated by Y. Porath 1972 for the Israel Dept. of Antiquities and Museums.

Y. Porath, "‘En Ha-Naṣiv," *IEJ* 23:4 (1973), pp. 259–260.

‘Erani, see ‘Areini

Erez

L. Y. Rahmani, "The Erez Mosaic Pavement," *IEJ* 25:1 (1975), pp. 21–24, pls. 3–4.

Esdar, Tell, Tell Isdar

Y. Aharoni, "Nothing Early and Nothing Late: Rewriting Israel's Conquest," *BA* 39:2 (1976), pp. 55–76, figs. 1–22; M. Kochavi, "Tell Esdar," *EAEHL* IV (1978), pp. 1169–1171, figs.; R. Cohen, "Tell Esdar, Stratum IV," *IEJ* 28:3 (1978), pp. 185–189, fig.

Eshtemo‘a

Excavated 1970 by Z. Yeivin for the Israel Dept. of Antiquities and Museums.

Z. Yeivin, "Es-Samo‘a (As-Samu‘)," *IEJ* 21:2–3 (1971), pp. 174–175; G. Foerster, "Ancient Synagogues in Eretz-Israel," *Qad.* 5:2 (1972), pp. 38–45, figs. (Hebrew); Z. Yeivin, "A Silver Hoard from Eshtemoa," *Qad.* 5:2 (1972), pp. 45–46, figs. (Hebrew); R. Hachlili, "The Niche and the Ark in Ancient Synagogues," *BASOR* 223 (1976), pp. 43–53, figs. 1–13; D. Barag, "Eshtemoa," *EAEHL* II (1976), pp. 386–389, figs.; Z. Yeivin, "The Synagogue of Eshtemoa," *ASR* (1981), pp. 120–122, figs.

Evron

Excavated 1976–77 by M. W. Prausnitz, A. Ronen for the Israel Dept. of Antiquities and Museums.

M. W. Prausnitz, A. Ronen, "Early Acheulian Site in the Evron Quarry," *IEJ* 27:2–3 (1977), pp. 162–163.

Far‘ah, Tell el- (N), Tirzah

S. W. Helms, Review of J. Mallet, *Tell el-Far‘ah (Région de Naplouse), 1973, PEQ* 106:2 (1974), p. 167; J. Mallet, "Tell el-Far‘ah (N) près de Naplouse: Remarques sur la Tombe A et le cylindre-sceau F 140," *RB* 81:3 (1974), pp. 422–431, 1 fig., pl. 23; R. de Vaux, "el-Far‘a, Tell, North," *EAEHL* II (1976), pp. 395–404, figs.; J. Mallet, "Tell el-Far‘ah près de Naplouse, l'empreinte de cylindre-sceau F 3863," *RB* 84:1 (1977) pp. 108–112, pl. 1; A. Ben-Tor, *Cylinder Seals of Third Millennium Palestine, BASOR Suppl.* 22 (1978), pp. 12, 102, 103, 106; H. Seeden, "A Small Clay Shrine in the AUB Museum," *Berytus* 27 (1979), pp. 7–25, 7 pls., esp. p. 25, n. 30, pl. 7:2; M. D. Fowler, "Cultic Continuity at Tirzah? A Re-examination of the Archaeological Evidence," *PEQ* 113:1 (1981), pp. 27–31.

Far'ah, Tell el-(S), Sharuḥen

W. P. Anderson, "Sharuḥen," *HBD* (1973), p. 669; A. Kempinski, "Tell el 'Ajjul-Beth-Aglayim or Sharuḥen?" *IEJ* 24:3–4 (1974), pp. 145–152; E. E. Platt, "Triangular Jewelry Plaques,"*BASOR* 221 (1976), pp. 103–111, figs. 1–6.

Excavated 1976 by R. Cohen for the Israel Dept. of Antiquities and Museums.
R. Cohen, "Tell el-Far'ah (South), *IEJ* 27:2–3 (1977), p. 170.

Site B was explored by D. Price-Williams 1972–1973 and excavated in 1976 for the British Western Negev Expedition, joined in 1976–1977 by I. Gilead, O. Bar-Yosef for Ben-Gurion University of the Negev.
D. Price-Williams, *The Tombs of the Middle Bronze Age II Period from the '500' Cemetery at Tell Fara (South) 1977;* J. F. Ross, Review, *PEQ* 112:1 (1980), pp. 66–67; I. Gilead, O. Bar-Yosef, "Prehistoric Site near Tell el-Far'ah 1977," *IEJ* 27:4 (1977), p. 236.
K. R. Maxwell-Hyslop, T. S. Wheeler, R. Maddin, J. D. Muhly, "An Iron Dagger from Tomb 240 at Tell Fara South," *Levant* 10 (1978), pp. 112–115, pls. 11–14; R. Gophna, "Sharuḥen, Tell," *EAEHL* IV (1978), pp. 1074–1082, figs., "Hazerim by Sharuḥen," p. 1082; K. R. Maxwell-Hyslop, "A Silver Earring from Tell el-Farah (South), *Archaeology in the Levant* (1978), pp. 179b–182, figs. 1–2, pl. 30 on p. 179b; W. H. Shea, "The Conquests of Sharuḥen and Megiddo Reconsidered," *IEJ* 29:1 (1979), pp. 1–5; I. Gilead, "A Middle Paleolithic Open-Air Site Near Tell Far'ah, Western Negev: Preliminary Report," *IEJ* 30:1–2 (1980), pp. 52–62, figs. 1–5, 4 tables; H. Liebowitz, "Military and Feast Scenes on Late Bronze Palestinian Ivories," *IEJ* 30:3–4 (1980), pp. 162–169, figs. 1–2, pl. 18 a–c.

Fiq

M. Avi-Yonah, *Gazetteer of Roman Palestine, Qedem* 5 (1976), p. 29; J. Kaplan, "Fejja," *EAEHL* II (1976), pp. 404–405, fig.; D. Urman, "Golan, Fiq," *EAEHL* II (1976), pp. 466–467, fig.; E. Epstein, "Hippos," *EAEHL* II (1976), pp. 521–523, esp. 523.

Fityan, Khirbet el-

S. T. Parker, "The Central Limes Arabicus Project: The 1980 Campaign," *ASOR Newsletter* 8 (June, 1981), pp. 8–20, figs.

Gadara, see Umm Qeis.

Gamla, Gamala Territory

Excavated 1976–78 by S. Guttman.
D. Urman, "Golan, Gamala," *EAEHL* II (1976), p. 457; E. M. Meyers, J. F. Strange, D. E. Groh, "The Meiron Excavation Project: Archaeological Survey in Galilee and Golan, 1976," *BASOR* 230 (1978), pp. 1–24, esp. pp. 2, 7; S. Guttman, H. Shanks, "Gamla, the Masada of the North," *BAR* 5:1 (1979), pp. 12–19, figs.; F. Josephus, "The Fall of Gamla," *BAR* 5:1 (1979), pp. 20–27, figs.; S. Guttman, "The Synagogue at Gamla," *ASR* (1981), pp. 30–34, figs.; Z. Ma'oz, "The Synagogue of Gamla and the Typology of Second-Temple Synagogues," *ASR* (1981), pp. 35–41, figs.

Gath, see 'Areini, Tell esh-Sheikh Aḥmed el-, see Safi

Gaza, Maiumas, Neapolis, Constantia

M. Barasch, "The David Mosaic at Gaza," *EI* 10 (1971), pp. 94–99; F. Vitto, "Région de Gaza," *RB* 82:2 (1975), pp. 240–245; E. Stern, "A Group of Cypriot Limestone Sculptures from the Gaza Region," *Levant* 7 (1975), pp. 104–107, fig. 1, pls. 19–20; A. Ovadiah, "Les Mosaïstes de Gaza dans l'antiquité chrétienne," *RB* 82:4 (1975), pp. 552–557, pls. 38–40; M. Avi-Yonah, "The Gaza School of Mosaicists in the Fifth-Sixth Centuries C. E.," *EI* 12 (1975), pp. 191–193, pls. 37–38 (Hebrew); A. Ovadiah, "Gaza," *EAEHL* II (1976), pp. 408–417, figs.; *id.*, "Gaza Maiumas, 1976," *IEJ* 27:2–3 (1977), pp. 176–178, fig. 1, pl. 24 b–c; *id.*, "Gaza Maiumas," *RB* 84:3 (1977), pp. 418–422, fig. 8, pl. 26; *id.*, "The Synagogue at Gaza," *ASR* (1981), pp. 129–132, figs., pl. 3; T. Watkins, "Levantine Bronzes from the Collections of the Rev. William Greenwell, now in the British Museum," *Levant* 13 (1981), pp. 119–155, figs. 1–12; A. F. Rainey, *ISBE* II (1982).

Gemme, see Jemmeh, Tell

Gerizim, Mount, Tell er-Râs

R. J. Bull, "A Tripartite Sundial from Tell er-Râs on Mt. Gerizim," *BASOR* 219 (1975), pp. 29–37, 6 figs., 4 pls.; *id.*, "Er-Ras, Tell, Mount Gerizim," *EAEHL* IV (1978), pp. 1015–1022, figs.; R. T. Anderson, "Mount Gerizim: Navel of the World," *BA* 43:4 (1980), pp. 217–221, figs.; J. Wilkinson, "Architectural Procedures in Byzantine Palestine," *Levant* 13 (1981), pp. 156–172, figs. 1–11.

Gezer

W. G. Dever et al., "Further Excavations at Gezer 1967–1971," *BA* 34:4 (1971), pp. 93–132, figs. 1–16; *id.*, "Gezer," *RB* 78:3 (1971), pp. 425–428, pls. 19–20 a;

Excavations continued 1972–73 by J. D. Seger for HUC, Jerusalem.

J. D. Seger, "Newly Discovered Burial Caves at Gezer," *Qad.* 5:1 (1972), pp. 15–18, figs. (Hebrew); R. Giveon, "An Egyptian Official in Gezer?" *IEJ* 22:2–3 (1972), pp. 143–144; W. G. Dever, "Tel Gezer," *IEJ* 22:2–3 (1972), pp. 158–160, pl. 28; J. D. Seger, "Gezer," *IEJ* 22:2–3 (1972), pp. 160–161; W. G. Dever, "Gezer," *RB* 79:3 (1972), pp. 413–418, pl. 39; J. D. Seger, "Tel Gezer," *IEJ* 22:4 (1972), pp. 240–242, pl. 54; Y. Yadin, *Hazor*, Schweich Lectures (1972), pp. 147–150; W. G. Dever, "The Gezer Fortifications and the 'High Place': An Illustration of Stratigraphic Methods and Problems," *PEQ* 105:1 (1973), pp. 61–70, figs. 1–3; K. M. Kenyon, Review of W. G. Dever, H. D. Lance, G. E. Wright, *Gezer I, 1970, PEQ* 105:2 (1973), pp. 170–171; W. G. Dever, "Tower 5017 at Gezer: A Rejoinder," *IEJ* 23:1 (1973), pp. 23–26, fig. 1; J. D Seger, "Tell Gezer," *RB* 80:3 (1973), pp. 408–412, pls. 14–15; *id.*, "Tel Gezer," *IEJ* 23:4 (1973), pp. 247–251, pl. 68 a–b; M. Hughes, Report on Gezer Dagger Found in 1934, *PEQ* 106:1 (1974), pp. 2–3; J. D. Seger, "Tel Gezer," *IEJ* 24:2 (1974), pp. 134–135; J. M. Weinstein, "A Statuette of the Princess Sobeknefru at Tell Gezer," *BASOR* 213 (1974), pp. 49–57, figs. 1–2; W. G. Dever et al., *Gezer* II (1974).

J. D. Seger, "Tell Gezer," *RB* 82:1 (1975), pp. 87–92, pls. 4–5, 9 a; *id.*, "The MB II Fortifications at Shechem and Gezer: A Hyksos Retrospective," *EI* 12 (1975), pp. 34–45, figs. 1–4, table; J. M. Weinstein, "Egyptian Relations with Palestine in the Middle Kingdom," *BASOR* 217 (1975), pp. 1–16, figs. 1–3; C. Graesser, Jr., "The Seal of Elijah," *BASOR* 220 (1975), pp. 63–66, figs. 1–4; A. Kempinski, Review of W. G. Dever et al., *Gezer II 1974, IEJ* 26:4 (1976), pp. 210–214; J. D. Seger, "The Search for Maccabean Gezer," *BA* 39:4 (1976), pp. 142–144, figs. 1–3; *id.*, "Reflections on the Gold Hoard from Gezer," *BASOR* 221 (1976), pp. 133–140, figs. 1–3.

W. G. Dever, "Gezer," *IDB-S* (1976), pp. 361–363, figs., *idem*, "Archaeology," pp. 44–52; *id.*, "Gezer," *EAEHL* II (1976), pp. 428–443, figs.; A. Ben-Tor, "Cult Scenes on Early Bronze Age Cylinder Seal Impressions from Palestine," *Levant* 9 (1977), pp. 90–100, figs. 1–28; R. Gophna, "An Early Bronze Age Cylinder-Seal from Gezer," *EI* 13 (1977), pp. 82–86 (Hebrew); K. M. Kenyon, Review of W. G. Dever et al., *Gezer II 1974, PEQ* 109:1 (1977), pp.

55–58; J. A. Callaway, Review of W. G. Dever et al., *Gezer II 1974*, *JBL* 96:2 (1977), pp. 279–281.

S. Izre'el, "Two Notes on the Gezer-Amarna Tablets," *TA* 4:3–4 (1977), pp. 159–167, pl. 18:5; E. E. Platt, "Bone Pendants," *BA* 41:1 (1978), pp. 23–28, figs.; C. M. Kraay, "Some Notes on the Abu Shusheh 'Hoard'," *IEJ* 28:3 (1978), pp. 190–192, pls. 29–30.

A. Ben-Tor, *Cylinder Seals of Third Millennium Palestine, BASOR Suppl.* 22 (1978), pp. 4, 11, 102, 103, 108; J. A. Sauer, "A Review of *Gezer II (HUC)*," *BASOR* 233 (1979), pp. 70–74; L. Y. Rahmani, "Palestinian Incense Burners of the Sixth to Eighth Centuries C. E.," *IEJ* 30:1–2 (1980), pp. 116–122, figs. 1–3, pls. 12–13; D. Cole, "How Water Tunnels Worked," *BAR* 6:2 (1980), pp. 8–29, figs.; P. Albenda, "Syrian Palestinian Cities on Stone," *BA* 43:4 (1980), pp. 222–229, figs.; J. N. Tubb, "A Bronze Arrowhead with Engraved Mark from Gezer in the British Museum Collection," *PEQ* 112:1 (1980), pp. 1–6, figs. 1–6, pl. 1; T. Watkins, "Levantine Bronzes from the Collections of the Rev. William Greenwell Now in the British Museum," *Levant* 13 (1981), pp. 119–155, figs. 1–12; A. F. Rainey, "Gezer," *ISBE* II (1982).

Ghadyan, 'Ain, see Yotvata

Ghassul, Teleilat el-

C. Elliott, "The Religious Beliefs of the Ghassulians c. 4000–3100 B. C.," *PEQ* 109:1 (1977), pp. 3–25, figs. 1–6, 2 tables; J. R. Lee, "Tuleilat el-Ghassul," *EAEHL* IV (1978), pp. 1205–1213, figs.; C. Elliott, "The Ghassulian Culture in Palestine: Origins, Influences, and Abandonment," *Levant* 10 (1978), pp. 37–54, figs. 1–6.

Ghazal

H. Kurdi, "A Brief Note on a Bronze Bowl and a Fibula from a Tomb in Ain Ghazal (Madaba Region, Jordan)," *ADAJ* 17 (1972), pp. 91–92, pls. 1–2.

Ghuweir, 'Ain el-

Excavated 1969 by P. Bar-Adon for the Hebrew University, the Israel Exploration Society and Dept. of Antiquities and Museums.

P. Bar-Adon, "Another Settlement of the Judean Desert Sect at 'Ain el-Ghuweir on the Dead Sea," *EI* 10 (1971), pp. 72–89, figs. 1–12, pls. 47–50 (Hebrew); *id.*, "Another Settlement of the Judean Desert Sect at 'En el-Ghuweir on the Shores of the Dead Sea," *BASOR* 227 (1977), pp. 1–25, figs. 1–24.

Gibeah, Tell el-Fûl

A. Demsky, "Geba, Gibeah, and Gibeon," *BASOR* 212 (1973), pp. 26–31; N. L. Lapp, "Casemate Walls in Palestine and the Late Iron II Casemate at Tell el-Fûl (Gibeah)," *BASOR* 223 (1976), pp. 25–42, figs. 1–12; L. A. Sinclair, "Gibeah," *EAEHL* II (1976), pp. 444–446, figs.; C. Graesser, Jr., "Gibeah," *IDB-S* (1976), pp. 363–364.

Gibeon, el-Jib

A. Demsky, "Geba, Gibeah, and Gibeon," *BASOR* 212 (1973), pp. 26–31; F. S. Frick, "Another Inscribed Jar Handle from el-Jîb," *BASOR* 213 (1974), pp. 46–48, 2 figs.; R. Amiran, "A Note on the 'Gibeon' Jar," *PEQ* 107:2 (1975), pp. 129–132, figs. 1–2, pl. 11; B. Bagatti, "L'edificio ecclesiastico di el-Gib (Gibeon)," *LA* 25 (1975), pp. 54–72, pls. 29–40; J. B. Pritchard, "Gibeon," *EAEHL* II (1976), pp. 446–447, 449–450, figs.; D. Cole, "How Water Tunnels Worked," *BAR* 6:2 (1980), pp. 8–29, figs.

Gil 'adi, Kefar

J. Kaplan, "Kefar Gil'adi," *EAEHL* III (1977), pp. 708–709, figs.

Gilat

Excavated by D. Alon for the Israel Dept. of Antiquities and Museums 1976.

D. Alon, "A Chalcolithic Temple at Gilat," *Qad.* 9:4 (1976), pp. 102–105, figs. (Hebrew); D. Saltz, "Gilat," *ASOR Newsletter* 10 (May 1977), pp. 11–12, fig.; D. Alon, "A Chalcolithic Temple at Gilath," *BA* 40:2 (1977), pp. 63–65, figs.

Gilgal

T. Noy, "Gilgal," *IEJ* 26:1 (1976), p. 48; *id.*, "Gilgal 1-A PrePottery Neolithic A Site in the Southern Jordan Valley," *Qad.* 10:2–3 (1977), pp. 60–61, figs. (Hebrew); T. Noy, J. Schuldenrein, E. Tchernov, "Gilgal, A Pre-pottery Neolithic A Site in the Lower Jordan Valley," *IEJ* 30:1–2 (1980), pp. 63–82, figs. 1–4, 5 tables, pls. 3–4.

Giscala, see Jish, el-

Giv'at ha-Parsa

Y. Olami, F. Burian, E. Friedman, "Giv'at ha-Parsa — A Neolithic Site in the Coastal Region," *EI* 13 (1977), pp. 34–47, pls. 1–5 (Hebrew).

Giv'at Sharett, see Beth-shemesh

Gush Ḥalav, see Jish, el-

Haditha

M. Avi-Yonah, "The Haditha Mosaic Pavement," *IEJ* 22:2–3 (1972), pp. 118–122, pls. 20–23; *idem, EI* 11 (1973), pp. 45–47 (Hebrew).

Haggag

A. Negev, "Inscriptions on Rock No. 5 in Wadi Haggag, Sinai," *EI* 12 (1975), pp. 132–141, figs. 1–3, pls. 28–30 (Hebrew); *id.* "The Inscriptions of Wadi Haggag, Sinai," *Qedem* 6 (1977).

Haifa

Excavated 1972–73 by M.W. Prausnitz for the University of Haifa, Israel Dept. of Antiquities and Museums.

M.W. Prausnitz, "Romema (Haifa)," *IEJ* 22:4 (1972), pp. 246–247; *idem, IEJ* 24:2 (1974), pp. 142–143, pl. 23 c; G. Foerster, "Some Menorah Reliefs from Galilee," *IEJ* 24:3–4 (1973), pp. 191–196, fig., pls. 39 b–41.

Haiyan, Khirbet see 'Ai

A. Ovadiah, C.G. de Silva, "Supplementum to the Corpus of the Byzantine Churches in the Holy Land," *Levant* 13 (1981), pp. 200–261, figs., esp. p. 235.

Hajar, Umm el-

Excavated by A. Biran et al., for the Israel Dept. of Antiquities and Museums.

A. Biran, "Tell er-Ruqeish to Tell er-Ridan," *IEJ* 24:2 (1974), pp. 141–142, pls. 24–25.

Ḥajjar, Khirbet el-

Excavated by H.O. Thompson 1972 for the American Center of Oriental Research, and the Jordan Dept. of Antiquities.

M.M. Ibrahim, "Two Ammonite Statuettes from Khirbet el-Ḥajjar," *ADAJ* 16 (1971), pp. 91–97, pls. 1–3; H.O. Thompson, "The 1972 Excavation of Khirbet el-Ḥajjar," *ADAJ* 17 (1972), pp. 47–72, pls. 1–11; *id.* "Khirbet el-Ḥajjar (Jordanie)," *RB* 81:1 (1974), pp. 77–80, pl. 5; *id.*, "The Ammonite Remains at Khirbet al-Ḥajjar," *BASOR* 227 (1977), pp. 27–34, figs. 1–4.

Ḥalif, Tell, Lahav

Excavated 1976–80 by J.D. Seger for the Albright Institute of Archaeological Research, University of Nebraska, Washington State University, N.G. School of Bib. Arch. HUC, Israel Dept. of Antiquities and Museums.

R. Gophna, "Kibboutz Lahav," *RB* 77:4 (1970), p. 578, pl. 41 a; J.D. Seger, "Tell Ḥalif (Lahav)," *IEJ* 22:2–3 (1972), p. 161; *id.*, "Lahav," *RB* 79:4 (1972), p. 585; R. Gophna, "Egyptian Immigration into Southern Canaan during the First Dynasty?" *TA* 3:1 (1976), pp. 31–37, fig. 1–3; J. D. Seger, "Tel Ḥalif (Lahav) 1976," *IEJ* 27:1 (1977), pp. 45–47, pl. 5 b-d; O. Borowski, "A Corinthian Lamp at Tell Ḥalif," *BASOR* 227 (1977), pp. 63–65, figs. 1–2; J.D. Seger, "Tell Ḥalif (Lahav)," *RB* 84:3 (1977), pp. 393–398, fig. 2, pls. 15–16; *id.*, "Tel Ḥalif: The 1977 Season," *ASOR Newsletter* 3 (Nov. 1977), pp. 1–4, figs.; J.D. Seger, O. Borowski, "The First Two Seasons at Tell Halif," *BA* 40:4 (1977), pp. 156–166, figs.; D.P. Cole, "Tell Ḥalif (Lahav) 1977," *IEJ* 28:1–2 (1978), pp. 119–121, fig. 1, pl. 24 a-b; J.D. Seger, "Tell Ḥalif 1977," *RB* 85:3 (1978), pp. 423–425, fig. 13, pls. 26–27; W.H. Shea, "The Inscribed Late Bronze Jar Handle from Tell Ḥalif," *BASOR* 232 (1978), pp. 78–80, figs. 1–3; J.D. Seger, "Tel Ḥalif (Lahav) 1979," *IEJ* 29:3–4 (1979), pp. 247–249, pls. 30 c-e, 31; *id.*, "Tell Ḥalif 1980," *IEJ* 30:3–4 (1980), pp. 223–226, pl. 30; D.P. Cole, "Tel Halif (Lahav) Israel 1980," *AJA* 85:2 (1981), p. 190; J.D. Seger, "Lahav Research Project: Excavations at Tell Ḥalif 1980," *BA* 44:3 (1981), pp. 183–186, figs.

Ḥaluza, see Khalasa

Ḥamadiya

J. Kaplan, "Ḥamadiya," *EAEHL* II (1976), pp. 468–469, figs.

Hammam 'Afrā

B. MacDonald, "The Hermitage of John the Abbot at Hammam 'Afrā, Southern Jordan," *LA* 30 (1980), pp. 351–364, figs. 59–70; *id.*, "The Wadi el-Ḥasa Survey: Fall, 1979," *ASOR Newsletter* 3 (Dec. 1980), pp. 5–7, 10–12, figs. 1–4.

Ḥammat-Gader, see Ḥammeh, Tell el-

Ḥammath near Tiberias

Excavated 1970 by E. Oren for the Israel Dept. of Antiquities and Museums.

E. Oren, "Ganei-Hamat (Tiberiade), *RB* 78:3 (1971), pp. 435–437, pls. 21 b, 23; *id.*, "Tiberias" (Hammat), *IEJ* 21:4 (1971), pp. 234–235; M. Avi-Yonah, "Hammath near Tiberias," *Gazetteer of Roman Palestine, Qedem* 5 (1976), p. 64; M. Dothan, "Tiberias, Hammath," *EAEHL* IV (1978), pp. 1178–1184, figs.; *id.*, "The Synagogue at Ḥammath-Tiberias," *ASR* (1981), pp. 63–69, figs.

Ḥammeh, Tell el-, Emmath, see also Umm Qeis

Excavated 1979–1980 by Y. Hirschfeld, G. Solar for the Hebrew University, and Israel Dept. of Antiquities and Museums.

M. Avi-Yonah, "Emmatha," *Gazetteer of Roman Palestine, Qedem* 5 (1976), p. 54; *id.*, "Ḥammat Gader," *EAEHL* II (1976), pp. 469–473, figs.; Y. Hirschfeld, G. Solar, "Ḥammat Gader (el-Ḥamma), Roman Thermae," *IEJ* 29:3–4, pp. 230–234, fig. 1, pl. a, b, d; Y. Hirschfeld, G. Solar, "The Roman Thermae at Ḥammath-Gader: Three Seasons of Excavations," *Qad.* 13:3–4 (1980), pp. 66–79, figs.; J. Naveh, Ancient Synagogue Inscriptions," *ASR* (1981), pp. 133–139, figs., esp. p. 138, fig.

Ḥanita

M. Barasch, "Animal Imagery in the Ḥanita Mosaics," *IEJ* 24:3–4 (1974), pp. 222–226, figs. 1–2, pl. 49; *id.*, "An Early Byzantine Relief at Ḥanita," *EI* 12 (1975), pp. 186–190, pls. 35–36 (Hebrew); D. Barag, *Ḥanita, Tomb XV: A Tomb of the Third and Early Fourth Century C.E., 'Atiqot* 13 (1978).

Ḥarif

A.E. Marks et al., "Prehistoric Sites near Har Harif, *IEJ* 22:2–3 (1972), pp. 73–85, figs. 1–7.

Haror, Tell

Y. Aharoni, "Tell Haror," *EI* 13 (1977), pp. 106–107, pl. 13 (Hebrew).

Harra Region, Jordan

V.A. Clark, "New Epigraphical Material from the Harra Region of Jordan," *ADAJ* 21 (1976), pp. 113–117, figs. 1–3.

Ḥatira

Excavated 1972 by Z. Meshel, R. Cohen for Tel Aviv University, Israel Dept. of Antiquities and Museums.

Z. Meshel, R. Cohen, "Refed and Ḥatira: Two Iron Age Fortresses in the Northern Negev," *TA* 7:1–2 (1980), pp. 70–81, figs. 1–5, pls. 24–27.

Hazerim, see Far'ah (S), Tell el-

Ḥazon, Ḥorvat

D. Bahat, "A Roof Tile of the Legio VI Ferrata and Pottery Vessels from Ḥorvat Ḥazon," *IEJ* 24:3–4 (1974), pp. 160–169, figs. 1–5, pl. 30 a-b.

Hazor

K.M. Kenyon, *Royal Cities of the Old Testament* (1971), pp. 53–58, 105–110, 127–128, figs. pls.; A. Malamat, "Hazor," *IEJ* 21:1 (1971), pp. 36–37; Y. Yadin, Y. Shiloh, "Hazor," *IEJ* 21:4 (1971), p. 230; *id.*, "Haṣor," *RB* 78:4 (1971), pp. 584–585, pl. 27a; Y. Yadin, *Hazor*, Schweich Lectures, (1972); H. Shanks, "An Incised Handle from Hazor Depicting a Syro-Hittite Deity," *IEJ* 23:4 (1973), pp. 234–235, pl. 63 c; Y. Yadin, "Haçor," *BTS* 156 (1973), pp. 8–14, figs.; *id.*, "The 1968–1969 Seasons of Excavations at Hazor," *EI* 11 (1973), pp. 134–143 (Hebrew); R. Reich, "The Persian Building at Ayyelet ha-Shaḥar: The Assyrian Palace at Hazor?" *IEJ* 25:4 (1975), pp. 233–237, figs. 1–2; Y. Yadin, *Hazor: The Rediscovery of a Great Citadel of the Bible* (1975); K.M. Kenyon, Review of Y. Yadin, *Hazor*, Schweich Lectures, 1972, *PEQ* 107:2 (1975), pp. 167–169; Y. Yadin, "Hazor," *IDB-S* (1976), pp. 387–391, figs.; *id.*, "Hazor," *EAEHL* II (1976), pp. 474–482, 485–495, figs.; W.W. Hallo, H. Tadmor, "A Lawsuit from Hazor," *IEJ* 27:1 (1977), pp. 1–11, fig. 1, pl. 1; J.M. Matthews, Review of Y. Yadin, *Hazor, The Rediscovery of a Great Citadel of the Bible*, 1975, *PEQ* 109:1 (1977), p. 68; H. Tadmor, "A Lexicographical Text from Hazor," *IEJ* 27:2–3 (1977), pp. 98–102, pl. 13; A. Ben-Tor, *Cylinder Seals of Third Millennium Palestine, BASOR Suppl.* 22 (1978), pp. 3, 7, 9, 10, 102, 103; D. Cole, "How Water Tunnels Worked," *BAR* 6:2 (1980), pp. 8–29, figs.; G.R.H. Wright, Review of M. Ottoson, *Temples and Cult Places in Palestine, 1980, PEQ* 113:1 (1981), pp. 69–70; A. F. Rainey, "Hazor," *ISBE* II (1982).

Hazorea, see Qiri, Tell

Hebron Area

N. Avigad, "Two Hebrew Inscriptions on Wine Jars," *IEJ* 22:1 (1972), pp. 1–9, figs. 1–4, pls. 1–3; D. Barag, "An Aramaic Synagogue Inscription from the Hebron Area," *IEJ* 22:2–3 (1972), pp. 147–149, fig. 1, pl. 24; A. Demsky, "Dark Wine from Judah," *IEJ* 22:4 (1972), pp. 233–234; R.R. Stieglitz, "The Seal of Ma'aseyahu," *IEJ* 23:4 (1973), pp. 236–237, pl. 63 d; W.G. Dever, M. Tadmor, "A Copper Hoard of the Middle Bronze Age I," *IEJ* 26:4 (1976), pp. 163–169, fig. table, pl. 30.

Ḥederah, Ḥadera

Y. Yadin, "Ḥederah," *EAEHL* II (1976), p. 496, fig.; A. Ronen, D. Kaufman, "Epi-Palaeolithic Sites near Nahal Hadera, Central Coastal Plain of Israel," *TA* 3:1 (1976), pp. 16–30, figs. 1–9; E. Siegelmann, "Naḥal Ḥadera (grotte funéraire) 1977," *RB* 85:1 (1978), pp. 103–104, fig. 7, pl. 11.

Ḥefer, Tell

Excavated 1979–1980 by S.M. Paley, Y. Porath, for the State University of New York, Buffalo, Israel Dept. of Antiquities and Museums.

S.M. Paley, Y. Porath, "The Regional Project in 'Emeq Ḥefer 1979," *IEJ* 29:3–4 (1979), pp. 236–239, pl. 28 c; *id.* "The Regional Project in 'Emeq Ḥefer 1980," *IEJ* 30:3–4 (1980), pp. 217–219.

Ḥefer, Valley, see Caesarea

Ḥenū, Rujm al-

P. McGovern, "Baq'ah Valley Project 1980," *BA* 44:2 (1981), pp. 126–128, figs.

Heptapegon, see Tabgha

Herodium, Jebel Fureidis

Excavated 1972 by E. Netzer for the Hebrew University.

E. Netzer, "Herodium," *IEJ* 22:4 (1972), pp. 247–249, fig. 1; G. Foerster, "The Synagogues at Masada and Herodium," *EI* 11 (1973), pp. 224–228, figs., pls. (Hebrew); A. Segal, "Herodium," *IEJ* 23:1 (1973), pp. 27–29, fig. 1, pls. 4–5; E. Netzer, "Herodium," *RB* 80:3 (1973), pp. 419–421, pl. 18; *id.*, "Recent Investigations at Lower Herodium," *Qad.* 6:3–4 (1973), pp. 107–110, figs. (Hebrew).

A. Segal, "Herodium and the Mausoleum of Augustus," *Qad.* 7:1–2 (1974), pp. 46–49, figs. (Hebrew); A. Segal, "The Stages of Construction of Herodium," *EI* 12 (1975), pp. 109–115, figs. 1–10, pls. 22–25 (Hebrew); G. Foerster, "Herodium," *EAEHL* II (1976), pp. 502–510, figs.; T.O. Hall, Jr., "Herodium," *IDB-S* (1976), pp. 409–410; J.F. Strange, "The Capernaum and Herodium Publications," *BASOR* 226 (1977), pp. 65–73; *ibid.* Part, 2 *BASOR* 233 (1979), pp. 63–69; A. Ovadiah, C.G. de Silva, "Supplementum to the Corpus of the Byzantine Churches in the Holy Land," *Levant* 13 (1981), pp. 200–261, figs.; G. Foerster, "The Synagogues at Masada and Herodium," *ASR* (1981), pp. 24–29, figs.

Ḥesa, Qal 'at el-

L. Copeland, C. Vita-Finzi, "Archaeological Dating and Geological Deposits in Jordan," *Levant* 10 (1978), pp. 10–25, figs. 1–5, pl. 6 a; B. MacDonald, "The Wadi el-Hasa Survey: Fall 1979," *ASOR Newsletter* 3 (Dec. 1980), pp. 5–7, 10–12, figs. 1–4.

Heshbon, see Ḥesbân

Ḥesbân, Tell (Heshbon)

Excavated by S.H. Horn 1968, 1971, 1973 for the American Center of Oriental Research, Andrews University, Jordan Dept. of Antiquities, et al.

A. Terian, "Coins from the 1968 Excavations at Heshbon," *AUSS* 9:2 (1971), pp. 147–160, pls. 1–2; S.H. Horn, "The Second Season of Excavations at Heshbon," *ASOR Newsletter* 4 (Nov. 1971), pp. 1–4; E.N. Lugenbeal, J.A. Sauer, "Seventh-Sixth Century B.C. Pottery from Area B at Heshbon," *AUSS* 10:1 (1972), pp. 21–69, pls. A-C, 1–11; R.G. Bullard, "Geological Study of the Heshbon Area," *AUSS* 10:2 (1972), pp. 129–141, pls. 12–16; S.H. Horn, "Heshbon (Jordanie)," *RB* 79:3 (1972), pp. 422–426, pls. 41–42 a; *id.*, "The 1971 Season of Excavations at Tell Ḥesban," *ADAJ* 17 (1972), pp. 15–22, pls. 1–5; C.-M. Bennett, Review of R.S. Boraas, S.H. Horn, "Heshbon 1968: The First Campaign at Tell Ḥesbân," *AUSS* 7:2, 1969, *PEQ* 104:2 (1972), p. 161.

R.S. Boraas, S.H. Horn, et. al., "Heshbon 1971," *AUSS* 11:1 (1973), pp. 1–144, figs., pls.; *ibid. AUM* 6 (1973); J.A. Sauer, "Heshbon Pottery 1971: A Preliminary Report on the Pottery from the 1971 Excavations at Tell Ḥesbân," *AUM* 7 (1973); S.H. Horn, "Ḥesbân," *ASOR Newsletter* 2 (Sept. 1973), pp. 1–4, figs.; *id.*, "The Excavations at Tell Ḥesbân 1973," *ADAJ* 18 (1973), pp. 87–88.

Excavated 1974, 1976, 1978 by L.T. Geraty for ACOR, Andrews University, Jordan Dept. of Antiquities, et al.

A. Terian, "Coins from the 1971 Excavations at Heshbon," *AUSS* 12:1 (1974), pp. 35–46, figs. 1–2, pls. 1–2; R.S. Boraas, S.H. Horn, "Ḥesbân," *PEQ* 106:1 (1974), pp. 5–6; M.F. Oakeshott, Review of R.S. Boraas, S.H. Horn, "Heshbon 1971," *AUM* 6 (1973), and J.A. Sauer, "Heshbon Pottery 1971," *AUM* 7 (1973), *PEQ* 106:1 (1974), p. 91; S.H. Horn, "The 1973 Season of Excavations at Tell Ḥesbân," *ADAJ* 19 (1974), pp. 151–156, 247–252, fig. 1, pls. 70–75; L.T. Geraty, "Hesban," *ASOR Newsletter* 5 (Nov. 1974), pp. 1–8; W.E. Rast, Review of J.A. Sauer, "Heshbon Pottery 1971," *AUM* 7, 1973, *AJA* 78 (1974), pp. 434–435.

R.S. Boraas, S.H. Horn et al., "Heshbon 1973," *AUM* 8 (1975); S.H. Horn, "Tell Ḥesbân," *RB* 82:1 (1975), pp. 100–105, pls. 7 b, 10; F.M. Cross, "Ammonite Ostraca from Heshbon, Ostraca IV–VIII," *AUSS* 13:1 (1975), pp. 1–20, figs. 1–3, pls. 1–2; B. Van Elderen, "A Greek Ostracon from Heshbon, Nine," *AUSS* 13:1 (1975), pp. 21–22, pl. 2; R.S. Boraas, S.H. Horn et al., "Heshbon 1973," *AUSS* 13:2 (1975), pp. 101–247, figs. 1–11, tables 1–4, pls. 1–16; L.T. Geraty, "Ḥesbân (Heshbon)," *RB* 82:4 (1975), pp. 576–586, fig. 2, pl. 48; *id.*, "The 1974 Season of Excavations at Tell Ḥesbân," *ADAJ* 20 (1975), pp. 47–56, pls. 13–20; S. La Bianca, "Pertinence and Procedures for Knowing Bones," *ASOR Newsletter* 1 (July 1975), pp. 1–6.

R.S. Boraas, L.T. Geraty, et al., "Heshbon 1974," *AUSS* 14:1 (1976), pp. 1–216, figs. 1–27, pls. 1–16; L.T. Geraty, "The 1976 Season of Excavation at Tell Ḥesbân," *ADAJ* 21 (1976), pp. 41–53, fig. 1, pls. 7–12; S.H. Horn, "Heshbon," *EAEHL* II (1976), pp. 510–514, figs.; *id.*, "Heshbon," *IDB-S* (1976), pp. 410–411, fig.; R.S. Boraas, L.T. Geraty, "Heshbon 1974," *AUM* 9 (1976); L.T. Geraty, "The Excavations at Tell Ḥesbân 1976," *ASOR Newsletter* 8 (Jan. 1977), pp. 1–15, figs.; M. Oakeshott, Review of R.S. Boraas, S.H. Horn, "Heshbon 1973," *AUM* 8, 1975, *PEQ* 109:1 (1977), p. 55; W.H. Shea, "Ostracon II from Heshbon," *AUSS* 15:2 (1977), pp. 217–222; L.T. Geraty, "Ḥesbân (Heshbon)," *RB* 84:3 (1977), pp. 404–408, fig. 4, pls. 19 b-20; W.G. Dever, Review of J.A. Sauer, "Heshbon Pottery 1971," *AUM* 7 (1973), *BASOR* 227 (1977), pp. 78–79; R.S. Boraas, L.T. Geraty, et al., "Heshbon 1976," *AUSS* 16:1 (1978), pp. 1–303, figs. 1–24, 4 tables, pls. 1–24.

Ḥesbân North Church excavated by J.I. Lawlor 1978 for the Baptist Bible College, ACOR, Jordan Dept. of Antiquities.

R.S. Boraas, L.T. Geraty, "Ḥesbân" *AUM* 10 (1978); J.A. Sauer, "Ḥesbân North Church," *ASOR Newsletter* 3 (Nov. 1978), pp. 11–12; R.S. Boraas, L.T. Geraty, "The Long Life of Tell Ḥesbân, Jordan," *Archaeology* 32:1 (1979), pp. 10–20, figs., pls.; J.I. Lawlor, "Ḥesbân (Heshbon) 1978," *RB* 86:1 (1979), pp. 115–117, pls. 5–6; R.R. Heginbottom, Review of R.S. Boraas, S.H. Horn, *Heshbon 1971, AUM* 6, 1973, *IEJ* 29:3–4 (1979), p. 257; J.I. Lawlor, "The 1978 Hesban North Church Project," *ASOR Newsletter* 4 (Jan. 1979), pp. 1–8, figs. 1–9; *id.*, "The Excavation of the North Church at Ḥesbân, Jordan," *AUSS* 18:1 (1980), pp. 65–76, fig., 3 pls.; J.A. Kritzeck, E.L. Nitowski, "The Rolling Stone Tomb F 1 at Tell Ḥesbân," *AUSS* 18:1 (1980), pp. 77–100, figs. 1–2, pls. 1–6; J.M. Reeves, "Parallels to a Rare Double-Spouted Early Roman Oil Lamp from TE 6, Tell Ḥesbân," *AUSS* 18:2 (1980), pp. 169–172, fig.; A. Terian, "Coins from the 1976 Excavation at Heshbon," *AUSS* 18:2 (1980), pp. 173–178, pls. 1–2; L.T. Geraty, "Heshbon," *ISBE* II (1982).

Ḥesi, Tell el-

Excavations continued by J.E. Worrell 1970–1973.

J.E. Worrell, "Tell el-Ḥesi," *ASOR Newsletter* 5 (Dec. 1970), pp. 1–4, 2 figs.; G.E. Wright, "A Problem of Ancient Topography: Lachish and Eglon," *HTR* 64:2–3 (1971), pp. 437–448, fig.; *ibid. BA* 34:3 (1971), pp. 76–86, figs. 1–4; L.E. Stager, "Climatic Conditions and Grain Storage in the Persian Period," *HTR* 64:2–3 (1971), pp. 448–450; *ibid, BA* 34:3 (1971), pp. 86–88, fig. 5; L.E. Toombs, "Tell el-Ḥesi," *IEJ* 21:2–3 (1971), pp. 177–178; J.E. Worrell, L.E. Toombs, "Tell el-Ḥesi," *IEJ* 21:4 (1971), pp. 232–233; *id.*, "Tell el-Ḥesi," *RB* 79:4 (1972), pp. 585–588; L.E. Toombs, "Tell el-Ḥesi 1970–71," *PEQ* 106:1 (1974), pp. 19–31, figs. 1–3, pls. 1–6; J.E. Worrell, "Tell el-Ḥesi," *IEJ* 24:2 (1974), pp. 139–141.

Excavated by D.G. Rose 1975–1979 for an international consortium of higher learning under the auspices of ASOR and AIAR.

D.G. Rose, L.E. Toombs, "Tell el-Ḥesi 1975," *IEJ* 25:2–3 (1975), pp. 172–174, pl. 18 a-b; M.D. Coogan, "A Cemetery from the Persian Period at Tell el-Ḥesi," *BASOR* 220 (1975), pp.

37–46, figs. 1–8; J.E. Worrell, "Tell el-Ḥesi," *RB* 82:2 (1975), pp. 268–270; D.G. Rose, L.E. Toombs, "Tell el-Ḥesi 1973 and 1975," *PEQ* 108:1 (1976), pp. 41–54, figs. 1–4, pls. 1–5; *id.*, "Tell el-Ḥesi," *RB* 83:2 (1976), pp. 257–260, pls. 28, 31 a; R. Amiran, J.E. Worrell, "Hesi, Tel," *EAEHL* II (1976), pp. 514–520, figs., A.F. Rainey, "Eglon (City)," D.G. Rose, "Tell el-Hesi?" *IDB-S* (1976), pp. 252–253; D.G. Rose, "The 1977 Season at Tell el-Ḥesi," *ASOR Newsletter* 3 (Nov. 1977), pp. 4–5; K.G. O'Connell, "An Israelite Bulla from Tell el-Ḥesi," *IEJ* 27:4 (1977), pp. 197–199, fig. 1, pl. 26 g-h; K.G. O'Connell, D.G. Rose, L.E. Toombs, "Tell el-Ḥesi 1977," *IEJ* 27:4 (1977), pp. 246–250, fig. 1, pl. 37 e; A. Ben-Tor, *Cylinder Seals of Third Millennium Palestine, BASOR Suppl.* 22 (1978), pp. 9, 37–40, 101–102; D.G. Rose, L.E. Toombs, "Four Seasons of Excavation at Tell el-Ḥesi: A Preliminary Report," *AASOR* 43 (1978), pp. 109–149, figs., pls.; K.G. O'Connell, D.G. Rose, L.E. Toombs, "Tell el-Ḥesi 1977," *PEQ* 110:2 (1978), pp. 75–90, figs. 1–7, pls. 5–9; *ibid. RB* 85:1 (1978), pp. 84–89, fig. 1, pl. 5 a; V.M. Fargo, K.G. O'Connell, "Five Seasons of Excavation at Tell el-Ḥesi 1970–77," *BA* 41:4 (1978), pp. 165–182, figs.; P.J. King, "Through the Ancient Near East with ASOR," *The Bible Today* 103 (1979), pp. 2113–2120, fig.; J.F. Ross, "Early Bronze Age Structures at Tell el-Ḥesi," *BASOR* 236 (1979), pp. 11–21, figs. 1–15; V.M. Fargo, "Early Bronze Age Pottery at Tell el-Ḥesi," *BASOR* 236 (1979), pp. 23–40, figs. 1–8; K.G. O'Connell, D.G. Rose, "Tell el-Ḥesi 1979," *PEQ* 112:2 (1980), pp. 73–91, figs. 1–6, pls. 4–7; J.K. Eakins, "Human Osteology and Archaeology," *BA* 43:2 (1980), pp. 89–96, figs.; K.G. O'Connell, D.G. Rose, "Tell el-Ḥesi 1979," *BA* 43:4 (1980), pp. 254–256, figs.; *ibid. IEJ* 30:3–4 (1980), pp. 221–223, pl. 29 b-c.

Ḥever, Naḥal

Y. Yadin, *Bar Kokhba* (1971); G. Howard, J.C. Shelton, "The Bar-Kokhba Letters and Palestinian Greek," *IEJ* 23:2 (1973), pp. 101–102; Y. Aharoni, "Judean Desert Caves, Naḥal Ḥever," *EAEHL* III (1977), pp. 670–675, figs.; Y. Yadin, "Judean Desert Caves, Cave of the Letters," *EAEHL* III (1977), pp. 652, 675–683, figs.

Hippos, Sûsitâ

C. Epstein, "Hippos (Sussita)," *EAEHL* II (1976), pp. 521–523. figs.

Ḥoferah, 'Ain el-

Excavated by I. Beit Arieh, R. Gophna 1977 for Tel Aviv University, Israel Dept. Antiquities and Museums.

I. Beit Arieh, R. Gophna, "A Note on a Chalcolithic Site in Wadi Araba," *TA* 4:3–4 (1977), pp. 105–109, figs. 1–5, pl. 7.

Holon

T. Noy, A. Issar, "Holon," *RB* 78:4 (1971), pp. 581–582, pl. 26 a,b.

Horvat Berachot, see Berachot

Ḥorvat Midras, see Midras

Ḥorvat Minha, see Munḥata

Ḥuderah, 'Ain, Sinai

O, Bar-Yosef, et al., "The Nawamis near 'Ein Ḥuderah," *IEJ* 27:2–3 (1977), pp. 65–88, figs. 1–5, 5 tables, pls. 9–12.

Ḥuṣn, Tell el-, Jordan

M. Kochavi, "El-Ḥuṣn," *EAEHL* II (1976), pp. 526–527, figs.

Ḥusifah, see 'Isfiya

Iktanu, Tell

K. Prag, "The Intermediate EB — MB Age," *Levant* 6 (1974), pp. 77–78, figs. 3–8; S. Richard, "Toward a Consensus of Opinion on the End of the Early Bronze Age in Palestine-Transjordan," *BASOR* 237 (1980), pp. 5–34, figs. 1–4.

'Ira, Tell

Excavated by A. Biran 1979 for the Israel Dept. of Antiquities and Museums, N. Glueck School of Bib. Arch., HUC.

Y. Aharoni, "Nothing Early and Nothing Late: Rewriting Israel's Conquest," *BA* 39:2 (1976), pp. 55–76, figs. 1–22; A. Biran, R. Cohen, "Tel 'Ira," *IEJ* 29:2 (1979), pp. 124–125, pl. 16 b-d; A. Biran, "Tell Ira 1979," *RB* 86:3 (1979), pp. 464–465, pl. 28; M. Kochavi, "Rescue in the Biblical Negev," *BAR* 6:1 (1980), pp. 24–27, figs.

'Irâq el-Barûd, see Carmel, Sefunim Caves.

'Iraq el-Emir, see 'Arâq el-Emir

Iraq ez-Zigan, Carmel Area

Excavated 1974–1975, 1977 by E.E. Wreschner for the Israel Dept. of Antiquities and Museums, Haifa University.

E.E. Wreschner, "Iraq ez-Zigan (Neve Sha'anan)," *IEJ* 25:2–3 (1975), pp. 160–161; E.E. Wreschner, A. Ronen, "Iraq ez-Zigan 1975," *IEJ* 25:4 (1975), pp. 254–255; E.E. Wreschner, M. Lamdan, "Iraq ez-Zigan 1977," *IEJ* 27:4 (1977), pp. 237–238.

Isbeiṭa, Shivta

A. Negev, "Subeita," *RB* 81 (1974), pp. 397–420; *ibid.* *EAEHL* IV (1978), pp. 1116–1122, 1124 figs.; M. Broshi, "The Population of Western Palestine in the Roman-Byzantine Period," *BASOR* 236 (1979), pp. 1–10, fig., 2 tables.

Isdar, see Esdar

'Isfiya

M. Avi-Yonah, "Ḥusifah," *EAEHL* II (1976), pp. 524–526, figs.

Iskander, Khirbet

K. Prag, "The Intermediate EB -MB Age: An Interpretation of the Evidence from Transjordan, Syria and Lebanon." *Levant* 6 (1974), pp. 69–116, figs. 1–9; M. Kochavi, "Iskander, Khirbet," *EAEHL* II (1976), pp. 531–532.

Iṣṭabah, Tell, near Beth-Shan

Excavated 1977 by V. Tsaferis for the Israel Dept. of Antiquities and Museums.

Y. Landau, V. Tsaferis, "Tel Iṣṭabah, Beth Shean: The Excavations and Hellenistic Jar Handles," *IEJ* 29:3–4 (1979), pp. 152–159, pls. 20–21.

'Izbet Ṣarteh, see Ṣarṭah

Jaffa

Excavated by J. Kaplan 1970–1974 for Hebrew and Tel Aviv Universities.

J. Kaplan, "Tel Aviv-Yafo," *IEJ* 20:3–4 (1970), pp. 225–226; *ibid. IEJ* 21:2–3 (1971), p. 174; J. Kaplan, "The Archaeology and History of Tel Aviv-Jaffa," *BA* 35:3 (1972), pp. 66–95, figs. 1–15; *id.*, "Jaffa," *RB* 80:3 (1973), pp. 415–417, pl. 17; *id.*, "Jaffa 1972–1973," *IEJ* 24:2 (1974), pp. 135–137, pl. 22 c–d; *id.*, "Tel Aviv-Yafo," *IEJ* 24:2 (1974), pp. 137–138, pl. 22 b; *id.*, "Jaffa," *RB* 82:2 (1975), pp. 257–260, pl. 24; J. and H. Kaplan, "Jaffa 1974," *IEJ* 25:2–3 (1975), p. 163, pl. 16 b; *id.*, "Jaffa," *RB* 83:1 (1976), pp. 78–79, pl. 10; *id.*, "Jaffa," *EAEHL* II (1976), pp. 532, 534–541, figs.

Janoah, see Abil, Tell

Japhia

D. Barag, "Japhia," *EAEHL* II (1976), pp. 541–543, figs.

Jarmouth, Khirbet Yarmouk

Excavated 1970 by A. Ben-Tor for Hebrew University.

A. Ben-Tor, "Jarmouth, Tel," *EAEHL* II (1976), pp. 544–545, fig.

Jâwa, Jordan

Excavated 1973–1975 by S.W. Helms for the British School of Archaeology in Jerusalem.

S.W. Helms, "Excavations at Jawa 1973," *ADAJ* 18 (1973), pp. 41–44, fig. 1; *id.*, "Jawa: An Early Bronze Age Fortress?" *Levant* 5 (1973), pp. 127–128, fig. 1; *id.*, Report on Jawa, *PEQ* 106:1 (1974), pp. 3–4; *id.*, "Jawa: A Fortified Town of the Fourth Millennium B.C.," *Archaeology* 27:2 (1974), pp. 136–137, figs; *id.*, "A Jordanian Ghost City," *ILN* (Aug. 1974), pp. 62–63, figs.; *id.*, "Jawa 1973: A Preliminary Report," *Levant* 7 (1975), pp. 20–38, figs. 1–13, pls. 8–9; *id.*, "Jawa (Transjordanie)," *RB* 82:1 (1975), pp. 79–80, fig. 2; *id.*, "Jawa (Transjordanie)," *RB* 82:4 (1975), pp. 559–561; fig. 1, pls. 42–43; S.W. Helms, L.A. Hunt, "Jawa Excavations 1974: A Preliminary Report," *Levant* 8 (1976), pp. 1–35, figs. 1–26, pls. 1–3; S.W. Helms, "Jawa Excavations 1975: Third Preliminary Report," *Levant* 9 (1977), pp. 21–35, figs. 1–8, pl. 7; *id.*, *Jawa, Lost City of the Black Desert* (1981).

Jbeyha

M. al Mhaisen, "Jbeyha Church 1976," *ADAJ* 21 (1976), pp. 9–11, 10 pls. (Arabic).

Jdur, Tell

S. Ben-Arieh, "A Late Bronze Age Temple at Tell Jdur," *Qad.* 11:2–3 (1978), p. 60, figs. (Hebrew).

Jebel Fureidis, see Herodium

Jebel Qafze, see Qafze

Jema 'in, Khirbet

S. Dar, "Khirbet Jema'in — A Village from the Period of the Monarchy," *Qad.* 13:3–4 (1980), pp. 97–100, figs. (Hebrew).

Jemmeh, Tell

Excavated by G.W. Van Beek 1972–1976 for the Smithsonian Institution.

L.Y. Rahmani, "Silver Coins of the Fourth Century B.C. from Tel Gamma," *IEJ* 21:2–3 (1971), pp. 158–160, figs. 1–6, pl. 31; G.W. Van Beek, "Tel Gamma," *IEJ* 22:4 (1972), pp. 245–246, pl. 55 b; *id.*, "Tell Gemmeh," *RB* 79:4 (1972), pp. 596–599; *id.*, "Assyrian Vaulted Buildings from Tell Gemme," *Qad.* 6 (1973), pp. 23–27, figs. (Hebrew); *id.*, "Tell Gemmeh," *RB* 80:4 (1973), pp. 572–576, pl. 26; *id.*, "Tell Gamma," *IEJ* 24:2 (1974), pp. 138–139, pl. 23 a–b; *id.*, "Tel Gamma," *IEJ* 24:3–4 (1974), pp. 274–275.

G.W. Van Beek, "Tel Jemmeh," *RB* 82:1 (1975), pp. 95–97, pl. 8; *id.*, "Tell Jemmeh," *RB* 82:4 (1975), pp. 573–576, pl. 47; E. Stern, "Bes Vases from Palestine and Syria," *IEJ* 26:4 (1976), pp. 183–187, figs. 1–3, pls. 32, 33 a–b; R. Amiran, G.W. Van Beek, "Jemmeh, Tel," *EAEHL* II (1976), pp. 545–549, figs.; G.W. Van Beek, "Tel Gamma 1975–1976," *IEJ* 27:2–3 (1977), pp. 171–176; E.E. Platt, "Bone Pendants," *BA* 41:1 (1978), pp. 23–28, figs.

Jenin, Tell

N. Tsori, "New Light on En-Gannim," *PEQ* 104:2 (1972), pp. 134–138, figs. 1–3, 2 maps; A.E. Glock, "Tell Jenin," *RB* 86:1 (1979), pp. 110–112, pls. 1–2; L.Y. Rahmani, "Palestinian Incense Burners of the Sixth to Eighth Centuries C.E.," *IEJ* 30:1–2 (1980), pp. 116–122, figs. 1–3, pls. 12–13.

Jerash, Gerasa, Jordan

A. Spijkerman, "A List of the Coins of Gerasa Decapoleos," *LA* 25 (1975), pp. 73–84, pls. 41–44; S. Applebaum, "Gerasa," *EAEHL* II (1976), pp. 417–428, figs.; C. Dauphin, "A New Method of Studying Early Byzantine Mosaic Pavements," *Levant* 8 (1976), pp. 113–149, figs. 1–21; M. Sartre, "Ti Iulius Iuliamus Alexander, Gouverneur d'Arabie," *ADAJ* 21 (1976), pp. 105–108, fig. 1; J. Pouilloux, "Deux inscriptions au theâtre sud de Gérasa," *LA* 27 (1977), pp. 246–254, pl. 44; H. Kalayan, "Restoration in Jerash (with observations about related monuments)," *ADAJ* 22 (1977–78), pp. 163–171, figs. 1–5, pls. 87–95; J. Pouilloux, "Une troisième dédicacc au théatre sud de Gérasa," *LA* 29 (1979), pp. 276–278, pl. 37; E.M. Meyers, "Ancient Synagogues in Galilee: Their Religious and Cultural Sctting," *BA* 43:2 (1980), pp. 97–108, figs.; J. Wilkinson, "Architectural Procedures in Byzantine Palestine," *Levant* 13 (1981), pp. 156–172, figs. 1–11.

Jericho, Tell es-Sultan

W.G. Dever, "The Peoples of Palestine in the Middle Bronze I Period," *HTR* 64:2–3 (1971), pp. 197–226; D. Kirkbride, "A Commentary on the Pottery Neolithic of Palestine," *HTR* 64:2–3 (1971), pp. 281–289; K.M. Kenyon, "Burial Customs at Jericho," *ADAJ* 16 (1971), pp. 5–30, figs. 1–17, pls. 1–13; A.M.T. More, "The Late Neolithic in Palestine," *Levant* 5 (1973), pp. 36–68, figs. 1–9; J.M. Weinstein, "Egyptian Relations with Palestine in the Middle Kingdom," *BASOR* 217 (1975), pp. 1–16, figs. 1–3; K.M. Kenyon, "Jericho,"

EAEHL II (1976), pp. 550–564, figs.; H. and M. Weippert, "Jericho in der Eisenzeit," *ZDPV* 92:2 (1976), pp. 105–148, figs. 1–9; K.M. Kenyon, in E. Bacon, ed., *The Great Archaeologists (1976)*, pp. 316–318, fig. 165, pl. 40; G.M. Landes, "Jericho," *IDB–S* (1976), pp. 472–473.

J. Birmingham, "Spectographic Analyses of Some Middle Bronze Age Metal Objects," *Levant* 9 (1977), pp. 115–120, fig. 1; J.N. Tubb, Review of H.J. Franken, *In Search of the Jericho Potters 1974, PEQ* 109:1 (1977), p. 58; H.A. Liebowitz, "Bone and Ivory Inlay from Syria and Palestine," *IEJ* 27;2–3 (1977), pp. 89–97, figs., 1–2; K. Yassine, "Pre-Second Millennium Dwellings in Palestine," *ADAJ* 22 (1977–78), pp. 14–19, fig. 1; A. Ben-Tor, *Cylinder Seals of Third Millennium Palestine, BASOR Suppl.* 22 (1978), pp. 4, 8, 102, 103; P. Dorell, "The Uniqueness of Jericho," *Archaeology in the Levant (1978)*, pp. 11–18; J.A. Callaway, "Dame Kathleen Kenyon," *BA* 42:2 (1979), pp. 122–125, fig.; K.M. Kenyon, R.A. Coughenour, "Jericho," *ISBE* II (1982).

Jericho, Tulûl Abū el- 'Alâyiq

Excavated 1973–1977 by E. Netzer, E.M. Meyers, for AIAR, Brandeis University, Israel Exploration Society, University of California in Israel at the Hebrew University.

E. Netzer, "Jericho," *IEJ* 23:4 (1973), p. 260, pl. 72 a–b; Z. Meshel, "A New Interpretation of the Finds at Herodian Jericho," *EI* 11 (1973), pp. 194–196, fig. (Hebrew); Y. Tsafrir, "Jericho in the Period of the Second Temple," *Qad.* 7:1–2 (1974), pp. 24–26, figs. (Hebrew); E. Netzer, "The Hasmonean and Herodian Winter Palaces at Jericho," *Qad.* 7:1–2 (1974), pp. 27–36, figs. (Hebrew); *id.*, "Jéricho," *RB* 82:2 (1975), pp. 270–274, fig. 3, pls. 26–27; *id.*, "The Hasmonean and Herodian Winter Palaces at Jericho," *IEJ* 25:2–3 (1975), pp. 89–100, figs. 1–4, pls. 8–9, 10 a–b.

E. Netzer, G. Foerster, G. Bacchi, *EAEHL* II (1976), pp. 552, 564–574, figs.; R. Hachlili, "The Niche and the Ark in Ancient Synagogues," *BASOR* 223 (1976), pp. 43–53, figs. 1–13; E. Netzer, "Jericho, les palais d'hiver hasmonéen et hérodien," *BTS* 189 (1977), pp. 8–16, fig.; *id.*, "The Winter Palaces of the Judean Kings at Jericho at the End of the Second Temple Period," *BASOR* 228 (1977), pp. 1–13, figs. 1–14; E. Netzer, E.M. Meyers, "Preliminary Report on the Joint Jericho Excavation Project," *BASOR* 228 (1977), pp. 15–27, figs. 1–11; R. Hachlili, "A Jerusalem Family in Jericho," *BASOR* 230 (1978), pp. 45–56, figs. 1–14.

E. Netzer, "Miqvaot (Ritual Baths) of the Second Temple Period at Jericho," *Qad.* 11:2–3 (1978), pp. 54–59, figs. (Hebrew); *id.*, "Herodian Jericho," *BAR* 4:4 (1978), pp. 10–14, figs.

Tombs excavated by R. Hachlili 1979 for the Israel Dept. of Antiquities and Museums.

R. Hachlili, "The Goliath Family in Jericho: Funerary Inscriptions from a First Century A.D. Jewish Monumental Tomb," *BASOR* 235 (1979), pp. 31–65, figs. 1–48, tables 1–3, with P. Smith, Genealogy, pp. 66–70, fig. 49, tables 1–2; R. Hachlili, "Ancient Burial Customs Preserved in Jericho Hills," *BAR* 5:4 (1979), pp. 28–35, figs.; E. Netzer, "The Hippodrome that Herod Built at Jericho," *Qad.* 13:3–4 (1980), pp. 104–107, figs.; R. Hachlili, "A Second Temple Period Jewish Necropolis in Jericho," *BA* 43:4 (1980), pp. 235–240, figs.; E. Netzer, "The Herodian Triclinia — a Prototype for the 'Galilean Type' Synagogue," *ASR* (1981), pp. 49–51, figs.; J. Naveh, "Ancient Synagogue Inscriptions," *ASR* (1981), pp. 133–139, esp. 138; R. Hachlili, "The *Nefeš*: the Jericho Column–Pyramid," *PEQ* 113:1 (1981), pp. 33–38, figs. 1–5, pls. 4–7.

Jerisheh, Tell el-

N. Avigad, "Jerishe, Tell," *EAEHL* II (1976), pp. 575–578, figs.; S. Geva, "Tell Jerishe," *IEJ* 27:1 (1977), p. 47, pl. 5 a.

Jerusalem

B. Mazar, "Le mur de l'esplanade du Temple," *BTS* 122 (170), pp. 8–15, figs.; R.H. Smith, "A Middle Bronze II Tomb from the Vicinity of Jerusalem," *ADAJ* 15 (1970), pp.

17–20, pls.; K.M. Kenyon, *Royal Cities of the Old Testament* (1971), pp. 13–52, 111–124, 134–150, figs. pls.; R. Amiran, "The First and Second Walls of Jerusalem Reconsidered in the Light of the New Wall," *IEJ* 21:2–3 (1971), pp. 166–167; M. Avi-Yonah, "The Newly-Found Wall of Jerusalem and Its Topographical Significance," *IEJ* 21:2–3 (1971), pp. 168–169; E. Oren, "Jerusalem: Colline 'française'," *RB* 78:3 (1971), pp. 429–430; N. Avigad, "The Burial Vault of a Nazirite Family on Mount Scopus," *IEJ* 21:4 (1971), pp. 185–200, figs. 1–10, pls. 33–43; J.F. Strange, "French Hill, Jerusalem," *IEJ* 21:4 (1971), pp. 233–234; Y. Margovsky, "Jérusalem: Bordj Kabrit et environs," *RB* 78:4 (1971), pp. 597–598, pl. 32; D. Bahat, "Jérusalem: Jardin arménien," *RB* 78:4 (1971), pp. 598–599.

R. Amiran, A. Eitan, "Herod's Palace," *IEJ* 22:1 (1972), pp. 50–51; U. Lux, "Jerusalem, Old City, Church of the Redeemer," *IEJ* 22:2–3 (1972), p. 171, pl. 34 a; D. Bahat, M. Broshi, "Jerusalem, Old City, the Armenian Garden," *IEJ* 22:2–3 (1972), pp. 171–172, pl. 34 b; E.D. Oren, "Jerusalem, the French Hill," *IEJ* 22:2–3 (1972), pp. 172–173; M. Avi-Yonah, "Excavations in Jerusalem — Review and Evaluation," *Qad.* 5:3–4 (1972), pp. 70–73, fig. (Hebrew).

B. Mazar, "Excavations near the Temple Mount," *Qad.* 5:3–4 (1972), pp. 74–90, figs. (Hebrew); N. Avigad, "Excavations in the Jewish Quarter of the Old City," *Qad.* 5:3–4 (1972), pp. 99–101, figs. (Hebrew); D. Bahat, M. Broshi, "Excavations in the Armenian Gardens," *Qad.* 5:3–4 (1972), pp. 102–103, figs. (Hebrew); M. Broshi, "Excavations in the House of Caiaphas, Mount Zion," *Qad.* 5:3–4 (1972), pp. 104–107, figs. (Hebrew); A. Kloner, "A Burial Cave of the Second Temple Period at Giv'at ha-Mivtar," *Qad.* 5:3–4 (1972), pp. 108–109, figs. (Hebrew); R. Reich, H. Gera, "Five Jewish Burial Caves on Mount Scopus," *Qad.* 5:3–4 (1972), pp. 110–111, figs. (Hebrew); M. Ben-Dov, "Excavations near the Temple Mount — the Early Islamic Periods (Ḥaram esh-Sherif)," *Qad.* 5:3–4 (1972), pp. 112–117, figs. (Hebrew).

D. Bahat, M. Ben-Ari, "Excavations in Zahal Square," *Qad.* 5:3–4 (1972), pp. 118–119, figs. (Hebrew); A. Mazar, "The Ancient Aqueducts of Jerusalem," *Qad.* 5:3–4 (1972), pp. 120–124, figs. (Hebrew); Y. Tsafrir, "The Location of the Seleucid Akra in Jerusalem," *Qad.* 5:3–4 (1972), pp. 125–126, figs. (Hebrew); *id.*, "The Archaeological Reconstruction of the Antonia Fortress," *Qad.* 5:3–4 (1972), pp. 127–129, figs. (Hebrew); Y. Yadin, "The Gate of the Essenes and the Temple Scroll," *Qad.* 5:3–4 (1972), pp. 129–130, fig. (Hebrew); N. Kenaan, "A Local Trend in Crusader Art in Jerusalem," *Qad.* 5:3–4 (1972), pp. 130–131, fig. (Hebrew).

E. Netzer, "Reconstruction of the Jewish Quarter in the Old City," *Qad.* 5:3–4 (1972), pp. 132–135, figs. (Hebrew); D. Cassuto, "Four Sephardi Synagogues in the Old City," *Qad.* 5:3–4 (1972), pp. 135–137, figs. (Hebrew); D. Tanai, "The Ben-Zakkai Synagogues: Reconstruction and Restoration," *Qad.* 5:3–4 (1972), pp. 138–139, figs. (Hebrew); N. Avigad, "Excavations in the Jewish Quarter of the Old City of Jerusalem, 1971," *IEJ* 22:4 (1972) pp. 193–200, figs. 1–4, pls. 41–46; M. Broshi, "Jerusalem: Quartier arménien," *RB* 79:4 (1972), pp. 578–581, pls. 48–49; U. Lux, "Jerusalem: Quartier du Lauristan," *RB* 79:4 (1972), pp. 577–578, pl. 47; B. Bagatti, "Nuove scoperte alla Tomba della Vergine a Getsemani," *LA* 22 (1972), pp. 236–290, figs. 1–25; M. Piccirillo, "L'edicola crociata sulla Tombe della Madonna," *LA* 22 (1972), pp. 291–314, figs. 1–10; U. Lux, "Vorläufiger Bericht über die Ausgrabung unter der Erlöserkirche im Muristan in her Altstadt von Jerusalem in den Jahren 1970 und 1971," *ZDPV* 88:2 (1972), pp. 185–201, figs. 1–7, pls. 18–23, plans 1–6.

Excavated 1973–1974 by S. Ben-Arieh and E. Netzer for the Hebrew University and Israel Dept. of Antiquities and Museums.

M. Avi-Yonah, "Excavations in Jerusalem: A Survey and an Evaluation," *CNI* 24:1 (1973), pp. 41–49, figs.; M. Burgoyne, "Tariq Bāb al-Hadid — A Mamlūk Street in the Old City of Jerusalem," *Levant* 5 (1973), pp. 12–35, figs. 1–12, pls. 9–25; S. Loffreda, "The Late Chronology of Some Rock-cut Tombs of the Selwan Necropolis, Jerusalem," *LA* 23 (1973), pp. 7–36; E.S. Rosenthal, "The Giv'at ha-Mivtar Inscription," *IEJ* 23:2 (1973), pp. 72–81, pl. 19; J. Naveh, "An Aramaic Tomb Inscription Written in Paleo-Hebrew Script," *IEJ* 23:2

(1973), pp. 82–91, fig. 1; A. Friendly, "Recent Excavations in Jerusalem," *Expedition* 15:3 (1973), pp. 15–24, figs.; S. Ben-Arieh, "Excavations Along the Third Wall in Jerusalem," *Qad.* 6:3–4 (1973), pp. 111–113, figs. (Hebrew); J. Naveh, "A New Tomb Inscription at Giv'at ha-Mivtar," *Qad.* 6:3–4 (1973), pp. 115–118, figs. (Hebrew); M. Sharon, "Arabic Inscriptions from the Excavations at the Western Wall," *IEJ* 23:4 (1973), pp. 214–220, pls. 55–56; N. Kenaan, "Local Christian Art in Twelfth Century Jerusalem," *IEJ* 23:4 (1973), pp. 221–229, pls. 57–62, 63 a–b; N. Avigad, "Jerusalem: Quartier Juif," *RB* 80:4 (1973), pp. 576–579, fig. 1, pls. 27–29 a; I. Lévy, "Jérusalem: Quartier Nord," *RB* 80:4 (1973), pp. 579–581, pls. 29 b–30; B. Bagatti, "Jerusalem: Tombeau de la Vierge," *RB* 80:4 (1973), pp. 581–582, pl. 31.

Y. Ben-Arieh, "The First Surveyed Maps of Jerusalem," *EI* 11 (1973), pp. 64–74 (Hebrew); M. Ben-Dov, "Building Techniques in the Omayyad Palace near the Temple Mount, Jerusalem," *EI* 11 (1973), pp. 75–91, figs., pl. (Hebrew); D. Barag, "A Jewish Burial Cave on Mount Scopus," *EI* 11 (1973), pp. 101–103, figs., pl., (Hebrew); A. Ovadiah, "A Crusader Church in the Jewish Quarter of Jerusalem," *EI* 11 (1973), pp. 208–212 (Hebrew); R. Amiran, A. Eitan, "Excavations in the Citadel, Jerusalem, 1968–1969," *EI* 11 (1973), pp. 213–218; B. Bagatti, "L'apertura della Tomba della Vergine a Getsemani," *LA* 23 (1973), pp. 318–321, figs. 1–3.

M.H. Burgoyne, "The Continued Survey of the Ribāt Kurd/Madrasa Jawhariyya Complex in Tarīq al-Ḥadīd, Jerusalem," *Levant* 6 (1974), pp. 51–64, figs. 1–8, pls. 18–23; D. Barag, J. Wilkinson, "The Monza-Bobbio Flasks and the Holy Sepulchre," *Levant* 6 (1974), pp. 179–187, figs. 1–8; C. Coüasnon, *The Church of the Holy Sepulchre in Jerusalem*, Schweich Lectures (1974); K.M. Kenyon, *Digging Up Jerusalem* (1974); N. Avigad, "More Evidence on the Judean Post-Exilic Stamp," *IEJ* 24:1 (1974), pp. 52–58, figs. 1–2, pl. 8; Y. Meshorer, "The Beginning of the Hasmonean Coinage," *IEJ* 24:1 (1974), pp. 59–61, pl. 9 b–k; D. Ussishkin, "The Rock Called Peristereon," *IEJ* 24:1 (1974), pp. 70–72, fig., pl. 10.

J. Wilkinson, "Ancient Jerusalem: Its Water Supply and Population," *PEQ* 106:1 (1974), pp. 33–51, figs. 1–11, 2 tables, pls. 7–12; R.H. Smith, "The Cross Marks on Jewish Ossuaries," *PEQ* 106:1 (1974), pp. 53–66, figs. 1–6; E. Puech, "L'inscription du tunnel de Siloé," *RB* 81:2 (1974), pp. 196–214, figs. 1–2; B. Bagatti, "Ritrovamento di una tomba pitturata sull'Oliveto," *LA* 24 (1974), pp. 170–187, figs. 1–18; V. Tsaferis, "A Tower and Fortress near Jerusalem," *IEJ* 24:2 (1974), pp. 84–94, figs. 1–4, pls. 14–16; S. Ben-Arieh, E. Netzer, "Excavations along the 'Third Wall' of Jerusalem, 1972–1974," *IEJ* 24:2 (1974), pp. 97–107, figs. 1–5, pls. 17–18; M. Gichon, B.H. Isaac, "A Flavian Inscription from Jerusalem," *IEJ* 24:2 (1974), pp. 117–123, pl. 19 a–b; M. Broshi, "Mount Zion," *IEJ* 24:3–4 (1974), p. 285.

Tomb excavated by A. Kloner 1975 for the Israel Dept. of Antiquities and Museums.

R.W. Hamilton, Review of C. Coüasnon, *The Church of the Holy Sepulchre, 1974, PEQ* 107:1 (1975), pp. 78–79; B. Mazar, *The Mountain of the Lord* (1975); J.B. Livio, "La Jerusalem Hérodienne," *BTS* 173 (1975), pp. 4–17, figs.; N. Avigad, "A Bulla of Jonathan the High Priest," *IEJ* 25:1 (1975), pp. 8–12, fig. 1, pl. 1; A. Kloner, "A Painted Tomb on the Mount of Olives," *Qad.* 8:1 (1975), pp. 27–30, figs. (Hebrew); Z. Yeivin, "A Third Century C.E. Mosaic from Shechem," *Qad.* 8:1 (1975), pp. 31–34, figs. (Hebrew); G. Barkai, A. Mazar, A. Kloner, "The Northern Cemetery of Jerusalem in First Temple times," *Qad.* 8:2–3 (1975), pp. 71–76, figs. (Hebrew); A. Ovadiah, "A Restored Crusader Church in the Jewish Quarter," *CNI* 25:3 (1975), pp. 150–153, figs.; A.G. Walls, "The Mausoleum of the Amir Kīlānī," *Levant* 7 (1975), pp. 39–76, figs. 1–25, pls. 10–14.

J.F. Strange, "Late Hellenistic and Herodian Ossuary Tombs at French Hill, Jerusalem," *BASOR* 219 (1975), pp. 39–67, figs. 1–16; B. Arensburg, Y. Rak, "Skeletal Remains of an Ancient Jewish Population from French Hill, Jerusalem," *BASOR* 219 (1975), pp. 69–71, figs. 1–3; L.T. Geraty, "A Thrice Repeated Ossuary Inscription from French Hill, Jerusalem," *BASOR* 219 (1975), pp. 73–78, figs. 1–2; J. Wilkinson, "The Streets of Jerusalem," *Levant* 7 (1975), pp. 118–136, figs. 1–12; D. Ussishkin, "The Original Length of the Siloam Tunnel in Jerusalem," *Levant* 8 (1975), pp. 82–95, figs. 1–3, pls. 12–13; I.L. Merker, "A

Greek Tariff Inscription in Jerusalem," *IEJ* 25:4 (1975), pp. 238–244, pl. 26 a; N. Avigad, "Jerusalem, the Jewish Quarter of the Old City, 1975," *IEJ* 25:4 (1975), pp. 260–261, pl. 28 b; Y. Tsafrir, "The Location of the Seleucid Akra in Jerusalem," *RB* 82:4 (1975), pp. 501–521, figs. 1–4, pls. 33–37.

K. Prag, Review of K.M. Kenyon, *Digging Up Jerusalem, 1974, PEQ* 108:1 (1976), p. 68; C. Katsimbinis, "New Findings at Gethsemani," *LA* 26 (1976), pp. 277–280, figs. 6–7, pls. 47–48; A. Mazar, "Iron Age Burial Caves North of the Damascus Gate, Jerusalem," *IEJ* 26:1 (1976), pp. 1–8, figs. 1–2; V. Møller-Christensen, "Skeletal Remains from Giv'at ha-Mivtar," *IEJ* 26:1 (1976), pp. 35–38, figs. 1–2; O. Goldwasser, J. Naveh, "The Origin of the Ṭet-Symbol," *IEJ* 26:1 (1976), pp. 15–19, figs. 1–4, pl. 3; G. Barkay, A. Kloner, "Burial Caves North of Damascus Gate, Jerusalem," *IEJ* 26:1 (1976), pp. 55–57; G. Barkay, "St. Andrew's Church, Jerusalem," *IEJ* 26:1 (1976), pp. 57–58.

J. Wilkinson, "Christian Pilgrims in Jerusalem during the Byzantine Period," *PEQ* 108:2 (1976), pp. 75–101, figs. 1–8; M. Avi-Yonah, "Gazetteer of Roman Palestine," *Qedem* 5 (1976); M. Broshi, "Recent Excavations along the Walls of Jerusalem," *Qad.* 9:2–3 (1976), pp. 75–78 (Hebrew); Y. Yadin, ed., *Jerusalem Revealed: Archaeology in the Holy City, 1968–1974*, (1976).

N. Avigad, "Un quartier résidential à Jérusalem au temps d'Hérode," *BTS* 182 (1976), pp. 6–13, figs.; M. Broshi, "Excavations on Mount Zion 1971–1972," *IEJ* 26:2–3 (1976), pp. 81–88, figs. 1–3, pls. 18–19; L.Y. Rahmani, "The Eastern Lintel of the Holy Sepulchre," *IEJ* 26:2–3 (1976), pp. 120–129, fig., pls. 26–27; A. Issar, "The Evolution of the Ancient Water Supply System in the Region of Jerusalem," *IEJ* 26:2–3 (1976), pp. 130–136, figs. 1–4; N. Avigad, "The Governor of the City," *IEJ* 26:4 (1976), pp. 178–182, fig., pl. 33 d; N. Avigad, *Archaeological Discoveries in the Jewish Quarter of Jerusalem*, (1976).

K.M. Kenyon, "David, city of," *IDB–S* (1976), pp. 207–209, fig. 1; R. Amiran, Y. Israeli, "Jerusalem," *IDB–S* (1976), pp. 475–477, fig.; Jerusalem, Plates, *EAEHL* II (1976), pp. 465, 483–484, 533; Articles, O. Bar-Yosef, pp. 579–580; B. Mazar, pp. 580–591, figs.; K.M. Kenyon, pp. 591–597, figs.; M. Avi-Yonah, pp. 597–627, figs.; N. Avigad, pp. 627–641, figs.; Y. Shiloh, pp. 642–647, figs. tables.

M. Broshi, "Les Murs de Jerusalem continuent de Livrer leurs secrets," *M d B* 1 (1977), pp. 48–53, figs., *id.*, "Along Jerusalem's Walls," *BA* 40:1 (1977), pp. 11–17, figs. 1–6; E.W. Hamrick, "The Third Wall of Agrippa I," *BA* 40:1 (1977), pp. 18–23, figs. 1–3; M. Broshi, Y. Tsafrir, "Excavations at the Zion Gate, Jerusalem 1974," *IEJ* 27:1 (1977), pp. 28–37, figs. 1–6, pls. 2–3.

N. Avigad, "Jerusalem, the Jewish Quarter of the Old City 1976," *IEJ* 27:1 (1977), pp. 55–57, pl. 8 a–b; K.J.H. Vriezen, "Jerusalem: Quartier du Mauristan," *RB* 84:2 (1977), pp. 275–278, pl. 12; M. Ben-Dov, "Discovery of the Nea Church — Jewel of Byzantine Jerusalem," *CNI* 26:2 (1977), pp. 86–90, figs.; P. Smith, "The Human Skeletal Remains from the Abba Cave," *IEJ* 27:2–3 (1977), pp. 121–124, pl. 15; N. Avigad, "A Building Inscription of the Emperor Justinian and the Nea in Jerusalem," *IEJ* 27:2–3 (1977), pp. 145–151, figs. 1–2, pls. 18–19; Y. Tsafrir, "Muqaddasi's Gates of Jerusalem — a New Identification Based on Byzantine Sources," *IEJ* 27:2–3 (1977), pp. 152–161, fig. 1; T.A. Holland, "A Study of Palestinian Iron Age Baked Clay Figurines, with Special Reference to Jerusalem: Cave 1," *Levant* 9 (1977), pp. 121–155, figs. 1–9; A.G. Walls, "The Mausoleum of the Amir Kīlanī: Restored Elevations," *Levant* 9 (1977), p. 168, figs. 1–5.

M. Hoberman, K.M. Kenyon, "A Note on the Siloam Tunnel — Hezekiah's Waterway from the Spring Gihon to the Siloam Pool," *Levant* 9 (1977), pp. 174–175; N. Avigad, "Jerusalem: Quartier Juif," *RB* 84:3 (1977), pp. 416–418, fig. 7, pl. 25; C. Katsimbinis, "The Uncovering of the Eastern Side of the Hill of Calvary and its Base," pp. 197–208, pls. 19–38, plans A–C; J. Gath, L.Y. Rahmani, "A Roman Tomb at Manaḥat, Jerusalem," *IEJ* 27:4 (1977), pp. 209–214, pls. 27–29.

D. Bahat, G. Solar, "Une église croisée récemment découverte à Jérusalem," *RB* 85:1 (1978), pp. 72–80, figs. 1–7, pl. 3; D. Bahat, "A propos de l'église des 'Sept. Douleurs' à

Jérusalem," *RB* 85:1 (1978), pp. 81–83, fig. 1, pl. 4; K.J.H. Vriezen, "Zweiter Vorläufiger Bericht über die Ausgrabung unter der Erlöserkirche im Muristan in der Altstadt von Jerusalem 1972–74," *ZDPV* 94:1 (1978), pp. 76–81, figs. 1–2, pls. 5–6; J. Wilkinson, "The Pool of Siloam," *Levant* 10 (1978), pp. 116–125, figs. 1–6; J. Folda, "Three Crusader Capitals in Jerusalem," *Levant* 10 (1978), pp. 139–155, fig. 1, pls. 15–22; A. Lemaire, "Les Ostraca Paleo-Hebreux des Fouilles de l'Ophel," *Levant* 10 (1978), pp. 156–161, fig. 1, pl. 23; K.M. Kenyon, "The Mystery of the Horses of the Sun at the Temple Entrance," *BAR* 4:2 (1978), pp. 8–9, fig.; G. Foerster, "Architectural Fragments from 'Jason's Tomb' Reconsidered," *IEJ* 28:3 (1978), pp. 152–156, figs. 1–2, pls. 27–28; N. Avigad, "Jerusalem, the Jewish Quarter of the Old City 1977," *IEJ* 28:3 (1978), pp. 200–201; D. Chen, S. Margalit, A. Solar, "Jérusalem (Quartier Chrétien 1977)," *RB* 85:3 (1978), pp. 419–421, fig. 10, pl. 24; N. Avigad, "Jérusalem (Quartier Juif) 1975–1977," *RB* 85:3 (1978), pp. 421–423, figs. 11–12, pl. 25; M. Ben-Dov, "Herodian Jerusalem Revisited," *CNI* 26:3–4 (1978), pp. 138–142, figs.; B. Mazar, "Herodian Jerusalem in the Light of the Excavations South and Southwest of the Temple Mount," *IEJ* 28:4 (1978), pp. 230–237, figs. 1–4, pls. 35–38.

City of David excavated 1978–1980 by Y. Shiloh for the Hebrew University, Israel Dept. of Antiquities and Museums.

Y. Shiloh, "Jerusalem: The City of David 1978," *IEJ* 28:4 (1978), pp. 274–276; L.Y. Rahmani, "Ossuaries and Bone Gathering in the Late Second Temple Period," *Qad.* 11:4 (1978), pp. 102–112, figs. (Hebrew); J. Prignaud, "Scribes et Graveurs à Jerusalem vers 700 av J.–C.," *Archaeology in the Levant* (1978), pp. 136–148, figs. 1–9, pls. 21–23; A.D. Tushingham, "Yerushalayim," *Archaeology in the Levant* (1978), pp. 183–193; R.W. Hamilton, "Jerusalem: Patterns of Holiness," *Archaeology in the Levant* (1978), pp. 194–201.

E.M. Yamauchi, "Archaeology of Palestine and Syria," *ISBE* I (1979), pp. 275, 279–281, figs.; Y. Shiloh, "New Excavations in the City of David," *Qad.* 12:1 (1979), pp. 12–19, figs. (Hebrew); A.D. Tushingham, "The Western Hill under the Monarchy," *ZDPV* 95:1 (1979), pp. 39–55, figs. 1–9, pl. 1; B. Pixner, "Noch einmal das Prätorium Versuch einer neuen Lösung," *ZDPV* 95:1 (1979), pp. 56–86, figs. 1–4, pls. 5–7; F. James, "The Revelation of Jerusalem, a Review of Archaeological Research," *Expedition* 22:1 (1979), pp. 33–43, figs.; Y. Shiloh, "Jerusalem (Ville de David) 1978," *RB* 86:1 (1979), pp. 126–130, figs. 5–6, pl. 12; A.S. Kaufman, "New Light on the Ancient Temple of Jerusalem," *CNI* 27:2 (1979), pp. 54–58, figs. 1–4; N. Avigad, "Jerusalem, the Jewish Quarter of the Old City 1978," *IEJ* 29:2 (1979), pp. 123–124.

H. Geva, "The Western Boundary of Jerusalem at the End of the Monarchy," *IEJ* 29:2 (1979), pp. 84–91, figs. 1–2; D. Adan (Bayewitz), "The 'Fountain of Siloam' and 'Solomon's Pool' in First Century C.E. Jerusalem," *IEJ* 29:2 (1979), pp. 92–100, figs. 1–3, pl. 11; N. Avigad, "The King's Daughter and the Lyre," *Qad.* 12:2–3 (1979), pp. 61–62, fig. (Hebrew); Y. Shiloh, "City of David: Excavation 1978," *BA* 42:3 (1979), pp. 165–171, figs.; D. Ussishkin, "The Camp of the Assyrians in Jerusalem," *IEJ* 29:3–4 (1979), pp. 137–142, fig.; G.S. Merker, "Boeotian Pottery in Collections in Jerusalem," *IEJ* 29:3–4 (1979), pp. 160–170, fig., pls. 22–23; D. Barag, "A New Source Concerning the Ultimate Borders of the Latin Kingdom of Jerusalem," *IEJ* 29:3–4 (1979), pp. 197–217, fig. 1, map; D. Chen, S. Margalit, G. Solar, "Jerusalem, Christian Quarter 1977," *IEJ* 29:3–4 (1979), pp. 243–244, pl. 32; Y. Shiloh, "Jerusalem, the City of David 1979," *IEJ* 29:3–4 (1979), pp. 244–246, pl. 33; M. Kaplan, Y. Shiloh, "Digging in the City of David," *BAR* 5:4 (1979), pp. 36–49, figs.; M.H. Burgoyne, A. Abul-Hajj, "Twenty-Four Mediaeval Arabic Inscriptions from Jerusalem," *Levant* 11 (1979), pp. 112–137, figs. 1–5, pls. 11–25; C.M. Kessler, "The Tashtimuriyya in Jerusalem in the Light of a Recent Architectural Survey," *Levant* 11 (1979), pp. 138–161, figs. 1–17, pls. 26–35; Y. Ben-Arieh, *The Rediscovery of the Holy Land in the Nineteenth Century* (1979); V. Corbo, "Problemi sul Santo Sepolcro di Gerusalemme in una recente pubblicazione," *LA* 29 (1979), pp. 279–292.

A. Kloner, "A Tomb of the Second Temple Period at French Hill, Jerusalem," *IEJ* 30:1–2 (1980), pp. 99–108, figs. 1–2, table, pls. 9–11 a–d; P. Smith, J. Zias, "Skeletal Remains from the Late Hellenistic French Hill Tomb," *IEJ* 30:1–2 (1980), pp. 109–115, 4 tables, pl. 11 e–h; D. Cole, "How Water Tunnels Worked," *BAR* 6:2 (1980), pp. 8–29, figs.; D. Bahat, "A Smithy in a Crusader Church," *BAR* 6:2 (1980), pp. 46–49, figs.; N. Avigad, "The Chief of the Corvée," *IEJ* 30:3–4 (1980), pp. 170–173, fig. 1, pl. 18 d–e; Z. Jacoby, "A Newly Discovered Crusader Fragment in Jerusalem," *IEJ* 30:3–4 (1980), pp. 202–204, pls. 22–24; Y. Shiloh, "Jerusalem, the City of David 1980," *IEJ* 30:3–4 (1980), pp. 220–221, pls. 28, 29a; B. Mazar, "Excavations near Temple Mount Reveal Splendors of Herodian Jerusalem," *BAR* 6:4 (1980), pp. 44–59, figs.; Y. Shiloh, "Excavating Jerusalem: The City of David," *Archaeology* 33:6 (1980), pp. 8–17, pls.; B.E. Schein, "The Second Wall of Jerusalem," *BA* 44:1 (1981), pp. 21–26, figs.

G. Edelstein, M. Kislev, "Mevasseret Yerushalayim," *BA* 44:1 (1981), pp. 53–56, figs.; A.S. Kaufman, "The Eastern Wall of the Second Temple at Jerusalem Revealed," *BA* 44:2 (1981), pp. 108–115, figs.; M.A. Zimmerman, "Tunnel Exposes New Areas of Temple Mount," *BAR* 7:3 (1981), pp. 34–41, figs.; M. Stein, "How Herod Moved Gigantic Blocks to Construct Temple Mount," *BAR* 7:3 (1981), pp. 42–46, figs.

T. Watkins, "Levantine Bronzes from the Collections of the Rev. William Greenwell, now in the British Museum," *Levant* 13 (1981), pp. 119–155, figs. 1–12; J. Wilkinson, "Architectural Procedures in Byzantine Palestine," *Levant* 13 (1981), pp. 156–172, figs. 1–11; A. Ovadiah, C.G. de Silva, "Supplementum to the Corpus of the Byzantine Churches in the Holy Land," *Levant* 13 (1981), pp. 200–261, figs., esp. 222–223; E.W. Hamrick, "The Fourth North Wall of Jerusalem: a 'Barrier Wall' of the First Century A.D.," *Levant* 13 (1981), pp. 262–266, fig.; C.E. Bosworth, "Some Observations on Jerusalem Arabic Inscriptions," *Levant* 13 (1981), pp. 266–267; Y. Shiloh, "The Rediscovery of Warren's Shaft," *BAR* 7:4 (1981), pp. 24–39, figs.; *id.*, "The City of David Archaeological Project, The Third Season 1980," *BA* 44:3 (1981), pp. 161–170, figs.

Jilah

A. Mazar, "A Site near Jerusalem from the Beginning of the Israelite Settlement," *Qad.* 13:1–2 (1980), pp. 34–39, figs. (Hebrew).

Jish, el-, Giscala, Gush Ḥalav

Excavated by E.M. Meyers 1977–1978 for ASOR, AIAR, Duke University, Garrett Evangelical Theological Seminary at Northwestern.

F. Vito, G. Edelstein, "The Mausoleum at Gush-Ḥalav," *Qad.* 7:1–2 (1974), pp. 49–55, figs. (Hebrew); F. Vitto, "Gush Ḥalav," *IEJ* 24:3–4 (1974), p. 282, pl. 55 e; *id.* "Gush Ḥalav," *RB* 82:2 (1975), pp. 277–278, pl. 30; E.M. Meyers, "Gush Ḥalav (el-Jish) 1977," *IEJ* 27:4 (1977), pp. 253–254, pl. 39 a–c; *id.*, "Meiron and Gush Ḥalav 1977," *ASOR Newsletter* 3 (Nov. 1977), pp. 8–9, fig.; *id.*, "Gush Ḥalav 1977," *RB* 85:1 (1978), pp. 112–113, pls. 15–16; M. Avi-Yonah, "Gush Ḥalav (Giscala)," *EAEHL* IV (1978), p. 1135; E.M. and C.L. Meyers, "Gush Ḥalav (el-Jish) 1978," *IEJ* 28:4 (1978), pp. 276–279, figs. 1–2, pl. 55 a–b.

E.M. and C.L. Meyers, J.F. Strange, R.S. Hanson, "Preliminary Report on the 1977 and 1978 Seasons at Gush Ḥalav (el-Jish)," *BASOR* 233 (1979), pp. 33–58, figs. 1–21; E.M. Meyers, "Gush Ḥalav 1978," *RB* 86:3 (1979), pp. 439–441, fig. 2, pl. 18; *id.* "Gush-Ḥalav," *Qad.* 13:1–2 (1980), pp. 41–43, figs. (Hebrew); *id.* "Ancient Synagogues in Galilee: Their Religious and Cultural Setting," *BA* 43:2 (1980), pp. 97–108, figs.; *id.* "Excavations at Gush Ḥalav in Upper Galilee," *ASR* (1981), pp. 75–77, figs.

Jisr, el-, see Yavneh–Yam

Jisr Banāt Ya 'qub

D. Gilead, "Jisr Banāt Ya 'aqub," *EAEHL* III (1977), pp. 653–655, figs.

Judean Desert Caves

D. Jeselsohn, "A New Coin Type with Hebrew Inscription," *IEJ* 24:2 (1974), pp. 77–78, pl. 11; P. Bar-Adon, "An Early Hebrew Inscription in a Judean Desert Cave," *IEJ* 25:4 (1975), pp. 226-232, figs. 1–2, pl. 25; D. Gilead, "Judean Desert Caves, Prehistoric Sites," *EAEHL* III (1977), pp. 658–665, figs.; J. Aviram, "Judean Desert Caves," *EAEHL* III (1977), pp. 665–666.

Judeideh, Tell ej-

M. Broshi, "Judeideh, Tell," *EAEHL* III (1978), pp. 694–696, figs.

Juḥadar, Tell el-

D. Urman, "Tell el-Juḥadar," *EAEHL* II (1976), pp. 457–458, figs.

Juheniyeh, Qasr el-, see Tamara

Kabri

Excavated 1976 by M.W. Prausnitz, A. Kempinski for Tel Aviv University, Israel Dept. of Antiquities and Museums.

M.W. Prausnitz, A. Kempinski, "Kabri," *IEJ* 27:2–3 (1977), pp. 165–166, pl. 22 a.

Kadesh-barnea, see Qudeirat, 'Ain el-

Kafr Kana

S. Loffreda, "Un lotto di ceramica da Karm er-Ras presso Kafr Kanna," *LA* 25 (1975), pp. 193–198, pls. 47–48; M. Avi-Yonah, "Synagogues," *EAEHL* IV (1978), pp. 1129–1138, esp. p. 1136, figs.

Kebara, see Carmel, Mount

Kedesh, Tell. Tell Abu Qudeis

E. Stern, "Kedesh, Tel," *EAEHL* III (1977), pp. 702–703, fig.; E. Stern, I. Beit Arieh, "Excavations at Tel Kedesh (Tell Abu Qudeis)," *TA* 6:1–2 (1979), pp. 1–25, figs. 1–11, pls. 1–3.

Kefire, Khirbet

K.J.H. Vriezen, "Ḫirbet Kefire — eine Oberflächenundersuchung," *ZDPV* 91:2 (1975), pp. 135–158, figs. 1–7, pls. 12–15; *id.*, "Khirbet Kefire," *RB* 84:3 (1977), pp. 412–416, fig. 6, pls. 23–24.

Keisan, Tell

Excavated 1971–1979 by R. de Vaux, P. Benoit, J. Briend, J.-B. Humbert for l'Ecole Biblique et Archéologique Française de Jérusalem.

J. Prignaud, J. Briend, A. Lemaire, M. Join-Lambert, A. Spycket, "Première campagne de fouilles à Tell Keisan, Israel," *RB* 79:2 (1972), pp. 227–274, figs. 1–11, pl. 3–17; J. Prignaud, "Tel Kison (Tell Keisan)," *IEJ* 22:2–3 (1972), pp. 177–178; *id.*, "Tel Kison (Tell Keisan)," *IEJ* 22:4 (1972), p. 249; A. Spycket, "Le culte du Dieu-Lune à Tell Keisan," *RB* 80:3 (1973), pp. 384–395, figs. 1–22, pl. 7; J. Prignaud, "Tell Kison," *IEJ* 23:4 (1973), p. 259; W.J. Fulco, "Monnaies de Tell Keisan 1971–1974," *RB* 82:2 (1975), pp. 234–239, pls. 18–19; J. Briend, "Tel Kison 1975," *IEJ* 25:4 (1975), pp. 258–260; *id.*, "Tell Keisan," *RB* 83:1 (1976), pp. 88–91, pls. 14–15; *id.*, "Tell Keisan, une eglise Byzantine," *BTS* 181 (1976), pp. 14–17, figs.; D. Saltz, "Tel Keisan," *ASOR Newsletter* 10 (May, 1977), pp. 3–4; J. Briend, "Tell Keisan," *RB* 84:3 (1977), pp. 409–412, fig. 5, pls. 21–22; P. Benoit, "Keisan, Tell," *EAEHL* III (1977), pp. 711–713, figs.; J.B. Humbert, E. Nobet, "Tell Keisan 1979," *RB* 86:3 (1979), pp. 444–449, figs. 4–5, table, pl. 19; J. Briend, J.-B. Humbert, *Tell Keisan 1971–1976, Une cité phénicienne en Galilée* (1980); A. Ovadiah, C.G. de Silva, "Supplementum to the Corpus of the Byzantine Churches in the Holy Land," *Levant* 13 (1981), pp. 200–261, esp. pp. 257–258.

Kfar Neburaya, see Nabratein

Khaḍr, el-

F.M. Cross, "Newly Found Inscriptions in Old Canaanite and Early Phoenician Scripts," *BASOR* 238 (1980), pp. 1–20, figs. 1–13.

Khalasa, Elusa

Excavated 1973 by A. Negev for Hebrew University.

G. Lombardi, "Khalasa–Elusa nella esplorazione archeologica," *LA* 22 (1972), pp. 335–368, figs. 1–7; A. Negev, "Nabataean Capitals in the Towns of the Negev." *IEJ* 24:3–4 (1974), pp. 153–159, pls. 27–29; *id.*, "Survey Excavations at Ḥaluṣa (Elusa) 1973," *Qad.* 7:3–4 (1974), pp. 94–97, figs. (Hebrew); *id.*, "Elusa," *BTS* 164 (1974), pp. 8–18, figs.; *id.* "Elusa (Halutza)," *RB* 82:1 (1975), pp. 109–113, pls. 12–16; *id.*, "Survey and Trial Excavations at Ḥaluza (Elusa) 1973)," *IEJ* 26:2–3 (1976), pp. 89–95, fig. 1, pls. 20–21; *id.*, "Elusa," *EAEHL* II (1976), pp. 359–360, figs.; M. Broshi, "The Population of Western Palestine in the Roman-Byzantine Period," *BASOR* 236 (1979), pp. 1–10, fig., 2 tables.

Khasfin

D. Urman, "Khasfin, Golan," *EAEHL* II (1976), pp. 458–459.

Kheleifeh, Tell el-

N. Glueck, "Incense Altars," H.T. Frank, W.L. Reed, eds., *Translating and Understanding the Old Testament* (1970), pp. 325–341, figs. 1–4, pls. 1–5; *id.*, "Incense Altars," *EI* 10 (1971), pp. 120–125, figs. 1–4, pls. 53–55; J.R. Bartlett, "The Rise and Fall of the Kingdom of Edom," *PEQ* 104:1 (1972), pp. 26–37; S.H. Horn, "A Seal from Amman," *BASOR* 205 (1972), pp. 43–45, fig.; H.O. Thompson, "Cosmetic Palettes," *Levant* 4 (1972), pp. 148–150, figs. 1–2, pl. 16 a–b; R. Hestrin, E. Stern, "Two 'Assyrian' Bowls from Israel," *IEJ* 23:3 (1973), pp. 152–155, figs. 1–3, pl. 46.

B. Mazar, "Ezion-geber and Ebronah," *EI* 12 (1975), pp. 46–48, figs. 1–2 (Hebrew); Z. Meshel, "On the Problem of Tell el-Kheleifeh, Elath and Ezion-geber," *EI* 12 (1975), pp. 49–56, figs. 1–3 (Hebrew); O. Goldwasser, J. Naveh, "The Origin of the Ṭet-Symbol," *IEJ* 26:1 (1976), pp. 15–19, figs. 1–4, pl. 3; E.K. Vogel, "Tell el-Kheleifeh," *IDB-S* (1976), pp. 869–870; J. Lindsay, "The Babylonian Kings and Edom, 605–550 B.C.," *PEQ* 108:1 (1976), pp. 23–39, fig. 1; N.L. Lapp, "Casemate Walls in Palestine and the Late Iron II Casemate at

Tell el-Fûl (Gibeah)," *BASOR* 223 (1976), pp. 25–42, figs. 1–12; N. Glueck, "Kheleifeh, Tell el-," *EAEHL* III (1977), pp. 713–717, figs.; E.E. Platt, "Bone Pendants," *BA* 41:1 (1978), pp. 23–28, figs.; C.-M. Bennett, "Some Reflections on Neo-Assyrian Influence in Transjordan," *Archaeology in the Levant* (1978), pp. 164–174, figs. 1–4; L.G. Herr, "The Formal Scripts of Iron Age Transjordan," *BASOR* 238 (1980), pp. 21–34, figs. 1–4.

Khiam, el-

D. Gilead, "Judean Desert Caves — Prehistoric Sites," *EAEHL* III (1977) pp. 658, 662–664.

Khirbet el-Kôm, see Qôm, Khirbet el-

Khirbet el-Mefjer, see Mefjer, Khirbet el-

Khirbet el-Minyeh, see Minya, Khirbet el-

Khirbet el-Meshash, see Masos

Khirbet Qumran, see Qumran

Khirbet Shema', see Shema', Khirbet

Khudriya, Khirbet, (east of 'Ai)

A. Ovadiah, C.G. de Silva, "Supplementum to the Corpus of the Byzantine Churches in the Holy Land," *Levant* 13 (1981), pp. 200–261, figs., esp. pp. 235–236;

Kinneret, Tell el- 'Oreimeh, see Beth-Yeraḥ

B. Mazar, R. Amiran, N. Haas, "An Early Bronze Age II Tomb at Beth-yeraḥ (Kinneret)," *EI* 11 (1973), pp. 176–193 (Hebrew); *id.*, "Kinneret (Tomb)," *EAEHL* III (1977), pp. 717–718, figs.; Y. Aharoni, "Kinneret, Tel," *EAEHL* III (1977), p. 719, fig.

Kiriat Tiv'on

F. Vitto, "Kiriat Tiv'on," *RB* 79:4 (1972), pp. 574–576, pl. 52 b.

Kirmil, Khirbet el-

S. Mittmann, "Die Mosaikinschrift einer altchristlichen Kirche in el-Kirmil," *ADAJ* 16 (1971), pp. 87–89, fig.; W.G. Dever, "A Middle Bronze I Cemetery at Khirbet el-Kirmil," *EI* 12 (1975), pp. 18–33, figs. 1–6.

Kishor, Khirbet Umm Kashram

A. Kloner, "A Lintel with a Menorah from Ḥorvat Kishor," *IEJ* 24:3–4 (1974), pp. 197–200, fig., pl. 39 a; *id.*, "A Lintel with a Menorah Relief from Ḥorvat Kishor, in the Shephelah," *Qad.* 9:2–3 (1976), pp. 81–82, figs. (Hebrew); *id.*, "A Lintel with Menorah Relief from Ḥorvat Kishor," *ASR* (1981), pp. 160–161, figs.

Kissufim

Excavated 1977 by R. Cohen for Israel Dept. of Antiquities and Museums.

R. Cohen, "Kissufim," *IEJ* 27:4 (1977), pp. 254–256, pl. 40 a; *id.*, "Kissufim 1977," *RB* 85:1 (1978), pp. 104–106; *id.*, "A Byzantine Church and Mosaic Floor near Kissufim," *Qad.* 12:1 (1979), pp. 19–24, figs. (Hebrew); *id.*, "The Marvelous Mosaics of Kissufim," *BAR* 6:1 (1980), pp. 17–23, figs.

Kittan, Tell

E. Eisenberg, "The Middle Bronze Age Temples at Tel Kittan," *Qad.* 9:4 (1976), pp. 105–109, figs. (Hebrew); *id.*, "The Temples at Tell Kittan," *BA* 40:2 (1977), pp. 77–81, figs., 1 pl.; D. Saltz, "Tel Kittan," *ASOR Newsletter* 10 (May, 1977), pp. 4–6, fig.

Kokhav ha-Yarden, see Belvoir, Kaukab el–Howa

M. Ben Dov, "The Synagogue at Kokhav ha-Yarden and the Identification of Grofina," *Qad.* 6:2 (1973), pp. 60–62, figs. (Hebrew).

Kudadi, Tell el-, Tell esh–Shûni

N. Avigad, "Kudadi, Tell," *EAEHL* III (1977), p. 720, fig.

Kufin, Khirbet

Excavated by R.H. Smith for ASOR.

R.H. Smith, "Excavations in the Cemetery at Khirbet Kufin, Palestine," *Colt Archaeological Institute Monograph I* (1962); D.C. Baramki, "Kufin, Khirbet," *EAEHL* I (1975), p. 309.

Kuntillet 'Ajrud

Excavated by Z. Meshel 1975–1976 for Tel Aviv University, Israel Dept. of Antiquities and Museums.

Z. Meshel, C. Meyers, "The Name of God in the Wilderness of Zin," *BA* 39:1 (1976), pp. 6–10, figs. 1–4; S. Singer, "Cache of Hebrew and Phoenician Inscriptions Found in the Desert," *BAR* 2:1 (1976), pp. 33–34, 3 figs.; Z. Meshel, "An Israelite Site on the Sinai Border," *Qad.* 9:4 (1976), pp. 119–124, figs. (Hebrew); *id.*, "Kuntilat 'Ajrud, 1975–1976," *IEJ* 27:1 (1977), pp. 52–53; *id.*, "Kuntilet 'Ajrud (Nord Sinai)," *RB* 84:2 (1977), pp. 270–273, fig. 1, pl. 11.

E. Stern, "New Types of Phoenician Style Decorated Pottery Vases from Palestine," *PEQ* 110:1 (1978), pp. 11–21, figs. 1–11, pls. 1–4; N. Avigad, "The King's Daughter and the Lyre," *IEJ* 28:3 (1978), pp. 146–151, figs. 1–17, pl. 26 c; Z. Meshel, *Kuntillet 'Ajrud* (1978); *id.*, "Kuntillet 'Ajrud: An Israelite Center in Northern Sinai," *Expedition* 20:4 (1978), pp. 50–54, figs.; *id.*, "Did Yahweh Have a Consort?" *BAR* 5:2 (1979), pp. 24–35, figs.

Kurnub, Mampsis

A. Negev, "The Nabataean Necropolis of Mampsis (Kurnub)," *IEJ* 21:2–3 (1971), pp. 110–129, figs. 1–10, pls. 21–28; *id.*, "The Staircase-Tower in Nabataean Architecture," *RB* 80:3 (1973), pp. 364–383, figs. 1–10, table, pls. 2–6; *id.*, "Nabataean Capitals in the Towns of the Negev," *IEJ* 24:3–4 (1974), pp. 153–159, pls. 27–29; R. Rosenthal, "On Nabataean Dolphins," *EI* 12 (1975), pp. 107–108, figs. 1–3, pl. 21 (Hebrew); A. Kloner, "Ancient Agriculture at Mamshit and the Dating of the Water-Diversion Systems in the Negev," *EI* 12 (1975), pp. 167–170 (Hebrew); R. Rosenthal, "Late Roman and Byzantine Bone Carvings from Palestine," *IEJ* 26:2–3 (1976), pp. 96–103, pls. 22–23 a–b; A. Negev, "Kurnub," *EAEHL* III (1977), pp. 722–735, figs., 721.

Kursi, Tell

Excavated 1970–1972 by V. Tsaferis, D. Urman for the Israel Dept. of Antiquities and Museums.

V. Tsaferis, "El-Koursi," *IEJ* 22:2–3 (1972), pp. 176–177, pls. 38 b–39; *id.*, "Kursi: monastère byzantin," *RB* 79:3 (1972), pp. 409–411, pl. 38; V. Tsaferis, D. Urman, "Excavations at Kursi," *Qad.* 6:2 (1973), pp. 62–64, figs. (Hebrew); D. Urman, "Kursi," *EAEHL* II (1976), pp. 459–460; A. Ovadiah, "Two Notes on the Early Byzantine Complex at Kursi," *PEQ* 109:2 (1977), pp. 123–124; A. Ovadiah, C.G. de Silva, "Supplementum to the Corpus of the Byzantine Churches in the Holy Land," *Levant* 13 (1981), pp. 200–261, figs., esp. pp. 238–240.

Lachish, Tell ed–Duweir

G.E. Wright, "A Problem of Ancient Topography: Lachish and Eglon," *BA* 34:3 (1971), pp. 76–86, figs. 1–4; *ibid.*, *HTR* 64:2–3 (1971), pp. 437–448, fig.

Excavated by D. Ussishkin 1973–1980 for Tel Aviv University, Israel Exploration Society.

T. Dothan, "Another Mourning Woman Figurine from the Lachish Region," *EI* 11 (1973), pp. 120–121 (Hebrew); A. Lemaire, "Un nouveau roi arabe de Qedar dans l'inscription de l'autel à encens de Lakish," *RB* 81:1 (1974), pp. 63–72, pl. 1; D. Ussishkin, "Tel Lachish," *IEJ* 24:3–4 (1974), pp. 272–273; Y. Aharoni, *Investigations at Lachish: The Sanctuary and the Residency (Lachish V)* (1975); D. Ussishkin, "Tel Lachish 1975," *IEJ* 25:2–3 (1975), pp. 166–168, pl. 18 c–d; B. Boyd, "Lachish," *IDB-S* (1976), p. 526; D. Ussishkin, "Tell Lakish," *RB* 83:2 (1976), pp. 260–266, pls. 29–30, 31 b; *id.*, "Royal Judean Storage Jars and Private Seal Impressions," *BASOR* 223 (1976), pp. 1–13, figs. 1–9; *id.*, "Lamelekh Store-Jars and the Excavations at Lachish," *Qad.* 9:2–3 (1976), pp. 63–68 (Hebrew); M. Gilula, "An Inscription in Egyptian Hieratic from Lachish," *TA* 3:3 (1976), pp. 107–108, pl. 5:1; A. Lemaire, "A Schoolboy's Exercise on an Ostracon at Lachish," *TA* 3:3 (1976), pp. 109–110, pl. 5:2; M. and Y. Aharoni, "The Stratification of Judahite Sites in the 8th and 7th Centuries B.C.E.," *BASOR* 224 (1976), pp. 73–90, figs.

D. Ussishkin, C. Clamer, "A Newly Discovered Canaanite Temple at Tel Lachish," *Qad.* 9:4 (1976), pp. 112–115, figs. (Hebrew); D. Ussishkin, "Lakish," *BTS* 194 (1977), pp. 6–14, figs.; *id.*, "Tel Lachish 1976," *IEJ* 27:1 (1977), pp. 48–51, fig. 1, pl. 6; O. Tufnell, "Lachish," *EAEHL* III (1977), pp. 735–746, figs.; D. Ussishkin, "Lachish, Solar Shrine," *EAEHL* III (1977), pp. 747–753, 756, 773 figs.; *id.*, "The Destruction of Lachish by Sennacherib and the Dating of the Royal Judean Storage Jars," *TA* 4:1–2 (1977), pp. 28–60, figs. 1–6; A. Horowitz, "Tel Lachish — A Geological Note," *TA* 4:1–2 (1977), pp. 61–65, figs. 1–2, pl. 2; C. Clamer, D. Ussishkin, "A Canaanite Temple at Tell Lachish," *BA* 40:2 (1977), pp. 71–76, figs., 1 pl.; D. Ussishkin, "Tel Lachish," *RB* 84:3 (1977), pp. 399–404, fig. 3, pls. 17–19 a; E.E. Platt, "Bone Pendants," *BA* 41:1 (1978), pp. 23–28, figs.

D. Ussishkin, "Excavations at Tel Lachish 1973–1977," *TA* 5:1–2 (1978), pp. 1–97, figs. 1–30, 1 table, pls. 1–32; *id.*, "Lachish: Renewed Archaeological Excavations," *Expedition* 20:4 (1978), pp. 18–28, figs.; P. Goldberg, "Geology of Late Bronze Age Mudbrick from Tel Lachish," *TA* 6:1–2 (1979), pp. 60–67, figs. 1–3, pls. 13 b, 14–16; D. Ussishkin, "Answers at Lachish," *BAR* 5:6 (1979), pp. 16–39, figs.; M. Shea, K.R. Maxwell–Hyslop, "A Gold Earring from the Great Shaft at Tell ed-Duweir (Lachish)," *Levant* 11 (1979), pp. 171–173, fig. 1, pl. 36 b–c; D. Ussishkin, "The Battle at Lachish, Israel," *Archaeology* 33:1 (1980), pp. 56–59, figs.; G.W. Ahlström, "Is Tell el-Duweir Ancient Lachish?" *PEQ* 112:1 (1980), pp. 7–9, fig. 1; A. Lemaire, "A Note on Inscription XXX from Lachish," *TA* 7:1–2 (1980), pp. 92–94, 1 fig., pl. 28.

D. Ussishkin, "The 'Lachish Reliefs' and the City of Lachish," *IEJ* 30:3–4 (1980), pp. 174–195, figs. 1–8, pls. 19–20; C. Clamer, "A Gold Plaque from Tel Lachish," *TA* 7:3–4 (1980), pp. 152–162, figs. 1–2, pl. 36; P. Albenda, "Syrian Palestinian Cities on Stone," *BA*

43:4 (1980), pp. 222–229, figs.; S.H. Horn, Review of K.M. Kenyon, *Archaeology in the Holy Land, 1979, BAR* 7:1 (1981), pp. 10, 12.

Lahav, see Ḥalif, Tell

Latroun

M. Ben-Dov, "The Fortress at Latroun," *Qad.* 7:3–4 (1974), pp. 117–120, figs. (Hebrew).

Lawieh, Golan

C. Epstein, "Early Bronze Age Seal Impressions from the Golan," *IEJ* 22:4 (1972), pp. 209–217, figs. 1–4, pls. 51–52 a–b; A. Ben-Tor, "Lawieh Enclosure," *Cylinder Seals of Third Millennium Palestine, BASOR Suppl.* 22 (1978), pp. 10, 11, 102, 103, 109.

Lehûn, el-

P. Naster, D. Homès-Fredericq, "Recherches archeologique à Lehun au Wadi Mojib," *ADAJ* 23 (1979), pp. 51–56, fig. 1.

Lejjûn, el-

N. Glueck, *The Other Side of the Jordan* (1970), pp. 150, 151, 153, 170, 171, figs.; S.T. Parker, "The 1976 Limes Arabicus Survey," *ASOR Newsletter* 5 (Feb. 1978), pp. 6–10, 1 table; J.M. Miller, "Archaeological Survey South of Wadi Mujib: Glueck's Sites Revisited," *ADAJ* 23 (1979), pp. 79–92, esp. p. 81.

Excavated by S.T. Parker 1981 for North Carolina State University.

S.T. Parker, "The Central Limes Arabicus Project: The 1980 Campaign," *ASOR Newsletter* 8 (June 1981), pp. 8–20, figs.; *id.* "The Central Limes Arabicus Project," *AJA* 85:2 (1981), p. 211.

Lod

J. Kaplan, "Neolithic and Chalcolithic Remains at Lod," *EI* 13 (1977), pp. 57–75, pls. 8–10 (Hebrew); *id.*, "Lod," *EAEHL* III (1977), pp. 753–754, fig.

Lohamei Hagetaot

G. Foerster, "Lohamei Hagetaot: Tombe byzantine," *RB* 78:4 (1971), p. 586, pl. 28.

Ma'abarot

R. Gophna, "Sharon Plain," *EAEHL* IV (1978), pp. 1071–1074, figs.

Ma'aḥaz, Tell

Excavated 1975 by R. Cohen et al. for Israel Dept. of Antiquities and Museums, Tel Aviv University.

R. Cohen, R. Amiran, R. Gophna, D. Alon, Y. Beit-Arieh, "Tell Ma'aḥaz," *IEJ* 23:2–3 (1975), p. 162, pl. 16 c; R. Gophna, "Egyptian Immigration into Southern Canaan during the First Dynasty?" *TA* 3:1 (1976), pp. 31–37, figs. 1–3.

Maaravim, Tell

Excavated by E.D. Oren, A. Mazar 1974 for the University of the Negev.

E.D. Oren, A. Mazar, "Tel Maaravim," *IEJ* 24:3–4 (1974), pp. 269–270.

Ma'ayan Barukh

A. Ronen, M.Y. Ohel, M. Lamdan, A. Assaf, "Acheulean Artifacts from Two Trenches at Ma'ayan Barukh," *IEJ* 30:1–2 (1980), pp. 17–33, figs. 1–8, 4 tables.

Machaerus, Qal'at el-Mishnaqa

Excavated 1978–1980 by V. Corbo for the Franciscan Biblical Institute, and Jordan Dept. of Antiquities.

A. Strobel, "Observations about the Roman Installations at Mukawer," *ADAJ* 19 (1974), pp. 101–127, figs. 1–17, pls. 39–56; *id.*, "Das römische Belagerungswerk um Machärus Topographische Untersuchungen," *ZDPV* 90:2 (1974), pp. 128–184, figs. 1–20, pls. 3–14; H.T. Frank, "Herodian Fortresses," *IDB-S* (1976), pp. 408–409.

S. Loffreda, "Mishnaqa (Macheronte)," *RB* 86:1 (1979), pp. 122–125, fig. 4, pl. 10 a; V. Corbo, "Macheronte. La Reggia — Fortezza Erodiana 1979," *LA* 29 (1979), pp. 315–326, figs. 38–48; M. Piccirillo, "First Excavation Campaign at Qal'at el-Mishnaqa-Meqawer 1978," *ADAJ* 23 (1979), pp. 177–183, fig. 1, pls. 76–82; V. Corbo, "La Fortezza di Macheronte (al Mishnaqa). Rapporto preliminare alla terza campagna di scavo 1980," *LA* 30 (1980), pp. 365–376, figs. 71–91; S. Loffreda, "Alcuni vasi ben datati della Fortezza di Macheronte," *LA* 30 (1980), pp. 377–402, figs. 92–102; M. Piccirillo, "Le monete di Macheronte," *LA* 30 (1980), pp. 403–414, fig. 103.

Madeba

Excavated 1972–1973 by B. Van Elderen for the Jordan Dept. of Antiquities.

B. Van Elderen, "The Salayta District Church in Madaba, Preliminary Report," *ADAJ* 17 (1972), pp. 77–80, pls. 1–6; *id.*, "Excavations of Byzantine Churches and Mosaics in 1973," *ADAJ* 18 (1973), pp. 83–84, pls. 51–54; G. Thümmel, "Zur Deutung der Mosaikkarte von Madeba," *ZDPV* 89:1 (1973), pp. 66–79.

C. Dauphin, "A Note on the Church of the Virgin at Madaba, Jordan," *PEQ* 107:2 (1975), pp. 155–157; M. Piccirillo, "Una tomba del Ferro I a Madaba (Madaba B, Moab)," *LA* 25 (1975), pp. 199–224, pls. 49–68; C. Dauphin, "A New Method of studying Early Byzantine Mosaic Pavements," *Levant* 8 (1976), pp. 113–149, figs. 1–21; M. Avi-Yonah, "Medeba," *EAEHL* III (1977), pp. 819–823, 825, figs.; C. Dauphin, "Mosaic Pavements as an Index of Prosperity and Fashion," *Levant* 12 (1980), pp. 112–134, figs. 1–11, pls. 16–19; R. North, Review of H. Donner, H. Cuppers, *Die Mosaikarte von Madeba I, 1977, Biblica* 62:1 (1981), pp. 127–129, figs. 1–2.

Mafraq

M. Piccirillo, "Una tomba del Ferro I a Mafraq (Giordania)," *LA* 26 (1976), pp. 27–30, pls. 13–16.

Magdala

V. Corbo, "Scavi archeologici a Magdala, 1971–73," *LA* 24 (1974), pp. 5–37, figs. 1–19; *id.*, "Piazza a villa urbana a Magdala," *LA* 28 (1978), pp. 232–240, pls. 71–76.

Magen

V. Tsaferis, "Magen, 1977–1978," *RB* 85:1 (1978), pp. 106–108, pl. 12.

Maḥruq, Khirbet el-

Excavated by Z. Yeivin 1974.

Z. Yeivin, "Israelite Towers at Khirbet Maḥrouq," *Qad.* 7:3–4 (1974), pp. 102–104, figs. (Hebrew); *id.*, "Khirbet el-Maḥruq," *IEJ* 24:3–4 (1974), pp. 259–260, pl. 55 c-d; *id.*, "Khirbet el-Maḥruq," *RB* 82:2 (1975), pp. 251–254, pl. 20; *id.*, "El-Maḥruq, Khirbet," *EAEHL* III (1977), pp. 766–768, figs.

Ma'in, ed-Deir

Excavated 1973 by B. Van Elderen, M. Russan for the Jordan Dept. of Antiquities.

B. Van Elderen, "Excavations of Byzantine Churches and Mosaics in 1973," *ADAJ* 18 (1973), pp. 83–84, pls. 51–54; M. Piccirillo, M. Russan, "A Byzantine Church at ed-Deir (Ma'in)," *ADAJ* 21 (1976), pp. 61–70, figs. 1–6, pls. 18–30.

Makhatet el-'Urj, see Sandahannah

Makmish, see Michal, Tell

Malfuf, Rujm el-

H.O. Thompson, "Rujm al-Malfuf Sud et Rujm al-Mekheizin (Transjordanie)," *RB* 82:1 (1975), pp. 97–100.

Malḥata, Tell, Tell el-Milḥ

Excavated 1971 by M. Kochavi for the Israel Dept. of Antiquities and Museums.

M. Kochavi, "The First Season of Excavations at Tell Malḥata," *Qad.* 3:1 (1970), pp. 22–24, figs. (Hebrew); *id.*, "Tell Malḥata," *RB* 79:4 (1972), pp. 593–596; Y. Aharoni, 'Nothing Early and Nothing Late: Rewriting Israel's Conquest," *BA* 39:2 (1976), pp. 55–76, figs. 1–22; M. Kochavi, "Malḥata, Tel," *EAEHL* III (1977), pp. 771–772, 774–775, figs.

Excavated 1979 by R. Amiran, C. Arnon for the Israel Dept. of Antiquities and Museums.

R. Amiran, C. Arnon, "Small Tel Malḥata," *IEJ* 29:3–4 (1979), pp. 255–256, pl. 35 a-b; M. Kochavi, "Rescue in the Biblical Negev," *BAR* 6:1 (1980), pp. 24–27, figs.

Mallaha, 'Einan

Excavated 1972 by J. Perrot, M. Lechevallier for the French Archaeological Mission.

M. Lechevallier, J. Perrot, "Eynan and Beisamoun," *IEJ* 23:2 (1973), pp. 107–108, pls. 23–24; *id.*, "Mallaḥa," *RB* 80:3 (1973), pp. 399–400, pl. 8; M. Lechevallier, "'Eynan," *IEJ* 23:4 (1973), p. 239, pl. 64 a; *id.*, "Mallaha," *RB* 82:1 (1975), pp. 70–71, pl. 1 a; F. R. Valla, "Note sur l'industrie lithique de Mallaḥa ('Eynan)," *IEJ* 25:1 (1975), pp. 1–7 figs. 1–3, table; M. Lechevallier, "'Eynan (Mallaḥa) 1974," *IEJ* 25:2–3 (1975), p. 161, pl. 16 a; J. Perrot, "Beisamoun in the Hula Valley," *Qad.* 8:4 (1975), pp. 114–117, figs. (Hebrew); M. Lechevallier, "Mallaḥa," *RB* 82:4 (1975), pp. 558–559, pl. 41; J. Perrot, "'Eynan (Mallaha) 1975," *IEJ* 26:1 (1976), pp. 47–48; *id.*, "Eynan," *EAEHL* II (1976), pp. 389–395, figs.; *id.*, "Mallaḥa ('Eynan)," *RB* 84:2 (1977), pp. 254–256, pl. 4; F.R. Valla, "'Eynan (Mallaḥ) 1976," *IEJ* 27:1 (1977), p. 42; K. Yassine, "Pre-Second Millennium Dwellings in Palestine," *ADAJ* 22 (1977–78), pp. 14–19, fig. 1.

Mambre, see Râmat el-Khalil

Mampsis, see Kurnub

Ma'on, Nirim

M. Avi-Yonah, "The Gaza School of Mosaicists in the Fifth-Sixth Centuries C.E.," *EI* 12 (1975), pp. 191–193, pls. (Hebrew); D. Barag, "Ma'on," *EAEHL* III (1977), pp. 779–781, figs. A. Kloner, "Ancient Synagogues in Israel," *ASR* (1981), pp. 11–18, esp. p. 17.

Ma'oz Ḥayyim

Excavated by V. Tsaferis 1974 for the Israel Dept. of Antiquities and Museums.

V. Tsaferis, "Ma'oz Ḥayyim," *IEJ* 24:2 (1974), pp. 143–144, pl. 26; *id.*, "The Synagogue at Ma'oz Hayim," *Qad.* 7:3–4 (1974), pp. 111–113, figs. (Hebrew); *id.*, "Maoz Haim," *RB* 83:1 (1976), pp. 87–88, pl. 136; *id.*, "The Synagogue at Ma'oz Ḥayim," *ASR* (1981), pp. 86–89, figs.

Maresha, see Sandahannah

Marisa, see Sandahannah

Marjamah, Tell, near 'Ain Samiyeh

Excavated by M. Zohar 1979–1980 for the Israel Dept. of Antiquities and Museums, and Hebrew University.

M. Zohar, "Tell Marjameh ('Ein Samiyeh)," *IEJ* 30:3–4 (1980), pp. 219–220.

Marwa, Jordan

S. Appelbaum, "Marwa," *EAEHL* III (1977), pp. 791–792, fig.

Masad, Khirbet

M. Fischer, "Ḥorbat Masad 1977–1978," *RB* 86:3 (1979), pp. 461–462, fig. 10, pl. 27 a.

Masada

G. Foerster, "The Synagogues at Masada and Herodium," *EI* 11 (1973), pp. 224–228, figs., pl. (Hebrew); Y. Yadin, "Masada," *IDB-S* (1976), pp. 577–580, figs.; *id.*, "Masada," E. Bacon, ed., *The Great Archaeologists," ILN 1842–1970* (1976), pp. 395–397, 422; Y. Yadin, "Masada," *EAEHL* III (1977), pp. 793–816, fig.; *id.*, "The Synagogue at Masada," *ASR* (1981), pp. 19–23, figs.; G. Foerster, "The Synagogues at Masada and Herodium," *ASR* (1981), pp. 24–29, figs.

Masos, Tell, Khirbet el-Meshâsh

Excavated 1972–1975 by Y. Aharoni, A. Kempinski, V. Fritz for the Universities of Mainz and Tel Aviv.

Y. Aharoni, A. Kempinski, V. Fritz, "Tel Masos (Khirbet el-Meshâsh)," *IEJ* 22:4 (1972), p. 243, pl. 55 a; *id.*, "Vorbericht über die Ausgrabungen auf der Ḥirbet el Mšaš (Tel Mâśôś), 1 Kampagne 1972," *ZDPV* 89:2 (1973), pp. 197–210, figs. 1–3, pls. 16–27, plans 1–4; F. Crüsemann, "Überlegen zur Identifikation der Ḥirbet el-Mšaš," *ZDPV* 89:2 (1973), pp. 211–224; A. Kempinski, "Tel Masos (Meshash). An Early Iron Age Site in the N. Negev," *Qad.* 6:3–4 (1973), pp. 104–106, figs. (Hebrew); Y. Aharoni, A. Kempinski, V. Fritz, "Tel Masos (Khirbet el-Meshâsh)," *RB* 81:1 (1974), pp. 89–91; *id.*, "Excavations at Tel Masos (Khirbet el-Meshâsh)," *TA* 1:2 (1974), pp. 64–74, figs. 1–3, pls. 11–15; R. Giveon, "A

Monogram Scarab from Tel Masos,"*TA* 1:2 (1974), pp. 75–76, pl. 15:1; Y. Aharoni, A. Kempinski, V. Fritz, "Tel Masos," *IEJ* 24:3–4 (1974), pp. 268–269, pl. 58 e.

E.K. Vogel, "Negev Survey of Nelson Glueck," *EI* 12 (1975), pp. 1–17, pls. 1–16, esp. p. 2; Y. Aharoni, V. Fritz, A. Kempinski, "Vorbericht über die Ausgrabungen auf der Ḥirbet el-Mšaš 1974," *ZDPV* 91:2 (1975), pp. 109–130, 1 fig., pls. 1–10, plans 1–4; V. Fritz, "Ein Ostrakon aus Ḥirbet el-Mšaš," *ZDPV* 91:2 (1975), pp. 131–134, pl. 11; Y. Aharoni, V. Fritz, A. Kempinski, "Excavations at Tel Masos (Khirbet el-Meshâsh) 1974," *TA* 2:3 (1975), pp. 97–124, figs. 1–4, pls. 18–23.

V. Fritz, A. Kempinski, "Tel Masos 1975," *IEJ* 26:1 (1976), pp. 52–54, pl. 9 c-e; *id.*, "Tel Masos," *RB* 83:1 (1976), pp. 67–72, pl. 5; *id.*, "Vorbericht über die Ausgrabungen auf der Ḥirbet el Mšaš 1975," *ZDPV* 92:2 (1976), pp. 83–104, figs. 1–7, pls. 7–12; Y. Aharoni, "Nothing Early and Nothing Late: Rewriting Israel's Conquest," *BA* 39:2 (1976), pp. 55–76, figs. 1–22; A. Sheffer, "Comparative Analysis of a 'Negev Ware' Textile Impression from Tel Masos," *TA* 3:2 (1976), pp. 81–88, figs. 1–2, pls. 2:3, 3–4; A Kempinski, V. Fritz, "Excavations at Tel Masos 1975," *TA* 4:3–4 (1977), pp. 136–158, figs. 1–7, pls. 13–17, 18:1–4; A. Kempinski, "Masos, Tel," *EAEHL* III (1977), pp. 816–819, figs.

F. Crüsemann, "Ein Israelitisches Ritual Bad aus vorexilischer Zeit," *ZDPV* 94:1 (1978), pp. 68–75, figs. 1–4, pls. 3–4; A. Kempinski, "Tel Masos," *Expedition* 20:4 (1978), pp. 29–37, figs.; C. -M. Bennett, "Some Reflections on Neo-Assyrian Influence in Transjordan, *Archaeology in the Levant*, P.R.S. Morrey, P.J. Parr, eds., (1978), pp. 164–171, figs. 1–4.

Excavated 1979–1980 by M. Kochavi for Tel Aviv University.

M. Kochavi, "Rescue in the Biblical Negev," *BAR* 6:1 (1980), pp. 24–27, figs.; V. Fritz, "Die Kulturhistorische Bedeutung der früheisenzeitlichen Siedlung auf der Ḥirbet el-Mšaš und das Problem der Landnahme," *ZDPV* 96:2 (1980), pp. 121–135, figs. 1–6; A. Kempinski, "Is Tel Masos an Amalekite Settlement?" *BAR* 7:3 (1981), pp. 52–53, fig.

Maṣṭabah, Tell el- see Iṣṭabah

Matta'

A. and R. Ovadiah, S. Gudovitz, "Une église byzantine à Matta'," *RB* 83:3 (1976), pp. 421–431, fig. 1, pls. 38–41.

Me'arat Hayonim

O. Bar-Yosef, "Me'arat Hayonim (la grotte des pigeons)," *RB* 78:3 (1971), pp. 411–412, pl. 12 b.

Medeibiyeh

Y. Shiloh, "The Proto-Aeolic Capital and Israelite Ashlar Masonry," *Qedem* 11 (1979).

Medeiyineh, Khirbet el- (on Wâdī Mojib)

Excavated by E. Olávarri 1976 for la Casa de Santiago de Jerusalén.

N. Glueck, *AASOR* 14 (1934), Site 141, pp. 52, 53, fig. 22, p. 98, plan pl. 12; *id.*, *The Other Side of the Jordan* (1970), p. 17, fig. 3; E. Olávarri, "Sondeo Arqueologico en Khirbet Medeineh junto a Smakieh (Jordania)," *ADAJ* 22 (1977–78), pp. 136–149, figs. 1–3, pl. 84; J.M. Miller, "Archaeological Survey of Central Moab 1978," *BASOR* 234 (1979), pp. 43–52, figs. 1–4; J.R. Kautz, "Tracking the Ancient Moabites," *BA* 44:1 (1981), pp. 27–35, figs.; B. Vawter, Review of E. Olávarri, *Studium Ovetense* 5 (1977), pp. 137–153, *OTA* 4:2 (June 1981), p. 100.

Medeiyineh, Khirbet el- (on Wâdī Themed)

N. Glueck, *AASOR* 14 (1934), Site 68, pp. 13–14, fig. 4; *id., The Other Side of the Jordan* (1970), pp. 142, 176–178, 188–189, figs. 85, 86, 96.

Mefjer, Khirbet el-

R.W. Hamilton, "Pastimes of a Caliph: Another Glimpse," *Levant* 4 (1972), pp. 155–156; M. Rosen-Ayalon, "Further Considerations Pertaining to Umayyad Art," *IEJ* 23: 2 (1973), pp. 92–100, figs. 1–2, pls. 20–22; E. Baer, "A Group of North Iranian Craftsmen among the Artisans of Khirbet el-Mefjer?" *IEJ* 24:3–4 (1974), pp. 237–240, pls. 52–53; R.W. Hamilton, "Al-Mafjar, Khirbet," *EAEHL* III (1977), pp. 754–755, 757–765, figs.; *id.*, "Khirbat al-Mafjar: The Bath Hall Reconsidered," *Levant* 10 (1978), pp. 126–138, 3 figs.

Megadim, Tell

M. Broshi, "Tell Megadim," *RB* 77:3 (1970), pp. 387–388; *id.*, "Megadim, Tel," *EAEHL* III (1977), pp. 823–824, 826, figs.

Megiddo

Excavated 1971 by Y. Yadin for Hebrew University.

Y. Aharoni, "The Stratification of Israelite Megiddo," *EI* 10 (1971), pp. 53–57, figs. 1–2; K.M. Kenyon, *Royal Cities of the Old Testament*, (1971), pp. 58–68, 93–105, 126–127, 130–131, figs., pls.; Y. Yadin,, Y. Shiloh, A. Eitan, "Megiddo," *IEJ* 22:2–3 (1972), pp. 161–164, pls. 29, 30b; Y. Yadin, *Hazor* (1972), pp. 150–164, figs., pls.; *id.*, "Megiddo," *RB* 79:4 (1972), pp. 571–574; I. Dunayevsky, A. Kempinski, "The Megiddo Temples," *ZDPV* 89:2 (1973), pp. 161–187, figs. 1–9, pls. 8–11; J. Briend, "Megiddo," *BTS* 153 (1973), pp. 8–18, figs.; I. Dunayevski, A. Kempinski, "The Megiddo Temples," *EI* 11 (1973), pp. 8–29 (Hebrew); C. Epstein, "The Sacred Area at Megiddo in Stratum XIX," *EI* 11 (1973), pp. 54–57, figs.; H.E. Kassis, "The Beginning of the Late Bronze Age at Megiddo," *Berytus* 22 (1973), pp. 5–22, 3 tables; O. Tufnell, "The Middle Bronze Age Scarab Seals from Burials on the Mound at Megiddo," *Levant* 5 (1973), pp. 69–82, figs. 1–3; Y. Yadin, "A Note on the Stratigraphy of Israelite Megiddo," *JNES* 32:3 (1973), p. 330; D. Ussishkin, "King Solomon's Palaces," *BA* 36:3 (1973), pp. 78–105, figs. 1–16; Y. Aharoni, "The Building Activities of David and Solomon," *IEJ* 24:1 (1974), pp. 13–16.

Excavated 1974 by A. Eitan for Hebrew University.

A. Eitan, "Megiddo," *IEJ* 24:3–4 (1974), pp. 275–276; O. Negbi, "The Continuity of the Canaanite Bronzework of the Late Bronze Age into the Early Iron Age," *TA* 1:4 (1974), pp. 159–172, 1 table, pls. 30b-32; J.M. Weinstein, "Egyptian Relations with Palestine in the Middle Kingdom," *BASOR* 217 (1975), pp. 1–16, figs. 1–3; Y. Shiloh, A. Horowitz, "Ashlar Quarries of the Iron Age in the Hill Country of Israel," *BASOR* 217 (1975), pp. 37–48, figs. 1–3, pls. 1–7; Y. Yadin, "The Megiddo Stables," *EI* 12 (1975), pp. 57–62, figs. 1–7, pl. 13 (Hebrew).

Y. Yadin, "Megiddo," *IDB-S* (1976), pp. 583–585, figs.; Y. Shiloh, "New Proto-Aeolic Capitals Found in Israel," *BASOR* 222 (1976), pp. 67–77, figs. 1–6, pls. 1–8; A. Siegelmann, "A Capital in the Form of a Papyrus Flower from Megiddo," *TA* 3:4 (1976), p. 141, fig. 1, pl. 10:3–4; Y. Aharoni, Y. Yadin, "Megiddo," *EAEHL* III (1977), pp. 830–856, figs.; Y. Shiloh, "The Proto-Aeolic Capital — the Israelite 'Timorah' (Palmette) Capital," *PEQ* 109:1 (1977), pp. 39–52, figs. 1–8, pls. 1–3; F.R. Brandfon, "The Earliest City Wall at Megiddo," *TA* 4:1–2 (1977), pp. 79–84, figs. 1–2.

E.E. Platt, "Bone Pendants," *BA* 41:1 (1978), pp. 23–28, figs.; A. Harif, "Middle Kingdom Architectural Elements in Middle Bronze Age Megiddo," *ZDPV* 94:1 (1978), pp. 24–31, figs. 1–4; Y. Shiloh, "Elements in the Development of Town Planning in the Israelite City," *IEJ* 28:1–2 (1978), pp. 36–51, figs. 1–10, pls. 13, 14, 15 a; A. Ben-Tor, *Cylinder Seals of Third Millennium Palestine, BASOR Suppl.* 22 (1978), pp. 4, 8–10, 12, 102, 103, 106; M. Artzy, I. Perlman, F. Asaro, "Imported and Local Bichrome Ware in Megiddo," *Levant* 10 (1978), pp. 99–111, figs. 1–4; W.H. Shea, "The Conquests of Sharuḥen and Megiddo Reconsidered," *IEJ* 29:1 (1979), pp. 1–5; C.J. Davey, "Some Ancient Near Eastern Pot Bellows," *Levant* 11 (1979), pp. 101–111, figs. 1–5; A. Harif, "Common Architectural Features at Alalakh, Megiddo and Shechem," *Levant* 11 (1979),pp. 162–167, figs. 1–8; P. Gerstenblith, "A Reassessment of the Beginning of the Middle Bronze Age in Syria-Palestine," *BASOR* 237 (1980), pp. 65–84, figs. 1–3, 2 tables; D. Cole, "How Water Tunnels Worked," *BAR* 6:2 (1980), pp. 8–29, figs.; Y. Shiloh, "Solomon's Gate as Recorded by its Excavator, R. Lamon, Chicago," *Levant* 12 (1980), pp. 69–76, figs. 1–3, pls. 8–10; J.D. Muhly, "Bronze Figurines and Near Eastern Metalwork," Review of O. Negbi, *Canaanite Gods in Metal, 1976, IEJ* 30:3–4 (1980), pp. 148–161; H. Liebowitz, "Military and Feast Scenes on Late Bronze Palestinian Ivories," *IEJ* 30:3–4 (1980), pp. 162–169, figs. 1–2, pl. 18 a—c; G.R.H. Wright, Review of M. Ottosson, *Temples and Cult Places in Palestine* (1980), pp. 69–70.

Meiron

Excavated 1971–1977 by C.L. and E.M. Meyers, J. F. Strange, for ASOR, AIAR, Duke University, et al.

E.M. Meyers, A.T. Kraebel, J.F. Strange, "Khirbet Shema‘ and Meiron," *IEJ* 22:2–3 (1972), pp. 174–176, figs. 2–3, pls. 37–38 a; C.L. and E.M. Meyers, J.F. Strange, "Excavations at Meiron, in Upper Galilee — 1971, 1972," *BASOR* 214 (1974), pp. 2–25, figs. 1–14; E.M. Meyers, J.F. Strange, "Meiron," *IEJ* 24:3–4 (1974), pp. 279–280, pl. 61 b-d; A. D. Ritterspach, "The Meiron Cistern Pottery," *BASOR* 215 (1974), pp. 19–29, fig. 1 a, pls. 1–3; E.M. and C.L. Meyers, J.F. Strange, "Meiron 1975," *IEJ* 25:2–3 (1975), pp. 174–176, pl. 20; E.M. Meyers, J.F. Strange, R.S. Hanson, "Meiron," *RB* 83:1 (1976), fig. 3, pls. 16–19.

D. Barag, "Meiron," *EAEHL* III (1977), pp. 856–860, figs., E.M. Meyers, "Meiron," *EAEHL* III (1977), pp. 856, 860, 862, figs.; *id.*, "Meiron and Gush Ḥalav 1977," *ASOR Newsletter* 3 (Nov. 1977), pp. 6–8, figs., E.M. Meyers et al., "Meiron 1974, 1975," *AASOR* 43 (1978), pp. 73–108, figs.; E.M. Meyers, "Meiron 1977," *RB* 85:1 (1978), pp. 109–112, pl. 14; E.M. and C.L. Meyers, J.F. Strange, "Meiron 1977," *IEJ* 28:1–2 (1978), pp. 126–128, pl. 24 c-d; C.L. and E.M. Meyers, "Digging the Talmud in Ancient Meiron," *BAR* 4:2 (1978), pp. 32–42, figs.; E.M. Meyers, J.F. Strange, D.E. Groh, "The Meiron Excavation Project: Archaeological Survey in Galilee and Golan 1976," *BASOR* 230 (1978), pp. 1–24, figs. 1–18; K. W. Russell, "The Earthquake of May 19, A.D. 363," *BASOR* 238 (1980), pp. 47–64, figs. 1–5; E.M. Meyers, "Ancient Synagogues in Galilee: Their Religious and Cultural Setting," *BA* 43:2 (1980), pp. 97–108, figs.; *id.*, "Early Meiron — Five Seasons of Excavations," *Qad.* 13:3–4 (1980), pp. 111–113, figs.; *id.*, "The Synagogue at Ḥorvat Shema‘," *ASR* (1981), pp. 70–74, figs.; E.M. Meyers, J.F. Strange, C.L. Meyers, *Excavations at Ancient Meiron* (1981).

Mekheizin, Rujm el-

H.O. Thompson, "Rujm al-Malfuf et Rujm al-Mekheizin (Transjordanie)," *RB* 82:1 1975), pp. 97–100, pl. 9 c.

Menahem, Kefar

D. Gilead, M. Israel, "An Early Palaeolithic Site at Kefar Menahem," *TA* 2:1 (1975), pp. –12, figs. 1–8, 3 tables, pl. 1.

Menorah, Tell, Tell Abu Faraj

Excavated 1975 by Z. Gal for the Israel Dept. of Antiquities and Museums.

Z. Gal, "An Early Iron Age Site near Tel Menorah in the Beth-shan Valley," *TA* 6:3–4 (1979), pp. 138–145, figs. 1–4, pl. 21.

Meqabelein, Amman

Excavated 1973 by A.J. 'Amr for the Jordan Dept. of Antiquities.

A.J. 'Amr, "Excavations at Meqabelein," *ADAJ* 18 (1973), pp. 73–74, pls. 43–46.

Meṣad Har Sa'ad

Excavated 1980 by R. Cohen for the Israel Dept. of Antiquities and Museums.

R. Cohen, "Meṣad Har Sa'ad," *IEJ* 30:3–4 (1980), pp. 234–235.

Meṣad Hashavyahu, see Yavneh Yam

Meṣad Tamar, see Tamara

Meṣer

M. Dothan, "Meṣer," *EAEHL* III (1977), pp. 864–865, figs.

Meshâsh, see Masos

Mesora, Khirbet

Excavated 1975, 1976 by R. Cohen for the Israel Dept. of Antiquities and Museums.

R. Cohen, "Ḥ. Mesora," *IEJ* 27:2–3 (1977), pp. 170–171.

Mevorakh, Tell

Excavated 1973–1976 by E. Stern for Hebrew University.

E. Stern, "Tel Meborach," *IEJ* 23:4 (1973), pp. 256–257, pl. 72 c; *id*, "Tel Mevorakh (Tel Meborach)," *IEJ* 24:3–4 (1974), pp. 266–268, pl. 58 A-D; *id*, "Tel Meborach," *RB* 82:2 (1975), pp. 254–257, pls. 21 b–23; *id*., "Tel Mevorach," *RB* 83:2 (1976), pp. 266–269, pls. 32–33; *id*., "Tel Mevorakh 1975," *IEJ* 26:1 (1976), pp. 49–50, pl. 10; *id*., "Bes Vases from Palestine and Syria," *IEJ* 26:4 (1976), pp. 183–187, figs. 1–3, pls. 32, 33 a–b; *id*., "Tel Mevorakh 1976," *IEJ* 26:4 (1976), pp. 199–200, pls. 32, 36 a–b; *id*., "A Late Bronze Age Temple at Tel Mevorakh," *Qad*. 9:4 (1976), pp. 109–111, figs. (Hebrew).

E. Stern, "The Excavation at Tell Mevorach and the Late Phoenician Elements in the Architecture of Palestine," *BASOR* 225 (1977), pp. 17–27, figs. 1–17; *id*., "Tel Mevorakh," *RB* 84:2 (1977), pp. 263–264, pls. 7 b–8; *id*., "A Late Bronze Age Temple at Tel Mevorakh," *BA* 40:2 (1977), pp. 89–91, figs., 1 pl.; *id*., "Tel Mevorakh 1976," *ASOR Newsletter* 2 (Aug. 1977), pp. 4–7, figs.; *id*., "Mevorakh, Tel," *EAEHL* III (1977), pp. 861, 866–871, figs.; *id*., "Excavations at Tel Mevorakh 1973–1976. Part One: From the Iron Age to the Roman Period." *Qedem* 9 (1978); E. Stern, D.L. Saltz, "Cypriote Pottery from the Middle Bronze Age Strata of Tel Mevorakh," *IEJ* 28:3 (1978), pp. 137–145, figs. 1–3, pls. 25, 26 a–b; E. Stern "Excavations at Tell Mevorakh Are Prelude to Tell Dor Dig," *BAR* 5:3 (1979), pp. 34–39 figs.; I. Perlman, J. Yellin, "The Provenience of Obsidian from Neolithic Sites in Israel," *IEJ* 30:1–2 (1980), pp. 83–88, fig. 1, 2 tables.

Michal, Tell, Makmish

Excavated 1977–1979 by J.D. Muhly, M. Kochavi, Z. Herzog et al., for the Universities of Tel Aviv, Brigham Young, Minnesota, Pennsylvania, Macquarie, Australia.

N. Avigad, "Makmish," *EAEHL* III (1977), pp. 768–770, figs.; Z. Herzog, "Tel Mikhal (Tell Makmish) 1977," *IEJ* 28:1–2 (1978), pp. 123–124, pl. 23 a–c; Z. Herzog, O. Negbi, S. Moshkovitz, "Excavations at Tell Michal 1977," *TA* 5:3–4 (1978), pp. 99–130, figs. 1–15, pls. 33–39; N. Bakler, "Geology of Tel Michal and the Herzliya Coast," *TA* 5:3–4 (1978), pp. 131–135, figs. 1–2, 1 table; R. Gophna, "Archaeological Survey of the Central Coastal Plain 1977," *TA* 5:3–4 (1978), pp. 136–147, figs. 1–7, pl. 40:1; A. R. Schulman, "Two Scarab Impressions from Tel Michal," *TA* 5:3–4 (1978), pp. 148–151, fig. 1, pl. 40:2–3; I. Mozel, "A Note on the Flint Implements from Tel Michal and Naḥal Poleg," *TA* 5:3–4 (1978), pp. 152–158, figs. 1–3; A. Kindler, "A Ptolemaic Coin Hoard from Tel Michal," *TA* 5:3–4 (1978), pp. 159–169, pls. 41–43.

Z. Herzog, S. Moshkowitz, O. Negbi, A.F. Rainey, "Tel Michal, "A Coastal Site in the Sharon Plain," *Expedition* 20:4 (1978), pp. 44–49, figs.; Z. Herzog, "Tel Mikhal (Tell Makmish) 1978," *IEJ* 29:2 (1979), pp. 120–122, pl. 15; S. Moshkovitch, "Tel Mikhal 1977–1978," *RB* 86:3 (1979), pp. 453–457, fig. 8, pls. 22 b–24.

Z. Herzog et al., "Excavations at Tel Michal 1978–1979," *TA* 7:3–4 (1980), pp. 111–151, figs. 1–14, pls. 29–35; C. Elliott, Review of Z. Herzog et al., *Excavations at Tel Michal 1977*, reprint of *TA* 5:3–4, 1978, *PEQ* 113:1 (1981), pp. 68–69.

Midras, Khirbet, Durusiya, Khirbet

Excavated 1976 by A. Kloner for the Israel Dept. of Antiquities and Museums.

A. Kloner, "Ḥ.Midras (Kh. Durusiya)," *IEJ* 27:4 (1977), pp. 251–253, pl. 39 d; *id.*, "Ḥorvat Midras," *Qad.* 11:4 (1978), pp. 115–119, figs. (Hebrew).

Minḥa, Ḥorvat, see Munḥata

Minya, Khirbet el-

O. Grabar, "Minya, Khirbet el-," *EAEHL* III (1977), pp. 875–876, fig.

Mirzbaneh, Dhahr, see Sâmiyeh, 'Ain es-

Mishmar, Naḥal, Judean Caves

P. Bar-Adon, "Judean Desert Caves, Naḥal Mishmar," *EAEHL* III (1977), pp. 683–690; *id.*, *The Cave of the Treasure* (1980).

Monash, Kfar

A. Ben-Tor, "The Date of the Kfar Monash Hoard," *IEJ* 21:4 (1971), pp. 201–206; T.F. Watkins, "The Date of the Kfar Monash Hoard Again," *PEQ* 107:1 (1975), pp. 53–63, figs. 1–4; R. Gophna, "Sharon Plain," *EAEHL* IV (1978), pp. 1071–1074.

Montfort Castle, Qal'at el-Qurain

M. Benvenisti, "Montfort," *EAEHL* III (1977), pp. 886–888, figs.

Mor, Tell

M. Dothan, "The Foundation of Tel Mor and of Ashdod," *IEJ* 23:1 (1973), pp. 1–17, figs. 1–7, pls. 1–3; *id.*, "Mor, Tel," *EAEHL* III (1977), pp. 889–890, fig. on p. 888.

Motza

E. Eisenberg, "Motsa," *RB* 82:4 (1975), p. 587; D. Bahat, "A Middle Bronze I Tomb-Cave at Motza," *EI* 12 (1975), pp. 18–23, figs. 1–5, table, pls. 9–12 (Hebrew).

Mount Gerizim, see Gerizim

Mount Tabor, see Tabor

Mughara, Jebel

J.L. Phillips, O. Bar-Yosef, "Jebel Maghara (Northern Sinai)," *IEJ* 23:2 (1973), pp. 106–107.

Mugharet Abu Shinjeh, see Dâliyeh, Wâdī edh-

Mughâret Abu Uṣba', see Carmel, Mount

Mukelik, Deir

Y. Blomme, E. Nodet, "Deir Mukelik, 1979," *RB* 86:3 (1979), pp. 462–464, fig. 11, pl. 27 b.

Mukhayyet, Khirbet el-, see Nebo, Mount

Munḥata, Ḥorvat Minḥa

E.M. Meyers, "Secondary Burials in Palestine," *BA* 33:1 (1970), pp. 1–29, figs. 1–14; E. Yeivin, I. Mozel," A *Fossil Directeur* Figurine of the Pottery Neolithic A," *TA* 4:3–4 (1977), pp. 194–200, figs. 1–3, pl. 20; H. de Contenson, "Jordan Valley," *EAEHL* III (1977), pp. 656–658, figs.; J. Perrot, N. Zori, "Minḥa, Ḥorvat," *EAEHL* III (1977), pp. 871–874, 900 figs.

Muqibleh, Jordan

H.O. Thompson, B. de Vries, "A Water Tunnel at Muqibleh," *ADAJ* 17 (1972), pp. 89–90, pls. 1–3.

Murabba'at

E. Stern, "Judean Desert Caves — Wâdī Murabba'at," *EAEHL* III (1977), pp. 691–694, figs.

Mûraq, Khirbet el-

E. Damati, "Khirbet el-Mûraq," *IEJ* 22:2–3 (1972), p. 173, pl. 35 a.

Musa, Wâdî

W.A. Ward, "A Possible New Link between Egypt and Jordan," *ADAJ* 18 (1973), pp. 45–46, pl. 27.

Na'aran, 'Ain Duq

M. Avi-Yonah, "Na'aran," *EAEHL* III (1977), pp. 891–894, figs.; J. Naveh, "Ancient Synagogue Inscriptions," *ASR* (1981), pp. 133–139, figs., esp. p. 136.

Nablus, Neapolis

C.M. Dauphin, "A Roman Mosaic Pavement from Nablus," *IEJ* 29:1 (1979), pp. 11–33, pls. 1–8 a.

Nablus, see Gerizim, Mount

Nablus, see Shechem

Nabratein, En, Neburaya, Kfar

N. Avigad, "Kefar Neburaya," *EAEHL* III (1977), pp. 710–711, figs.

Excavated 1980–1981 by E. Meyers et al., for ASOR, National Geographic Society and others.
E.M. Meyers, "Excavations at En-Nabratein, Upper Galilee: The 1980 Season," *ASOR Newsletter* 2 (Sept. 1980), pp. 3–7, 10–11, figs.; J.N. Wilford, *The New York Times* (Aug. 2, 1981), p. 22; *Newsweek* (Aug. 17, 1981), p. 61.

Nagila, Tell

M. Artzy, F. Asaro, I. Perlman, "The Tel Nagila Bichrome Krater as a Cypriote Product," *IEJ* 25:2–3 (1975), pp. 129–134, figs. 1–2, table; R. Amiran, A. Eitan, "Nagila, Tel," *EAEHL* III (1977), pp. 894–898, figs.

Naḥal David Caves

N. Avigad, "Judean Desert Caves, Naḥal David," *EAEHL* III (1977), pp. 666–670, fig.

Naḥf

Excavated 1978 by F. Vitto for the Israel Dept. of Antiquities and Museums.
F. Vitto, "Potter's Kilns at Kfar Naḥf," *IEJ* 30:3–4 (1980), pp. 205–206, pl. 25 a.

Naḥal Ḥever, see Ḥever

Naḥal Mishmar, see Mishmar

Naḥal Seelim, see Seelim

Nahariya

D. Barag, "Glass Vessels from the Roman Cemetery at Nahariya," *Qad.* 4:3 (1971), pp. 96–98, figs. (Hebrew).

Excavated 1972, 1974, 1976 by G. Edelstein and C. Dauphin for the Israel Dept. of Antiquities and Museums.
G. Edelstein, "Nahariya," *RB* 81:1 (1974), pp. 100–102, pl. 14 a; J. M. Weinstein, "Egyptian Relations with Palestine in the Middle Kingdom," *BASOR* 217 (1975), pp. 1–16,

figs. 1–3; G. Edelstein, C. Dauphin, "A Byzantine Church at Nahariya," *Qad.* 8:4 (1975), pp. 128–132, figs. (Hebrew); *id.*, "Nahariya 1976," *IEJ* 26:2–3 (1976), pp. 141–142; *id.*, "Nahariya," *RB* 84:2 (1977), pp. 278–281, figs. 2–3; M. Dothan, "Nahariya," *EAEHL* III, (1977), pp. 908–912, 917, figs.; A. Harif, "Coastal Buildings of Foreign Origin in Second Millennium B. C. Palestine," *PEQ* 110:2 (1978), pp. 101–106, figs. 1–2; A. Ovadiah, C. G. de Silva, "Supplementum to the Corpus of the Byzantine Churches in the Holy Land," *Levant* 13 (1981), pp. 200–261, figs., esp. pp. 246–248, fig.

Naharon, Tell

Excavated 1977–1978 by F. Vitto for the Israel Dept. of Antiquities and Museums.

F. Vitto, "Two Marble Heads from Tel Naharon at Scythopolis," *Qad.* 11:2–3 (1978), pp. 67–70, figs. (Hebrew); *id.*, "Tel Naharon," *IEJ* 30:3–4 (1980), p. 214, pl. 27 b.

Naṣbeh, Tell en-

M. Broshi, "Naṣbeh, Tell en-," *EAEHL* III (1977), pp. 912–916, 918, figs.; M. Aharoni, "The Askos: Is it the Biblical Nĕbel?" *TA* 6:1–2 (1979), pp. 95–97, fig. 1.

Na'ur

S. 'Abbadi, "A Byzantine Tomb from Na'ur," *ADAJ* 18 (1973), pp. 69–71, figs. 1–2, pls. 41–42.

Natosh, 'En

D. Urman, "'En Natosh," *EAEHL* II (1976), pp. 466.

Nazareth

Excavated 1970 by B. Bagatti for the Franciscan Custody of the Holy Land.

R. Rosenthal, Review of B. Bagatti, *Excavations in Nazareth I, 1969, IEJ* 21:2–3 (1971), p. 181; B. Bagatti, "Scavo presso la chiese di S. Giuseppe a Nazaret (agosto 1970)," *LA* 21 (1971), pp. 5–32, figs. 1–23; J. Prawer, "A Crusader Tomb of 1290 from Acre and the Last Archbishops of Nazareth," *IEJ* 24:3–4 (1974), pp. 241–251, figs. 1–3, pl. 54; S. Loffreda, "Ceramica del Ferro I trovata a Nazaret," *LA* 27 (1977), pp. 135–144, pls. 13–18; B. Bagatti, "Nazareth," *EAEHL* III (1977), pp. 919–922, figs.; A. Ovadiah, C. G. de Silva, "Supplementum to the Corpus of the Byzantine Churches in the Holy Land," *Levant* 13 (1981), pp. 200–261, p. 248, figs.

Neapolis, see Nablus

Nebi Rubin, see Yavneh Yam

Nebi Samwil

K. Baltzer, J. Conrad, F. Rehkopf, H. F. Schmid, S. Wagner, "Die Besiedlungsreste und Grabanlagen zwischen Bet Hanina und en-Nabi Samwil," *ZDPV* 87:1 (1971), pp. 23–41, figs. 1–4, pls. 1–3.

Nebo, Mount, Khirbet el-Mukhayyet, Siyâgha

Excavated 1973, 1976 by M. Piccirillo for the Franciscan Custody of the Holy Land.

V. Corbo, "Scavi archeologici sotto i mosaici della basilica del Monte Nebo (Siyagha)," *LA*

20 (1970), pp. 273–298, figs. 1–13, 4 plans; M. Piccirillo, "Campagna archeologica a Khirbet Mukhayyet (Città del Nebo) 1973," *LA* 23 (1973), pp. 322–358, figs. 1–30, 1 plan; *id.*, "Campagna archeologica nella basilica di Mosè profeta a sul Monte Nebo-Siyagha 1976," *LA* 26 (1976), pp. 281–318, 2 figs., 8 plans, pls. 49–80; *id.*, "New Discoveries on Mount Nebo," *ADAJ* 21 (1976), pp. 55–59, figs. 1–2, pls. 13–17; B. Bagatti, "Nebo, Mount," *EAEHL* III (1977), pp. 923–926, figs.; R. Hachlili, "The Zodiac in Ancient Jewish Art: Representation and Significance," *BASOR* 228 (1977), pp. 61–77, figs. 1–18; M. Piccirillo, "Les découvertes du Nebo: Aout 1976," *BTS* 188 (1977), pp. 6–19, figs.; *id.*, "Campagne archéologique dans la basilique du mont Nébo-Siyâgha," *RB* 84:2 (1977), pp. 246–253, fig. 1, pls. 2–3; S. S. Weinberg, "A Moabite Shrine Group," *Muse* 12 (1978), pp. 30–48, figs. 1–19.

Nekheileh, 'Ain Abu

D. Kirkbride, "The Neolithic in Wadi Rumm," *Archaeology in the Levant* (1978), pp. 1–10, figs. 1–5, pl. 1.

Nessana, 'Auja el-Ḥafir, Nitsanah

M. Avi-Yonah, "Nessana," *EAEHL* III (1977), pp. 927–930, figs.

Netopha, Bedd Faluh, Khirbet

K. Kob, "Noch einmal Netopha," *ZDPV* 94:2 (1978), pp. 119–134, figs. 1–4, pls. 9–10.

Nicopolis, see Emmaus

Nirim, see Ma'on

Nitsanah, see Nessana

Nizzanim

E. Yeivin, Y. Olami, "Nizzanim — A Neolithic Site in Naḥal Evtah," *TA* 6:3–4 (1979), pp. 99–135, figs. 1–19, pls. 17–20:1–3; R. Gophna, "Two Early Bronze Age Basalt Bowls from the Vicinity of Nizzanim," *TA* 6:3–4 (1979), pp. 136–137, fig. 1, pl. 20:4.

Numeira

R. T. Schaub, W. E. Rast, "Bab edh-Dhra' and Numeira," *ASOR Newsletter* 6 (March 1978), p. 4; H. Shanks, "Have Sodom and Gomorrah been Found?" *BAR* 6:5 (1980), pp. 26–36, figs.; W. E. Rast, R. T. Schaub, "Expedition to the Southeastern Dead Sea Plain, Jordan 1979," *ASOR Newsletter* 8 (June 1980), pp. 12–17, figs., esp. pp. 15–16.

Oboda, see 'Abdah

Orda, see Kissufim

'Oreimeh, Tell el-

V. Fritz, "Kinneret und Ginnosar Voruntersuchung für eine Ausgrabung auf dem Tell el-Oreme am See Genezareth," *ZDPV* 94:1 (1978), pp. 32–45, figs. 1–3, pl. 2.

Oren, Naḥal, Carmel, Mount

T. Noy, E. Higgs, "Naḥal Oren," *IEJ* 21:2–3 (1971), pp. 171–172; T. Noy, "A House and Tombs from the Pre-Pottery Neolithic Period," *Qad.* 6:1 (1973), pp. 18–19, figs.; *id.*, "Naḥal Oren," *EAEHL* III (1977), pp. 898–899, 901–907, figs.

Ostracina, Ostrakine

E. Oren, "A Christian Settlement at Ostracina in Northern Sinai," *Qad.* 11:2–3 (1978), pp. 81–87, figs. (Hebrew), E. D. Oren, M. A. Morrison, "Excavations at Ostrakine," Part I, *ILN* (Nov. 1981), pp. 76–77, figs.; *ibid., Part II, ILN* (Dec. 1981), p. 90, figs.

Pella, Tabaqat Faḥil, Tell el-Ḥusn, Piḥilum

R. H. Smith, "A Refuge for Christians," *ILN* (March 16, 1968), pp. 26–27, figs. 1–7; *id.*, "The Sectioning of Potsherds as an Archaeological Method," *Berytus* 21 (1972), pp. 39–53, figs. 1–3, pls. 1–2; *id.*, "A Sarcophagus from Pella: New Light on Earliest Christianity," *Archaeology* 26:4 (1973), pp. 250–256, figs.; *id.*, *Pella of the Decapolis I* (1973); J. A. Sauer, Review of *Pella of the Decapolis I, ADAJ* 19 (1974), pp. 169–172; R. H. Smith, "Pella of the Decapolis," *IDB-S* (1976), pp. 651–652, fig.; L. I. Levine, "Pella," *EAEHL* IV (1978), pp. 939–943, figs.

Excavated 1979–1981 by R. H. Smith, J. B. Hennessy, for The College of Wooster, University of Sydney, Jordan Dept. of Antiquities.

E. S. Kindig, "Return to Pella," *The Cleveland Plain Dealer Magazine* (Sept. 9, 1979), pp. 58–59, 61, 63, 67–68, 71, figs.; R. H. Smith, "Pella," *ASOR Newsletter* 7 (April, 1980), pp. 22–26, figs.; *id.*, "Pella of the Decapolis," *Jordan* 5:3 (1980), pp. 13–15, 18–19, figs.; *id.*, "Excavations at Pella of the Decapolis, Jordan," *AJA* 85:2 (1981), p. 218; *id.*, "Pella of the Decapolis," *ASOR Newsletter* 7 (May, 1981), pp. 7–10, figs.; *id.*, "Pella of the Decapolis: An American-Australian Expedition Reconstructs 7000 Years of History in the Jordan Valley," *Archaeology* 34:5 (1981), pp. 46–53, figs., cover.

Petra, Reqem

M. Lindner, ed., *Petra und das Königreich der Nabatäer* (1970); A. Negev, "A Nabataean Epitaph from Trans-Jordan," *IEJ* 21:1 (1971), pp. 50–52, pl. 4; K. Schmitt-Korte, "A Contribution to the Study of Nabataean Pottery," *ADAJ* 16 (1971), pp. 47–60, figs. 1–14, 1 table; *id.*, "Die Entwicklung des Granatapfel-Motivs in der nabatäischen Keramik," *Naturhistorische Gesellschaft* (1972), pp. 40–44, figs. 1–8; A. Negev, "Nabataean Sigillata," *RB* 79:3 (1972), pp. 381–398, figs. 1–5, pls. 32–34; G. R. H. Wright, "Petra: Some Unusual Views," *ZDPV* 88:2 (1972), pp. 182–184, pls. 15–17.

C.-M. Bennett, "Umm el-Biyarah," *The Archaeological Heritage of Jordan* I (1973), p. 21; P. C. Hammond, "Pottery from Petra," *PEQ* 105:1 (1973), pp. 27–49, 8 figs., 3 pls.; G. R. H. Wright, "The Date of the Khaznet Firʿaun at Petra in the Light of an Iconographic Detail," *PEQ* 105:1 (1973), pp. 83–90, figs. 1–3, pl. 4; A. Negev, "The Staircase-Tower in Nabataean Architecture," *RB* 80:3 (1973), pp. 364–383, figs. 1–10, table, pls. 2–6; P. C. Hammond, *The Nabataeans: Their History, Culture and Archaeology* (1973); C.-M. Bennett, "An Unusual Cup from Petra (Southern Jordan)," *Levant* 5 (1973), pp. 131–133, fig. 1, pl. 45 c.

Excavated 1973 by F. Zayadine, M. Lindner for the Jordan Dept. of Antiquities and Naturhistorische Gesellschaft, Nürnberg.

F. Zayadine, "Excavations at Petra (April 1973)," *ADAJ* 18 (1973), pp. 81–82, pl. 50:2–3; A. Negev, "Petra and the Nabataeans," *Qad.* 7:3–4 (1974), pp. 71–93, figs. (Hebrew); *id.*, *The Nabataean Potter's Workshop at Oboda* (1974); F. Zayadine, "Excavations at Petra, 1973–1974," *ADAJ* 19 (1974), pp. 135–150, figs. 1–5, pls. 57–69; P. C. Hammond, "Magnetometer/

Resistivity Survey at Petra, Jordan — 1973," *BASOR* 214 (1974), pp. 39–41, 1 fig.

Y. Meshorer, "Nabataean Coins," *Qedem* 3 (1975); P. C. Hammond, "Survey and Excavation at Petra, 1973–1974," *ADAJ* 20 (1975), pp. 5–30, 5 figs., pls. 1–10.

Excavated 1973–1974 by P. C. Hammond, F. Zayadine for the Jordan Dept. of Antiquities.

S. Perowne, Review of I. Browning, *Petra, 1973, PEQ* 107:1 (1975), pp. 80–81; P. J. Parr, K. B. Atkinson, E. H. Wickens, "Photogrammetic Work at Petra 1965–1968, an Interim Report," *ADAJ* 20 (1975), pp. 31–45, figs. 1–3, pls. 11–12; P. C. Hammond, *The Excavations of the Main Theater at Petra 1961–1962* (1975); J. T. Milik, J. Starcky, "Inscriptions récemment découvertes à Pétra," *ADAJ* 20 (1975), pp. 111–130, pls. 37–47; P. C. Hammond, *A History of the Nabataeans: Studies in Mediterranean Archaeology.* (1975).

A. Negev, "The Nabataean Necropolis at Egra," *RB* 83:2 (1976), pp. 203–236, figs. 1–6, tables, pls. 20–25; M. Gory, "Travaux effectués par l'Institut Géographique National de France," *ADAJ* 21 (1976), pp. 79–85, pls. 33–38; *id.*, "Etablissement d'un Photoplan," *ADAJ* 21 (1976), pp. 87–91, pls. 39–40; F. Zayadine, P. Hottier, "Relevé Photogrammétrique à Pétra," *ADAJ* 21 (1976), pp. 93–104, figs. 1–5, pls. 41–53; J. T. Milik, "Une inscription bilingue nabatéenne et grecque à Petra," *ADAJ* 21 (1976), pp. 143–152, fig.

M. J. Price, Review of Y. Meshorer, "Nabataean Coins," *Qedem* 3, 1973, *IEJ* 27:1 (1977), pp. 59–61; R. Sivan, "Notes on Some Nabataean Pottery Vessels," *IEJ* 27:2–3 (1977), pp. 138–144, figs. 1–2, pl. 14; P. C. Hammond, "The Capitals from 'The Temple of the Winged Lions' Petra," *BASOR* 226 (1977), pp. 47–51, figs. 1–7; *id.*, "Excavations at Petra 1975–1977," *ADAJ* 22 (1977–78), pp. 81–101, pls. 43–62; D. F. Graf, "The Saracens and the Defense of the Arabian Frontier," *BASOR* 229 (1978), pp. 1–26; P. C. Hammond, Review of I. Browning, *Petra, 1973, BASOR* 229 (1978), pp. 75–76; *id.*, "New Light on Petra," *ILN* (July 1978), pp. 64–65, figs.; C.-M. Bennett, D. L. Kennedy, "A New Roman Military Inscription from Petra," *Levant* 10 (1978), pp. 163–165, fig. 1, pl. 25 b.

A. Negev, "Petra," *EAEHL* IV (1978), pp. 943–959, figs.; P. J. Parr, "Pottery, People and Politics," *Archaeology in the Levant* (1978), pp. 202–209, fig. 1; F. Zayadine, "Petra (Nécropole de Khutbha) 1973–1978," *RB* 86:1 (1979), pp. 133–136, figs. 8–9, pl. 10 b, c.

Excavated 1976–1978 by F. Zayadine for the Jordan Dept. of Antiquities.

F. Zayadine, "Excavations at Petra 1976–78," *ADAJ* 23 (1979), pp. 185–197, figs. 1–5, pls. 83–94; N. I. Khairy, "Ink-wells of the Roman Period from Jordan," *Levant* 12 (1980), pp. 155–162, figs. 1–5, pl. 25; L. G. Herr, "The Formal Scripts of Iron Age Transjordan," *BASOR* 238 (1980), pp. 21–34, figs. 1–4; K. W. Russell, "The Earthquake of May 19, A. D. 363," *BASOR* 238 (1980), pp. 47–64, figs. 1–5; P. C. Hammond, "New Evidence for the 4th-century A. D. Destruction of Petra," *BASOR* 238 (1980), pp. 65–67; N. I. Khairy, "A New Dedicatory Nabataean Inscription from Wadi Musa," *PEQ* 113:1 (1981), pp. 19–26, figs. 1–3, pl. 3; P. C. Hammond, "Cult and Cupboard at Nabataean Petra," *Archaeology* 34:2 (1981), pp. 27–34, figs.; P. C. Hammond, "New Light on the Nabataeans, Recent Excavations at Petra," *BAR* 7:2 (1981), pp. 22–41, figs., *id.*, "A Kingdom of Traders," *Aramco World Magazine* (March-April 1981), pp. 36–41, figs.

Petra, see Beidha, Wâdī

Petra, see Musa, Wâdī

Poleg, Tell

R. Gophna, "The Middle Bronze Age II Fortifications at Tel Poleg," *EI* 11 (1973), pp. 111–119 (Hebrew); *id.*, "Poleg, Tel," *EAEHL* IV (1978), pp. 959–960, figs.; *id.*, "Archaeological Survey of the Central Coastal Plain 1977," *TA* 5:3–4 (1978), pp. 136–147, figs. 1–7, pl. 40:1; I Mozel, "A Note on the Flint Implements from Tel Michal and Naḥal Poleg," *TA* 5:3–4

(1978), pp. 152–158, figs. 1–3; M. Kochavi, R. Gophna, "Aphek-Antipatris, Tel Poleg, Tel Zeror and Tel Burga: Four Fortified Sites in the Sharon Plain," *ZDPV* 95:2 (1979), pp. 121–165, figs. 1–18, pls. 8–9 a.

Poran, Tell

R. Gophna, "Fortified Settlements from the Early Bronze and Middle Bronze II at Tel Poran," *EI* 13 (1977), pp. 87–90, pl. 11 (Hebrew).

Ptolemais, see Acco

Qa 'a Mejalla, Jordan

A. Betts, "Evidence of the Stone Age," *ILN* (Nov. 1980), pp. 88–89, figs.

Qa 'aqir, Jebel

E. Meyers, "Secondary Burials in Palestine," *BA* 33:1 (1970), pp. 1–29, figs. 1–14; W.G. Dever, "Jebel Qa'aqir," *IEJ* 21:4 (1971), pp. 229–230; *id.*, "Djebel Qa'aqir," *RB* 78:4 (1971), pp. 595–597, pl. 31 a; *id.*, "The Peoples of Palestine in the Middle Bronze I Period," *HTR* 64:2–3 (1971), pp. 197–226; S. Gitin, "Middle Bronze I 'Domestic' Pottery at Jebel Qa'aqir: A Ceramic Inventory of Cave G 23," *EI* 12 (1975), pp. 46–62, figs. 1–5, tables 1–13; W.G. Dever, "New Vistas on the EB IV ('MB I') Horizon in Syria-Palestine," *BASOR* 237 (1980), pp. 35–64, figs. 1–6.

Qadeis, 'Ain

R. Cohen, "'Ein Qedeis," *IEJ* 27:2–3 (1977), p. 171.

Qadesh-barnea, see Qudeirat, 'Ain el-

Qafze, Jebel

B. Vandermeersch, "Qafzeh," *RB* 77:4 (1970), pp. 561–564, pl. 32; M. Stekelis, "El-Qafze Cave," *EAEHL* IV (1978), pp. 961–962, figs.

Qanafid, Umm el-

W.J. Fulco, "A Seal from Umm el-Qanafid, Jordan," *Orientalia* 48:1 (1979), pp. 107–108, fig.

Qanatir, Umm el-

M. Avi-Yonah, "Synagogues," *EAEHL* IV (1978), pp. 1129–1138, figs.

Qarnaim, Kfar

S. Goldschmidt, "Synagogue Remains at the Mound of Kefar Qarnaim," *EI* 11 (1973), pp. 39–40 (Hebrew).

Qaryat el-'Anab, see Abu Ghosh

Qashish, Tell

A. Ben-Tor, "Yoqne'am Regional Project Looks Beyond the Tell," *BAR* 6:2 (1980), pp. 30–44, figs.

Qasile, Tell el-

Excavated 1971–1974 by A. Mazar, 1976 by H. Ritter–Kaplan, for Tel Aviv and Hebrew Universities, Israel Exploration Society.

A. Mazar, "A Philistine Temple at Tell Qasile," *Qad.* 6:1 (1973), pp. 20–23 (Hebrew); *ibid. BA* 36:2 (1973), pp. 42–48, figs. 1–2; A. Mazar, "Excavations at Tell Qasile 1971–72," *IEJ* 23:2 (1973), pp. 65–71, fig. 1, pls. 13–18; *id.*, "Tell Qasilé," *RB* 80:3 (1973), pp. 412–415, pl. 16; *id.*, "Excavations at Tell Qasile 1973–1974," *IEJ* 25:2–3 (1975), pp. 77–78, figs. 1–4, pls. 5–7; *id.*, "Tel Qasilé," *RB* 82:2 (1975), pp. 263–266, pl. 25; *id.*, A. Mazar, "Further Philistine Temples at Tell Qasile," *Qad.* 9:4 (1976), pp. 115–118, figs. (Hebrew); *ibid. BA* 40:2 (1977), pp. 82–87, figs., pl. B.

T. Dothan, I. Dunayevsky, "Qasile, Tell," *EAEHL* IV (1978), pp. 963–968, figs., A. Mazar, "Qasile, Tell," *EAEHL* IV (1978), pp. 968–975, figs.; H. Ritter–Kaplan, "Tel Qasileh 1976," *RB* 85:3 (1978), pp. 415–416, pl. 23 a; *id.*, "Remains on the Northern Slope of Tell Qasile 1976," *IEJ* 28:3 (1978), pp. 199–200; A. Mazar, "Excavations at Tell Qasile I: The Philistine Sanctuary," *Qedem* 12 (1980).

Qasr 'Amra, see 'Amra

Qaṣr el-'Abd, see 'Araq el-Emir

Qasta, Khirbet, see Haifa

Qatifa, Tell

A. Biran "Tell er-Ruqeish to Tell er-Ridan," *IEJ* 24:2 (1974), pp. 141–142, pls. 24–25.

Qedesh

M. Tadmor, "A Cult Cave of the Middle Bronze Age I near Qedesh," *IEJ* 28:1–2 (1978), pp. 1–30, figs. 1–11, pls. 1–12.

Qelt, Wâdî el-, see Jericho, Herodian

J. Wilkinson, "The Way from Jerusalem to Jericho," *BA* 38:1, (1975), pp. 10–24, figs. 5–20; Y.E. Meimaris, "The Hermitage of St. John the Chozebite," *LA* 28 (1978), pp. 171–192, pls. 35–46; A. Ovadiah, C.G. de Silva, "Supplementum to the Corpus of the Byzantine Churches in the Holy Land," *Levant* 13 (1981), pp. 200–261, figs., esp. 213–214, fig.

Qiri, Tell, Hazorea, Abu–Zureiq

Excavated by E. Anati 1970–1971 for Tel Aviv University.

E. Anati, "Hazorea," *IEJ* 21:2–3 (1971), pp. 172–173; *id.*, "Abu–Zureiq (Hazorea)," *RB* 78:4 (1971), pp. 582–584, pl. 26 c.

Excavated 1975–1978 by A. Ben–Tor for Hebrew University and Israel Dept. of Antiquities and Museums.

A. Ben–Tor, "Tell Qiri (Hazorea)," *IEJ* 25:2–3 (1975), pp. 168–169, pl. 19 e; *id.*, "Tell

Qiri," *RB* 83:2 (1976), pp. 272–274, pl. 36; *id.*, "Excavations at Tell Qiri (ha–Zore'a) 1975–76," *ASOR* Newsletter 6 (Nov. 1976), pp. 10–12, figs. *id.*, "Tell Qiri (Hazorea) 1976," *IEJ* 26:4 (1976), pp. 200–201, pl. 36 c; *id.*, "Excavations at Tell Qiri in Kibbutz Hazorea," *Qad.* 10:1 (1977), pp. 24–27, figs. (Hebrew); *id.*, "Tel Qiri 1976–1977," *RB* 85:1 (1978), pp. 100–102, fig. 6, pls. 9–10; B. Brandl, A. Schwarzfeld, "Tell Qiri (Hazorea) 1977," *IEJ* 28:1–2 (1978), pp. 124–125; A. Ben–Tor, "Tell Qiri, a Look at Village Life," *BA* 42:2 (1979), pp. 105–113, figs.; *id.*, "Yoqne'am Regional Project Looks Beyond the Tell," *BAR* 6:2 (1980), pp. 30–44, figs.

Qiryat Tiv'on, see Beth She'arim

Qishyon

Excavated by R. Amiran, C. Cohen 1977 for Tel Aviv University and Israel Dept. of Antiquities and Museums.

R. Amiran, C. Cohen, "Tel Qishyon," *IEJ* 27:2–3 (1977), pp. 164–165, pl. 21 c–d.

Qisrin

Excavated 1971–1972 by D. Urman for Israel Dept. of Antiquities and Museums.

D. Urman, "Qisrin," *EAEHL* II (1976), pp. 460–462, figs.

Qla' et-Twal

W.A. Ward, "A Possible New Link between Egypt and Jordan," *ADAJ* 18 (1973), pp. 45–56, pl. 27.

Qôm, Khirbet el-

Excavated 1971 by J.S. Holladay, Jr., for the Hebrew Union College and Canada Council.

J.S. Holladay, "Khirbet el–Qôm," *IEJ* 21:2–3 (1971), pp. 175–177; W.G. Dever, "Inscriptions from Khirbet el-Kom," *Qad.* 4:3 (1971), pp. 90–92 (Hebrew); J.S. Holladay, "Khirbet el-Kôm," *RB* 78:4 (1971), pp. 593–595, pl. 30; L.T. Geraty, "The Khirbet el Kôm Bilingual Ostracon," *BASOR* 220 (1975), pp. 55–61, figs. 1–2; A. Lemaire, "Les inscriptions de Khirbet el–Qôm et l'Ashérah de Yhwh," *RB* 84:4 (1977), pp. 595–608, fig., pl. 31; W.G. Dever, "El–Qôm, Khirbet," *EAEHL* IV (1978), pp. 976–977, figs.; A. Skaist, "A Note on the Bilingual Ostracon from Khirbet el–Kôm," *IEJ* 28:1–2 (1978), pp. 106–108; G. Barkay, "A Group of Iron Age Scale Weights," *IEJ* 28:4 (1978), pp. 209–217, fig. 1, pls. 33–34.

Qoshet, Ḥorvat, see Haifa

Qubur el–Walayda, see Walaida, Qubur el-

Qudeirât, 'Ain el-, Kadesh–barnea

Excavated 1975–1979 by R. Cohen for the Israel Dept. of Antiquities and Museums.

I. Gilead, P. Goldberg, "Prehistoric Survey in the Kadesh–Barnea Area," *IEJ* 26:2–3 (1976), p. 137; I. Beit Arieh, R. Gophna, "Early Bronze Age II Sites in Wâdī el-Qudeirat (Kadesh–barnea)," *TA* 3:4 (1976), pp. 142–150, figs. 1–9, pls. 11–12; R. Cohen, "Kadesh–Barnea 1976," *IEJ* 26:4 (1976), pp. 201–202; C. Meyers, "Kadesh Barnea: Judah's Last Outpost," *BA* 39:4 (1976), pp. 148–151, figs. 1–3; D. Saltz, "Tel Qadesh Barnea," *ASOR Newsletter* 10 (May 1977), pp. 13–14; M. Dothan, "Kadesh–Barnea," *EAEHL* III (1977), pp. 697–698, figs.

R. Cohen, "Kadesh–Barnea 1978," *IEJ* 28:3 (1978), p. 197, pl. 31 c–d; *id.*, "The Iron Age Fortresses in the Central Negev," *BASOR* 236 (1979), pp. 61–79, figs. 1–14; *id.*, "Kadesh–Barnea 1979," *IEJ* 30:3–4 (1980), pp. 235–236, pls. 31b, 32; *id.*, "Excavations at Kadesh–barnea 1976–1978," *BA* 44:2 (1981), pp. 93–107, figs.; *id.*, "Did I Excavate Kadesh–Barnea?" *BAR* 7:3 (1981), pp. 20–33, figs.

Qumran, Khirbet

E.M. Yamauchi, *The Stones and the Scriptures* (1972), pp. 126–145, figs.; P. Benoit, "Note sur les Fragments grecs de la grotte 7 de Qumran," *RB* 79:3 (1972), pp. 321–324, pl. 27 a; A. Strobel, "Die Wasseranlagen der Ḥirbet Qumran," *ZDPV* 88:1 (1972), pp. 55–86, figs. 1–4, pls. 1–10; J. Briend, "Qumran," *BTS* 137 (1972), pp. 8–14, figs.; J. de Croix, "Une journée chez les Esséniens," *BTS* 137 (1972), pp. 14–19, figs.; C.M. Martini, "Note sui papiri della grotta 7 di Qumrân," *Biblica* 53:1 (1972), pp. 101–104; M. Baillet, "Les Manuscrits de la Grotte 7 de Qumrân et le Nouveau Testament," *Biblica* 53:4 (1972), pp. 508–516; G.E. Wright, "Scrolls, the Dead Sea," *HBD* (1973), pp. 653–655, 2 figs.; R. de Vaux, *Archaeology and the Dead Sea Scrolls* (1973); J.A. Sanders, "The Dead Sea Scrolls — A Quarter Century of Study," *BA* 36:4 (1973), pp. 109–148, figs. 1–13; J.C. Trever, *Scrolls from Qumran Cave I* (1972); M. Knibb, Review of J.C. Trever, *Scrolls from Qumran Cave I* (1972), *PEQ* 106:2 (1974), p. 170; J. Murphy–O'Connor, "The Essenes and their History," *RB* 81 (1974), pp. 215–244.

F.M. Cross, S. Talmon eds., *Qumran and the History of the Biblical Text* (1975); J.A. Fitzmyer, *The Dead Sea Scrolls: Major Publications and Tools for Study* (1975); G. Vermes, "Dead Sea Scrolls," *IDB–S* (1976), pp. 210–219, 563–564.

R. de Vaux, J.T. Milik, *Qumran Grotte 4, II, Discoveries in the Judean Desert* VI (1977); P.R. Ackroyd, Review of the book in *PEQ* 110:2 (1978), p. 140; J. Murphy–O'Connor, "The Essenes in Palestine," *BA* 40:3 (1977), pp. 100–124, figs.; D. Graf, "The Pagan Witness to the Essenes," *BA* 40:3 (1977), pp. 125–129, figs.; Y. Yadin, *The Temple Scroll* (1977); D. Flusser, Review of the book in *CNI* 26:3–4 (1978), pp. 168–171; J. Milgrom, "The Temple Scroll," *BA* 41:3 (1978), pp. 105–120, figs.; E. Qimron, "New Readings in the Temple Scroll," *IEJ* 28:3 (1978), pp. 161–172; B.A. Levine, "The Temple Scroll: Aspects of its Historical Provenance and Literary Character," *BASOR* 232 (1978), pp. 5–23; J.A. Sanders, "History and Archeology of the Qumran Community," Review of E.–M. Laperrousaz, *Qoumran 1976, BASOR* 231 (1978) pp. 79–80; R. de Vaux, "Qumran, Khirbet," *EAEHL* IV (1978), pp. 978–986, 988, figs., 1005; S.H. Horn, *Biblical Archaeology After 30 Years 1948–1978* (1978), pp. 14–18, 28–29.

E.M. Yamauchi, "Archaeology of Palestine and Syria," *ISBE* I (1979), p. 282, pls. 13–17; W.S. LaSor, "Dead Sea Scrolls," *ISBE* I (1979), pp. 883–897, figs.; J. Licht, "An Ideal Town Plan from Qumran — the Description of the New Jerusalem," *IEJ* 29:1 (1979), pp. 45–59, figs. 1–3; M. Sharabani, "Monnaies de Qumran au Musée Rockefeller de Jerusalem," *RB* 87:2 (1980), pp. 274–284, pls. 3–5.

K.W. Russell, "The Earthquake of May 19, A.D. 363," *BASOR* 238 (1980), pp. 47–64, figs. 1–5; N.I. Khairy, "Inkwells of the Roman Period from Jordan," *Levant* 12 (1980), pp. 155–162, figs. 1–5, pl. 25; F.M. Cross, J.C. Trever, *Introduction, Three Scrolls from Qumran Cave I* (1981); D.J. Shenhav, "Saving the Dead Sea Scrolls for the Next 2000 Years," *BAR* 7:4 (1981), pp. 44–51, figs.

Qumran, see *Revue de Qumran*

Qumran, see Buqêʿah

Quweira

G. Osborn, J.M. Duford, "Geomorphological Processes in the Inselberg Region of S.W. Jordan," *PEQ* 113:1 (1981), pp. 1–17, figs. 1–3, pls. 1–2.

Rabah, Wâdî

J. Kaplan, "Rabah, Wadi," *EAEHL* IV (1978), p. 994, figs.

Rabbah, Rabbath–Ammon, Rabbat–Moab

F. Zayadine, "Deux Inscriptions grecques de Rabbat Moab (Areopolis)," *ADAJ* 16 (1971), pp. 71–76, pls. 1–6; *id.*, "Un Séisme à Rabbat Moab (Jordanie) d'apres une Inscription grecque du VIe S.," *Berytus* 20 (1971), pp. 139–141, fig.; V.E.G. Kenna, "An LB Stamp Seal from Jordan," *ADAJ* 18 (1973), p. 79, pl. 50:1; G.M. Landes, "Rabbah," *IDB–S* (1976), p. 724; M. Avi–Yonah, E. Stern, "Rabbath–Ammon," *EAEHL* IV (1978), pp. 987, 989–993, figs.

Rabbath–Ammon, see 'Ammân

Rabud, Khirbet, Debir

M. Kochavi, "Khirbet Rabud = Debir," *TA* 1:1 (1974), pp. 2–33, figs. 1–12, pls. 1–4; J. Briend, "La ville de Debir," *BTS* 176 (1975), pp. 4–10, figs.; M. Kochavi, "Debir (City)," *IDB–S* (1976), p. 222; *id.*, "Rabud, Khirbet," *EAEHL* IV (1978), p. 995; A.F. Rainey, "Debir," *ISBE* I (1979), pp. 901–904, fig. 1.

Raddana, Khirbet, 'Ai

Excavated 1969 by R.E. Cooley for Evangel College, Southern Baptist Theological Seminary.

J.A. Callaway, R.E. Cooley, "A Salvage Excavation at Raddana, in Bireh," *BASOR* 201 (1971), pp. 9–19, figs. 1–7; F.M. Cross, Jr., D.N. Freedman, "An Inscribed Jar Handle from Raddana," *BASOR* 201, (1971), pp. 19–22, figs. 1–3; Y. Aharoni, "Khirbet Raddana and Its Inscription," *IEJ* 21:2–3 (1971), pp. 130–135, figs. 1–4; J.A. Callaway, "Khirbet Raddana," *RB* 81:1 (1974), pp. 91–94, pls. 8–9; F.M. Cross, Jr., "Early Alphabetic Scripts," *Symposia*, F.M. Cross, ed. (1979), pp. 97–111.

Rafid, Er-

D. Urman, "Er–Rafid," *EAEHL* II (1976), p. 467.

Raḥba, Khirbet Umm et–Tin

Excavated 1974 by R. Cohen for Israel Dept. of Antiquities and Museums.

R. Cohen, "Ḥ. Raḥba," *IEJ* 25:2–3 (1975), pp. 171–172.

Rajib

G. Bisheh, "Rock-Cut Tombs at Rajib," *ADAJ* 18 (1973), pp. 63–67, fig. 1, pls. 36–40.

Ramat-Aviv

J. Kaplan, "Ramat–Aviv," *RB* 84:2 (1977), pp. 284–285, pl. 14.

Râmat el-Khalîl, Mambre

S. Appelbaum, "Mamre," *EAEHL* III (1977), pp. 776–778, figs.

Ramat Maṭred

M. Hopf, G. Zachariae, "Determination of Botanical and Zoological Remains from Ramat Maṭred and Arad," *IEJ* 21:1 (1971), pp. 60–64, figs. 1–3, pls. 5b–6; Y. Aharoni, "Ramat Matred," *EAEHL* IV (1978), p. 999, figs.

Excavated 1979 by R. Cohen for Universities Tel Aviv, Hebrew, Beersheba, and Israel Dept. of Antiquities and Museums.

R. Cohen, "Ramat Maṭred Excavations," *IEJ* 30:3–4 (1980), pp. 231–234.

Ramat Raḥel, Beth–haccherem

E. Stern, "Seal Impressions in the Achaemenid Style in the Province of Judah," *BASOR* 202 (1971), pp. 6–16, figs. 1–15; N. Avigad, "Bullae and Seals from a Post–Exilic Archive," *Qedem* 4 (1976); Y. Aharoni, "Beth Haccherem," *IDB–S* (1976), p. 97; Y. Shiloh, "New Proto-Aeolic Capitals Found in Israel," *BASOR* 222 (1976), pp. 67–77, figs. 1–6, pls. 1–8; Y. Aharoni, "Ramat Raḥel," *EAEHL* IV (1978), pp. 1000–1004, 1006–1009, figs.

Rameh, Kafr er-

V. Tsaferis, T. Shai, "Excavations at Kafr er-Rameh," *Qad.* 9:2–3 (1976), pp. 83–85, figs. (Hebrew).

Ramla

M. Rosen-Ayalon, "The First Mosaic Discovered in Ramla," *IEJ* 26:2–3 (1976), pp. 104–119, figs. 1–6, pls. 23 c–d, 24–25; *id.*, "A Muslim Mosaic Pavement at Ramle," *Qad.* 10:4 (1977), pp. 116–117, figs.; *id.*, "Ramla," *EAEHL* IV (1978), pp. 1010–1015, figs.

Ramm, Wâdî, Rumm, Iram

A. Negev, "Nabataean Capitals in the Town of the Negev," *IEJ* 24:3–4 (1974), pp. 153–159, pls. 27–29; N.P.S. Price, A.N. Garrard, "A Prehistoric Site in the Rum Area of the Hisma," *ADAJ* 20 (1975), pp. 91–93, fig. 1; D.F. Graf, "The Saracens and the Defense of the Arabian Frontier," *BASOR* 229 (1978), pp. 1–26, 2 maps; A. Negev, "Er-Ram," *EAEHL* IV (1978), pp. 996–998, figs.; J.E. Clarke, "Jordan's Diverse Lands," *Jordan* (Spring 1981), pp. 12–15, figs., cover.

Raphia

D. Barag, "The Borders of Syria-Palaestina on an Inscription from the Raphia Area," *IEJ* 23:1 (1973), pp. 50–52, pl. 12 b; *id.*, "An Epitaph of the Early Fifth Century A.D. from the Raphia Area," *IEJ* 24:2 (1974), pp. 128–131, pl. 19 c.

Raqiq, Ḥorvat, Khirbet Abu Ruqaiyiq

J. Naveh, "A Nabataean Incantation Text," *IEJ* 29:2 (1979), pp. 111–119, fig., pl. 14.

Ras 'Ali, Khirbet

A. Kuschke, "Kleine Beiträge zur Siedlungsgeschichte der Stämme Asser und Juda," *HTR* 64:2–3 (1971), pp. 291–313, figs.

Râs el-'Ain, see Apheq

Ras el-Jami'-'Isawiyeh

C. Graesser, Jr., "Ras el-Jami'-'Isawiyeh," *RB* 77:4 (1970), pp. 576–577, pls. 38 b–40a.

Râs en-Nâqb

D.O. Henry, "Palaeolithic Sites within the Râs en-Nâqb Basin, Southern Jordan," *PEQ* 111:2 (1979), pp. 79–85, figs. 1–3; *ibid.*, *ADAJ* 23 (1979), pp. 93–99, figs. 1–3; G. Osborn, J.M. Duford, "Geomorphological Processes in the Inselberg Region of SW Jordan," *PEQ* 113:1 (1981), pp. 1–17, figs. 1–3, pls. 1–2.

Râs en-Naqura, see Rosh ha-Niqra

Refed, Ras Mudeifi

Excavated 1972 by Z. Meshel, R. Cohen for Tel Aviv University, Israel Dept. of Antiquities and Museums.

Z. Meshel, R. Cohen, "Refed and Ḥatira: Two Iron Age Fortresses in the Northern Negev," *TA* 7:1–2 (1980), pp. 70–81, figs. 1–5, pls. 24–27.

Regev, Tell

M. Prausnitz, "Accho, Plain of," *EAEHL* I (1975), pp. 23–25, fig.

Reḥov

Excavated 1976–1980 by F. Vitto for Israel Dept. of Antiquities and Museums.

D. Bahat, "A Synagogue Chancel-Screen from Tel Reḥob," *IEJ* 23:3 (1973), pp. 181–183, pl. 48; N. Tsori, "Middle Bronze I and Early Iron I Tombs near Tel Reḥov in the Beth-Shean Valley," *EI* 12 (1975), pp. 9–17, figs. 1–5, 3 tables, pls. 5–8 (Hebrew); F. Vitto, "The Synagogue at Reḥob," *Qad.* 8:4 (1975), pp. 119–123, figs. (Hebrew); J. Sussman, "The Inscription in the Synagogue at Reḥob," *Qad.* 8:4 (1975), pp. 123–128, figs. (Hebrew); A. Demsky, "The Permitted Villages of Sebaste in the Reḥov Mosaic," *IEJ* 29:3–4 (1979), pp. 182–193, fig. 1; F. Vitto, "The Synagogue of Rehov 1980," *IEJ* 30:3–4 (1980), pp. 214–217, fig. 1, pl. 27a, c; *id.*, "The Synagogue at Reḥob," *ASR* (1981), pp. 90–94, figs.; J. Sussmann, "The Inscription in the Synagogue at Reḥob," *ASR* (1981), pp. 146–151, figs., (translation) 152–153.

Reḥovot, see Ruḥeibeh

Rekhmeh, Khirbet

E.K. Vogel, "Negev Survey of Nelson Glueck: Summary," *EI* 12 (1975), pp. 1–17, pls. 1–16, esp. pp. 3, 4.

Reqem, see Petra

Resisim, Be'er

Excavated 1978–1980 by R. Cohen, W.G. Dever for AIAR, University of Arizona, Israel Dept. of Antiquities and Museums.

R. Cohen, W.G. Dever, "Ḥ. Be'er Resisim," *IEJ* 28:4 (1978), pp. 263–264, pl. 52 a; *id.*, "Be'er Resisim 1979," *IEJ* 29:3–4 (1979), pp. 254–255, fig. 1, pl. 36 a; *id.*, "Preliminary Report of the Second Season of the Central Negev Highlands Project," *BASOR* 236 (1979), pp. 41–60, figs. 1–18; W.G. Dever, "New Vistas on the EB IV (MB I) Horizon in Syria-Palestine," *BASOR* 237 (1980), pp. 35–64, figs. 1–6; R. Cohen, W.G. Dever, "Be'er Resisim, 1980," *IEJ* 30:3–4 (1980), pp. 228–231, fig. 1; W.G. Dever, "The 1980 Season of the Central Negev Highlands Project, Israel," *AJA* 85:2 (1981) p. 192.

Ridan, Tell er-

Excavated by A. Biran et al. for Israel Dept. of Antiquities and Museums.

A. Biran, "Tell er–Ruqeish to Tell er–Ridan," *IEJ* 24:2 (1974), pp. 141–142, pls. 24–25.

Rimmon, Khirbet

Excavated by A. Kloner 1978–1979 for Israel Dept. of Antiquities and Museums.

A. Kloner, "Ḥurvat Rimmon 1979," *IEJ* 30:3–4 (1980), pp. 226–228, pl. 31a.

Ritma, Khirbet, Kiteity

Excavated by R. Cohen, Z. Meshel 1969–1972 for Tel Aviv University and Israel Dept. of Antiquities and Museums.

Z. Meshel, "Ḥorvat Ritma — an Iron Age Fortress in the Negev Highlands," *TA* 4:3–4 (1977), pp. 110–135, figs. 1–9, pls. 8–12.

Roded, Naḥal

U. Avner, "Naḥal Roded," *IEJ* 22:2–3 (1972), p. 158, pl. 27 c.

Romema, see Haifa

Rosh ha-Niqra, Râs en–Naqura

C. Epstein, "Early Bronze Age Seal Impressions from the Golan," *IEJ* 22:4 (1972), pp. 209–217, figs. 1–4, pls. 51–52 a–b; M. Tadmor, "A Middle Bronze Age I Tomb-Group from the Rosh Haniqra Ridge," *EI* 11 (1973), pp. 286–289 (Hebrew); S.W. Helms, "The Early Bronze Gate at Râs en–Naqura," *ZDPV* 92:1 (1976), pp. 1–9, figs. 1–4; A. Ben–Tor, "Cult Scenes on Early Bronze Age Cylinder Seal Impressions from Palestine," *Levant* 9 (1977), pp. 90–100, figs. 1–28; A. Ben–Tor, *Cylinder Seals of Third Millennium Palestine, BASOR Suppl.* 22 (1978), pp. 3, 7, 11, 43–45, 102, 103; M. Tadmor, "Rosh ha–Niqra, Tel," *EAEHL* IV (1978), pp. 1023–1024, figs.

Rosh Zin

D.O. Henry, "The Natufian Site of Rosh Zin: A Preliminary Report," *PEQ* 105:2 (1973), pp. 129–140, figs. 1–7.

Ruhama

M.Y. Ohel, "Upper Acheulean Handaxes from Ruhama, Israel," *TA* 3:2 (1976), pp. 49–56, figs. 1–5, tables 1–2.

Ruḥeibeh, Khirbet, Reḥovot

Excavated 1976 by R. Cohen for Israel Dept. of Antiquities and Museums; churches excavated 1976–1979 by Y. Tsafrir.

E.K. Vogel, "Negev Survey of Nelson Glueck: Summary," *EI* 12 (1975), pp. 1–17, pls. 1–16, esp. pp. 13, 17; Y. Tsafrir, "Reḥovot (Kh. Ruḥeibeh)," *RB* 84:3 (1977), pp. 422–427, pls. 27–28a; *id.*, "Reḥovot in the Negev: Four Seasons of Excavations," *Qad.* 12:4 (1979), pp. 124–132, figs. (Hebrew); R. Cohen, "The Iron Age Fortresses in the Central Negev," *BASOR* 236 (1979), pp. 61–79, figs. 1–14.

Rumeith, Tell er-

P.W. Lapp, *The Tale of the Tell* (1975), pp. 111–119.

Rupin, Kfar

R. Gophna, "A Middle Bronze Age II Village in the Jordan Valley," *TA* 6:1–2 (1979), pp. 28–33, figs. 1–3, pls. 4–5.

Ruqeish, Tell er-

Excavated 1973 by A. Biran et al. for Israel Dept. of Antiquities and Museums.

A. Biran, "Tell er–Ruqeish to Tell er–Ridan," *IEJ* 24:2 (1974), pp. 141–142, pls. 24–25.

Rushmiya, Khirbet

M.W. Prausnitz, "Rosh Maya (Kh. Rushmiya) Haifa," *RB* 82:4 (1975), pp. 591–594.

Sabiya, Khirbet

Excavated 1974 by E. Ayalon for Israel Dept. of Antiquities and Museums.

E. Ayalon, "The Jar Installation of Khirbet Sabiya," *IEJ* 29:3–4 (1979), pp. 175–181, figs. 1–2, pl. 24.

Sadaqah

H. Kurdi, "A New Nabataean Tomb at Sadaqah," *ADAJ* 17 (1972), pp. 85–87, pls. 1–4.

Ṣaf

R. Gophna, M. Kislev, "Tel Ṣaf 1977–1978," *RB* 86:1 (1979), pp. 112–114, pl. 3.

Ṣafadi, Bir eṣ-, Beersheba

C. Elliott, "The Religious Beliefs of the Ghassulians c. 4000–3100 B. C.," *PEQ* 109:1 (1977), pp. 3–25, figs. 1–6, 2 tables.

Ṣâfi, Tell eṣ-, Gath

N. Na'aman, "Sennacherib's 'Letter to God' on his Campaign to Judah," *BASOR* 214 (1974), pp. 25–39, fig.; A. F. Rainey, "The Identification of Philistine Gath: A Problem in Source Analysis for Historical Geography," *EI* 12 (1975), pp. 63–76, figs. 1–2; E. Stern, "Phoenician Masks and Pendants," *PEQ* 108:2 (1976), pp. 109–118, figs. 1–12, pls. 9–11; A. F. Rainey, "Gath," *IDB-S* (1976), p. 353; E. Stern, "Es-Safi, Tell," *EAEHL* IV (1978), pp. 1024–1027, figs.; A. F. Rainey, "Gath," *ISBE* II (1982).

Ṣafuṭ, Tell

M. Weippert, "Ein Siegel vom Tell Ṣafuṭ," *ZDPV* 95:2 (1979), pp. 173–177, figs. 1–2, pl. 9 b.

Sahab, near Amman

Excavated 1968 by R. W. Dajani, 1972–1975 by M. M. Ibrahim for the Jordan Dept. of Antiquities.

R. W. Dajani, "A Late Bronze-Iron Age Tomb Excavated at Sahab 1968," *ADAJ* 15 (1970), pp. 29–34, 23 pls.; S. H. Horn, "Three Seals from Sahab Tomb C," *ADAJ* 16 (1971), pp. 103–106, figs.; M. M. Ibrahim, "Archaeological Excavations at Sahab," *ADAJ* 17 (1972), pp. 23–36, pls. 1–7; *id.*, "Second Season of Excavation at Sahab 1973," *ADAJ* 19 (1974), pp. 55–61, pls. 12–23; *id.*, "Third Season of Excavation at Sahab 1975," *ADAJ* 20 (1975), pp. 69–82, figs. 1–5, pls. 25–34; *id.*, "The Collared Rim of the Early Iron Age," *Archaeology in the Levant* (1978), pp. 116–126, fig. 1, pls. 18–20.

Sa'idiyeh, Tell es-, Zarethan

W. P. Anderson, "Zarethan," *HBD* (1973), pp. 835–836; O. Negbi, "The Continuity of the Canaanite Bronzework of the Late Bronze Age into the Early Iron Age," *TA* 1:4 (1974), pp. 159–172, 1 table, pls. 30 b—32; T. L. McClellan, "Zarethan," *IDB-S* (1976), pp. 978–979, figs.; J. B. Pritchard, "Tell es-Sa'idiyeh," *EAEHL* IV (1978), pp. 1028–1032, figs.; *id.*, *The Cemetery at Tell es-Sa'idiyeh, Jordan,* (1980).

Šalbit

D. Barag, "Sha'albim," *EAEHL* IV (1978), pp. 1070–1071, figs.

Salmonah, see Abu Hawam, Tell

Salt, es-

A. Hadidi, "Es-Salt 1977," *RB* 86:3 (1979), pp. 458–459, pl. 26 b; *id.*, "A Roman Family Tomb at es-Salt," *ADAJ* 23 (1979), pp. 129–137, figs. 1–4, pls. 47–58.

Samaria, Sebaste

A. D. Tushingham, "A Royal Israelite Seal (?) and the Royal Jar Handle Stamps (Part One)," *BASOR* 200 (1970), pp. 71–78, figs. 1–3; *ibid.*(Part Two), *BASOR* 201 (1971), pp. 23–35; K. M. Kenyon, *Royal Cities of the Old Testament* (1971), pp. 71–89, 90–91, 124–125, figs., pls.; A. R. Millard, "An Israelite Royal Seal?" *BASOR* 208 (1972), pp. 5–9; M. Gichon, "The Plan of a Roman Camp Depicted upon a Lamp from Samaria," *PEQ* 104:1 (1972), pp. 38–58, figs. 1–17; A. D. Tushingham, "A Hellenistic Inscription from Samaria-Sebaste," *PEQ* 104:1 (1972), pp. 59–63, pl.; H. O. Thompson, "Cosmetic Palettes," *Levant* 4 (1972), pp. 148–150, figs. 1–2, pl. 16 a–b.

M. Tadmor, "Fragments of a Throne of the Persian Period from Samaria," *Qad.* 6:2 (1973), pp. 57–60, figs. (Hebrew); R. Hestrin, E. Stern, "Two 'Assyrian' Bowls from Israel," *IEJ* 23:3 (1973), pp. 152–155, figs. 1–3, pl. 46; M. Tadmor, "Fragments of an Achaemenid Throne from Samaria," *IEJ* 24:1 (1974), pp. 37–43, fig. 1, 2 tables, pls. 3–7; D. Flusser, "The Great Goddess of Samaria," *IEJ* 25:1 (1975), pp. 13–20, pl. 2; Y. Shiloh, A. Horowitz, "Ashlar Quarries of the Iron Age in the Hill Country of Israel," *BASOR* 217 (1975), pp. 37–48, figs. 1–3, pls. 1–7.

R. J. Bull, "An Archaeological Context for Understanding John 4:20," *BA* 38:2 (1975), pp. 54–59, figs. 10–13; Y. Shiloh, "New Proto-Aeolic Capitals Found in Israel," *BASOR* 222 (1976), pp. 67–77, figs. 1–6, pls. 1–8, J. B. Hennessy, "Samaria," *IDB-S* (1976), pp. 771–772; R. W. Klein, "Samaria Papyri," *IDB-S* (1976), p. 772; I. J. Winter, "Phoenician and North Syrian Ivory Carving in Historical Context: Questions of Style and Distribution," *Iraq* 38:1 (1976), pp. 1–22, figs. 1–2, pls. 1–6.

W. H. Shea, "The Date and Significance of the Samaria Ostraca," *IEJ* 27:1 (1977), pp. 16–27; R. T. Anderson, *Studies in Samaritan Manuscripts and Artifacts* (1978); E. E. Platt, "Bone Pendants," *BA* 41:1 (1978), pp. 23–28, figs.; S. Applebaum, S. Dar, Z. Safrai, "The Towers of Samaria," *PEQ* 110:2 (1978), pp. 91–100, figs. 1–2, pls. 10–12; N. Avigad, "Samaria," *EAEHL* IV (1978), pp. 1032–1050, figs.; V. Sussman, "Samaritan Lamps of the Third-Fourth Centuries A.D." *IEJ* 28:4 (1978), pp. 238–250, pls. 39–46; Y. Yadin, "The House of Ba'al in Samaria, and that of Athalia in Judah," *Archaeology in the Levant* (1978), pp. 127–135; M. Mallowan, "Samaria and Calah Nimrud: Conjunctions in History and Archaeology," *Archaeology in the Levant* (1978), pp. 155–163, pls. 24–26; P. R. S. Moorey, "Kathleen Kenyon and Palestinian Archaeology," *PEQ* 111:1 (1979), pp. 3–10.

A. F. Rainey, "The *Sitz im Leben* of the Samaria Ostraca," *TA* 6:1–2 (1979), pp. 91–94; D. Eitam, "Olive Presses of the Israelite Period: Rock-cut Installations in the Samarian Hills," *TA* 6:3–4 (1979), pp. 146–155, figs. 1–4, 1 table, pls. 22–23; M. Baillet, "Trois inscriptions samaritaines au musée de l'Ecole Biblique de Jérusalem," *RB* 86:4 (1979), pp. 583–593, pls. 29–31; R. T. Anderson, "Mount Gerizim: Navel of the World," *BA* 43:4 (1980), pp. 217–221, figs.

Samaria Papyri, see Wâdī edh-Dâliyeh

Samaria, see Reḥov

Sâmiyeh, 'Ain es-, Khirbet es-Sâmiyeh

B. Shantur, Y. Labadi, "Tomb 204 at 'Ain -Samiya," *IEJ* 21:2–3 (1971), pp. 73–77, figs. 1–4, pls. 9–10; Z. Yeivin, "A Silver Cup from Tomb 204a at 'Ain Samiya," *IEJ* 21:2–3 (1971), pp. 78–81, figs. 1–2, pl. 9; Y. Yadin, "A Note on the Scenes Depicted on the 'Ain-Samiya Cup," *IEJ* 21:2–3 (1971), pp. 82–85, fig. 1; Z. Yeivin, "'Ain Samiyeh," *RB* 78:3 (1971), p. 424; R. Grafman, "Bringing Tiamat to Earth," *IEJ* 22:1 (1972), pp. 47–49, figs. 1–2; W. G. Dever, "Middle Bronze Age I Cemeteries at Mirzbâneh and 'Ain-Samiya," *IEJ* 22:2–3 (1972), pp. 95–112, figs. 1–7.

Excavated by A. Mazar for the Hebrew University 1975.

W. G. Dever, "MB II A Cemeteries at 'Ain es-Sâmiyeh and Sinjil," *BASOR* 217 (1975), pp. 23–36, figs. 1–3, pls. 1–2; Z. Yeivin, "Ein Samiya and Dhahr Mirzbaneh," *EAEHL* II (1976), pp. 357–358, 361, figs.; W. G. Dever, "The Beginning of the Middle Bronze Age in Syria/Palestine," in F. M. Cross, W. E. Lemke, P. D. Miller, eds., *Magnalia Dei: The Mighty Acts of God. Essays on the Bible and Archaeology in Memory of G. Ernest Wright* (1976).

A. Mazar, "Khirbet Marjame ('Ain Samiya)," *IEJ* 26:2–3 (1976), pp. 138–139; M. F. Kaplan, "Another Slaying of Tiamat," *IEJ* 26:4 (1976), pp. 174–177, fig. 1, pl. 33 c. A. Mazar, "An Israelite Fortress-City near 'Ain Samiya," *Qad.* 10:4 (1977), pp. 111–113, figs.; S. S. Weinberg, "A Two-Storey Lamp from Palestine," *IEJ* 29:3–4 (1979), pp. 143–147, fig. 1, pl. 17; W. G. Dever, "New Vistas on the EB IV ('MB I') Horizon in Syria-Palestine," *BASOR* 237 (1980), pp. 35–64, figs. 1–6.

Sâmiyeh, 'Ain es-, see Dhahr Mirzbâneh

Sâmiyeh, 'Ain es-, see Marjameh, Tell

Samra, Qataret es-

Excavated by A. Leonard, Jr. for ACOR and Jordan Dept. of Antiquities 1978.

A. Leonard, Jr., "Preliminary Notes on the 1978 Season at Kataret es-Samra," *ASOR Newsletter* 3 (Oct. 1979), pp. 1–3, fig.; *id.*, "Kataret es-Samra: A Late Bronze Age Cemetery in Transjordan?" *BASOR* 234 (1979), pp. 53–65, figs. 1–9.

Sandahannah, Tell, Beit Jibrin, Eleutheropolis, Marisa

B. Bagatti, "Il cristianesimo ad Eleuteropoli (Beit Gebrin)," *LA* 22 (1972), pp. 108–129, figs. 1–8; D. C. Baramki, "A Byzantine Church at Mahatt el Urdi, Beit Jibrin 1941–1942," *LA* 22 (1972), pp. 130–152, figs. 1–18; A. Spijkerman, "The Coins of Eleutheropolis Iudaeae," *LA* 22 (1972), pp. 369–384, pls. 1–4.

Cave excavated 1972 by A. Kloner for the Israel Dept. of Antiquities and Museums.

A. Kloner, "A Columbarium at Marissa," *Qad.* 6:3–4 (1973), pp. 113–115, figs. (Hebrew); R. Ovadiah, "Jonah on a Mosaic Pavement at Beth Guvrin," *IEJ* 24:3–4 (1974), pp. 214–215, pl. 46.

M. Avi-Yonah, "Beth Govrin," *EAEHL* I (1975), pp. 194–197, figs.; T. O. Hall, Jr., "Mareshah (City)," *IDB-S* (1976), pp. 566–567; M. Avi-Yonah, "Mareshah," *EAEHL* III (1977), pp. 782–790, figs.; A. Kloner, "Marisa," *EAEHL* III (1977), pp. 790–791, figs.; G. Horowitz, "Town Planning of Hellenistic Marisa: A Reappraisal of the Excavations after Eighty Years," *PEQ* 112:2 (1980), pp. 93–111, figs. 1–15.

Ṣarṭah, ʿIzbet

Excavated 1976 by M. Kochavi for the Dept. of Antiquities and Museums et al.

M. Kochavi, "An Ostracon of the Period of Judges from ʿIzbet Ṣarṭah," *TA* 4:1–2 (1977), pp. 1–13, figs. 1–4, pl. 1; A. Demsky, "A Proto-Canaanite Abecedary," (ʿIzbet Ṣarṭah)," *TA* 4:1–2 *(1977), pp. 14*–27, figs. 1–4; J. Naveh, "Some Considerations on the Ostracon from ʿIzbet Ṣarṭah," *IEJ* 28:1–2 (1978), pp. 31–35, figs. 1–2; M. Garsiel, I. Finkelstein, "The Westward Expansion of the House of Joseph in the Light of the ʿIzbet Ṣarṭah Excavations," *TA* 5:3–4 (1978), pp. 192–198, fig. 1; M. Kochavi, A. Demsky, "A Proto-Canaanite Abecedary from ʿIzbet-Sartah," *Qad.* 11:2–3 (1978), pp. 61–67, figs. (Hebrew).

M. Kochavi, I. Finkelstein, "Izbet Ṣarṭah 1976–1978," *IEJ* 28:4 (1978), pp. 267–268; *ibid.*, *RB* 86:1 (1979), pp. 114–115, fig. 1, pl. 4; J. Naveh, "The Greek Alphabet: New Evidence," *BA* 43:1 (1980), pp. 22–25, figs.; M. Kochavi, A. Demsky, "An Israelite Village from the Days of the Judges," *BAR* 4:3 (1978), pp. 18–21, figs.; *id.*, "An Alphabet from the Days of the Judges," *BAR* 4:3 (1978), pp. 22–30, figs.; F. M. Cross, "Newly Found Inscriptions in Old Canaanite and Early Phoenician Scripts," *BASOR* 238 (1980), pp. 1–20, figs. 1–13.

Sebaste, see Reḥov

Ṣeelim, Naḥal

Y. Aharoni, "Judean Desert Caves, Naḥal Ḥever, Naḥal Ṣeelim," *EAEHL* III (1977), pp. 670–675, fig.

Sefunim, see Carmel, Mount

Selaʿ, es-

A. F. Rainey, "Selaʿ," *IDB-S* (1976), p. 800.

Sepphoris

N. Avigad, "The 'Tomb of Jacob's Daughters' near Sepphoris," *EI* 11 (1973), pp. 41–44 (Hebrew); M. Avi-Yonah, "Sepphoris," *EAEHL* IV (1978), pp. 1051–1055, figs.

Sera', Tell, Tell esh-Shari'a

Excavated 1972–1976 by E. D. Oren for the Israel Exploration Society, and Ben Gurion, Negev, Hebrew Universities.

E. D. Oren, "Tel Ser' (Tell esh-Shari'a)," *IEJ* 22:2–3 (1972), pp. 167–169, pl. 31; E. Oren, E. Netzer, "A Cult-Building in the Excavation at Tel Sera'," *Qad.* 6:2 (1973), pp. 53–56, figs. (Hebrew); S. Groll, "A Note on the Hieratic Texts from Tel Sera'," *Qad.* 6:2 (1973), pp. 56–57, figs. (Hebrew); E. D. Oren, "Tel Sera'," *RB* 80:3 (1973), pp. 401–405, pls. 10 b, 11 a; E. D. Oren, E. Netzer, "Sera', Tell esh-Shari'a," *IEJ* 23:4 (1973), pp. 251–254, pls. 68 c, 69, 70; *ibid.*, *IEJ* 24:3–4 (1974), pp. 264–266, pl. 57; E. D. Oren, "Esh-Shari'a, Tell (Tel Sera')," *EAEHL* IV (1978), pp. 1057, 1059–1069, figs.

Serâbit el-Khâdem

Excavated 1974 by I. Beit Arieh for Tel Aviv University.

I. Beit Arieh, "A Chalcolithic Work Station near Serabit el-Khadem," *Qad.* 8:2–3 (1975), pp. 62–64, figs. (Hebrew); I. Beit Arieh, R. Giveon, B. Saas, "Explorations at Serâbit el-Khadim 1977," *TA* 5:3–4 (1978), pp. 170–187, figs. 1–10, pls. 44–52:1; I. Beit Arieh, "A Chalcolithic Site near Serabit el-Khâdim," *TA* 7:1–2 (1980), pp. 45–64, figs. 1–10, pls. 15–21.

Seyl Aqlat, see Beidha, Wâdī

Sha'albim, see Šalbit

Sha'ar ha-Golan

M. Stekelis, *The Yarmukian Culture of the Neolithic Period* (1972); E. Yeivin, I. Mozel, "A *Fossil Directeur* Figurine of the Pottery Neolithic A," *TA* 4:3–4 (1977), pp. 194–200, figs. 1–3, pl. 20; M. Stekelis, "Sha'ar ha-Golan," *EAEHL* IV (1978), pp. 1055–1056, 1058, figs.

Sha'ar Ramon

Z. Meshel, Y. Tsafrir, "The Nabataean Road from 'Avdat to Sha'ar-Ramon, I" *PEQ* 106:2 (1974), pp. 103–118, figs. 1–5, pls. 15–18; *ibid.*, II, *PEQ* 107:1 (1975), pp. 3–21, figs. 1–6, pls. 1–2.

Shadud, 'En-

E. Braun, "'En-Shadud," *IEJ* 29:3–4 (1979), pp. 234–235, pl. 27 f.

Shalem, Tell

N. Tsori, "An Inscription of the Legio VI Ferrata from the Northern Jordan Valley," *IEJ* 21:1 (1971), pp. 53–54, pl. 5 a.

Shamir

D. Bahat, "The Date of the Dolmens near Kibbutz Shamir," *IEJ* 22:1 (1972), pp. 44–46, fig. 1; *ibid.* *EI* 11 (1973), pp. 58–63 (Hebrew); A. Ben-Tor, Cylinder Seals of Third Millennium Palestine, *BASOR Suppl.* 22(1978), pp. 4, 6, 102, 103.

Shari'a, see Sera', Tell

D. Saltz, "Shari'a," *ASOR Newsletter* 10 (May 1977), pp. 9–11.

Sharuḥen, see Far'ah (S)

Shave-Ziyyon

E. Linder, "A Cargo of Phoenicio-Punic Figurines," *Archaeology* 26:3 (1973), pp. 182–187, figs.; W. Culican, "A Votive Model from the Sea," *PEQ* 108:2 (1976), pp. 119–123, pls. 12–14.

Shechem, Tell Balâṭah

E. F. Campbell, J. F. Ross, L. E. Toombs, "The Eighth Campaign at Balâṭah (Shechem)," *BASOR* 204 (1971), pp. 2–17, figs. 1–7, 8 (on p. 40); G. R. H. Wright, "Pre-Israelite Temples in the Land of Canaan," *PEQ* 103:1 (1971), pp. 17–32, figs. 1–7; L. E. Toombs, "The Stratigraphy of Tell Balaṭah (Ancient Shechem)," *ADAJ* 17 (1972), pp. 99–110, pls. 1–2; J. D. Seger, "Shechem Field XIII, 1969," *BASOR* 205 (1972), pp. 20–35 figs. 1–7; W. G. Dever, "Shechem," *IEJ* 22:2–3 (1972), pp. 156–157, pl. 25; *id.*, "Shechem," *IEJ* 22:4 (1972), pp. 239–240, pl. 53 b; B. W. Anderson, "Shechem," *HBD* (1973), pp. 670–671; G. R. H. Wright, "Co-ordinating the Survey of Shechem over Sixty Years 1913–1973," *ZDPV* 89:2 (1973), pp. 188–196, figs. 1–7, 1 drawing, pls. 12–15; S. H. Horn, "Scarabs and Scarab Impressions from Shechem III," *JNES* 32:3 (1973), pp. 281–289, figs. 1–2.

W. G. Dever, "Shechem," *IEJ* 23:4 (1973), pp. 243–245, fig., pls. 66 b, 67 a; *id.*, "Sichem," *RB* 80:4 (1973), pp. 567–570, pls. 23 b-24; W. G. Dever, "Excavations at Shechem and Mt. Gerizim," *Archaeological Convention, 1972, of the Israel Exploration Society* (1973); *id.*, "The MB II C Stratification in the Northwest Gate Area at Shechem," *BASOR* 216 (1974), pp. 31–52, figs. 1–14.

J. D. Seger, "The Middle Bronze IIC Date of the East Gate at Shechem," *Levant* 6 (1974), pp. 117–130, figs. 1–6; G. R. H. Wright, "Temples at Shechem — a Detail," *ZAW* 87:1 (1975), pp. 56–64, figs. 1 a, 1 b, 2–4; W. G. Dever, "Sichem," *RB* 82:1 (1975), pp. 81–83, pl. 3 a; J. D. Seger, "The MB II Fortifications at Shechem and Gezer: A Hyksos Retrospective," *EI* 12 (1975), pp. 34–45, figs. 1–4, table; L. E. Toombs, "The Stratification of Tell Balâṭah (Shechem)," *BASOR* 223 (1976), pp. 57–59, chart.

M. H. Wiencke, "Clay Sealings from Shechem, the Sudan, and the Aegean," *JNES* 35:2 (1976), pp. 127–130, fig.; E. F. Campbell, "Shechem," *IDB-S* (1976), pp. 821–822; C. Clamer, "A Burial Cave near Nablus (Tell Balata)," *IEJ* 27:1 (1977), p. 48; E. Otto, "Survey archäologische Ergebnisse zur Geschichte der früheisenzeitlichen Siedlung Janoah (Jos. 16:6–7)." *ZDPV* 94:2 (1978), pp. 108–118, figs. 1–3, pls. 7–8; G. E. Wright, "Shechem," *EAEHL* IV (1978), pp. 1083–1094, figs.; *id.*, "A Characteristic North Israelite House," *Archaeology in the Levant* (1978), pp. 149–154, figs. 1–4; L. E. Toombs, "Shechem: Problems of the Early Israelite Era," *Symposia*, F. M. Cross, ed., (1979), pp. 69–83, figs. 1–7.

A. Zeron, "The Seal of 'M-B-N' and the List of David's Heroes," *TA* 6:3–4 (1979), pp. 156–157; A. Harif, "Common Architectural Features at Alalakh, Megiddo and Shechem," *Levant* 11 (1979), pp. 162–167, figs. 1–8; E. Stern, "Achaemenian Tombs from Shechem," *Levant* 12 (1980), pp. 90–111, figs. 1–10, pls. 13–15; *ibid. Qad.* 13:3–4 (1980), pp. 101–103, figs.; S. Geva, "A Fragment of a Tridacna Shell from Shechem," *ZDPV* 96:1 (1980) pp. 41–47, figs. 1–4, pl. 1; K. W. Russell, "The Earthquake of May 19, A. D. 363," *BASOR* 238 (1980), pp. 47–64, figs. 1–5.

Sheikh Muḥsin

I. Beit Arieh, "Sheikh Muḥsin," *RB* 82:2 (1975), pp. 245–246.

Sheikh Nebi Ṣaleḥ

I. Beit Arieh, D. Gilead, "Sheikh Nebi Ṣaleḥ," *RB* 79:4 (1972), pp. 603–604; I. Beit Arieh, "Sheikh Nebi Ṣaleḥ," *RB* 81:1 (1974), p. 85.

Shelomi

Excavated 1976–1978 by C. Dauphin for the Israel Dept. of Antiquities and Museums, St. Andrews, University of Edinburgh, École Biblique.

C. Dauphin, "Shelomi," *IEJ* 26:2–3 (1976), pp. 140–141, pl. 28 a; *ibid.*, *RB* 84:2 (1977), pp. 281–284, pl. 13; *ibid. IEJ* 27:4 (1977), pp. 256–259, fig., pl. 40 b–d; *ibid.*, *RB* 85:1 (1978), pp. 108–109, fig. 8, pl. 13; *ibid.*, *IEJ* 28:4 (1978), pp. 279–280. pl. 55 c–d; C. Dauphin, "A Monastery Farm of the Early Byzantine Period at Shelomi," *Qad.* 12:1 (1979), pp. 25–29, figs. (Hebrew); *id.*, "Shelomi 1978," *RB* 86:3 (1979), pp. 437, pl. 17.

Shema', Khirbet, see Meiron

Excavated 1970–1972 by E. M. Meyers et al., for ASOR, AIAR, Luther College, Drew, Dropsie, Duke, Harvard, Minnesota Universities.

A. T. Kraabel, E. M. Meyers, "Khirbet Shema' (Meiron)," *RB* 78:3 (1971), pp. 418–419, pls. 16–17; E. M. Meyers, A. T. Kraabel, J. F. Strange, "Archaeology and Rabbinic Tradition at Khirbet Shema', 1970 and 1971 Campaigns," *BA* 35:1 (1972), pp. 1–31, figs. 1–13; E. M. Meyers, "Ḥurvat Shema', the Settlement and the Synagogue," *Qad.* 5:2 (1972), pp. 58–61, figs. (Hebrew); E. M. Meyers, A. T. Kraabel, J. F. Strange, "Khirbet Shema' and Meiron," *IEJ* 22:2–3 (1972), pp. 174–176, figs. 2–3, pls. 37–38 a; E. M. Meyers, "Khirbet Shema' (Meiron)," *RB* 79:3 (1972), pp. 408–409, pl. 37.

A. T. Kraabel, "Khirbet Shema' et Meiron," *RB* 80:4 (1973), pp. 585–587, pls. 34–35; E. Meyers, "Tomb," *IDB-S* (1976), pp. 905–908, figs.; E. M. Meyers et al., *Ancient Synagogue Excavations at Khirbet Shema', Upper Galilee, Israel, 1970–72, AASOR* 42 (1976); E. M. Meyers, "Shema', Khirbet," *EAEHL* IV (1978), pp. 1094–1097, figs.; K. W. Russell, "The Earthquake of May 19, A. D. 363," *BASOR* 238 (1980), pp. 47–64, figs. 1–5. E. M. Meyers, "Ancient Synagogues in Galilee: Their Religious and Cultural Setting," *BA* 43:2 (1980), pp. 97–108, figs.; *id.*, "The Synagogue at Ḥorvat Shema'," *ASR* (1981), pp. 70–74, figs.

Shiloh, Seilun, Tell

F. Zayadine, Review of M. L. Buhl, S. Holm-Nielsen, *Shiloh: The Danish Excavations at Tall Sailun, Palestine, 1969, Berytus* 19 (1970), pp. 159–161; Y. Shiloh, Review of *Shiloh, IEJ* 21:1 (1971), pp. 67–69; W. P. Anderson, "Shiloh," HBD (1973), pp. 676–677, fig., S. Holm-Nielsen, "Shiloh," *IDB-S* (1976), pp. 822–823; A. Kempinski, "Shiloh," *EAEHL* IV (1978), pp. 1098–1100, figs.

Shinjeh, see Daliyeh, Wâdī edh-

Shiqmona

Excavated 1970–1979 by J. Elgavish for the Haifa Museum of Ancient Art.

J. Elgavish, "Shiqmona," *RB* 78:3 (1971), pp. 419–422, pl. 18 a; E. Stern, Review of J. Elgavish, *Archaeological Excavations at Shikmona*(1968), *PEQ* 104:2 (1972), pp. 157–158; J. Elgavish, "Shiqmona," *IEJ* 22:2–3 (1972), p. 167; *id.*, "Shiqmona," *IEJ* 23:2 (1973), pp. 117–118, pls. 30 e, 31; *id.*, *Archaeological Excavations at Shiqmona II* (1974), (Hebrew); *id.*, "Shiqmona," *RB* 81:1 (1974), pp. 98–100; A. Spycket, "Nouveaux Documents pour illustrer le culte du dieu-lune," *RB* 81:2 (1974), pp. 258–259, pl. 15; J. Elgavish, "Shiqmona," *IEJ* 24:3–4 (1974), pp. 283–284, pl. 62.

J. Elgavish, "Shiqmona," *IEJ* 25:4 (1975), pp. 257–258, pl. 28 c–d; *ibid. RB* 82:4 (1975), pp. 587–591, pls. 49–50; *ibid., RB* 83:2 (1976), pp. 270–272, pls. 34–35; *id.*, "Pottery from the Hellenistic Stratum at Shiqmona," *IEJ* 26:2–3 (1976), pp. 65–76, figs. 1–6, pls. 13–16; *id.*, "Shiqmona," *RB* 84:2 (1977), pp. 264–266, pls. 9 a–b, 10; D. Saltz, "Shiqmona," *ASOR Newsletter* 10 (May 1977), p. 4; J. Elgavish, "Shiqmona 1976," *IEJ* 27:2–3 (1977), pp. 166–167, pl. 22 b–d; *id.*, "Shiqmona 1977," *IEJ* 28:1–2 *(1978), pp. 122–123*, pl. 22 c–d; *id.*, "Shikmona 1977," *RB* 85:3 (1978), pp. 408–409, pl. 21 b.

J. Elgavish, "Shiqmona 1978," *IEJ* 28:4 (1978), pp. 280–281, pl. 52 c; *id.*, "Shiqmona, Tel," *EAEHL* IV (1978), pp. 1101–1109, figs.; *id.*, "Shiqmona 1978," *RB* 86:3 (1979), pp. 449–450; *id.*, "Shiqmona 1979," *IEJ* 30:3–4 (1980), pp. 208–209.

Shivta, see Isbeita

Shuqba Cave, see Carmel, Mount

Sinai, St. Catherine's Monastery

G. H. Forsyth, K. Weitzman, *The Monastery of Saint Catherine at Mount Sinai* (1973); N. Liphschitz, Y. Waisel, "Dendroarchaeological Investigations (St. Catherine's Monastery)," *IEJ* 26:1 (1976), pp. 39–44, fig. 1, table, pls. 7–8; Y. Tsafrir, "St. Catherine's Monastery in Sinai, Drawings by I. Dunayevsky," *IEJ* 28:4 (1978), pp. 218–229, figs. 1–7, pls. 47–51; J. H. Charlesworth, "The Manuscripts of St. Catherine's Monastery," *BA* 43:1 (1980), pp. 26–34, figs.

Sinjil

W. G. Dever, "MB II A Cemeteries at 'Ain es-Sâmiyeh and Sinjil," *BASOR* 217 (1975), pp. 23–36, figs. 1–3, pls. 1–2.

Ṣippor, Tell, Tell eṭ-Ṭuyur

E. Stern, "Phoenician Masks and Pendants," *PEQ* 108:2 (1976), pp. 109–118, figs. 1–12, pls. 9–11; A. Biran, "Ṣippor, Tell," *EAEHL* IV (1978), pp. 1111–1113, figs.

Siran, Tell

Excavated 1972 by H. O. Thompson for the University of Jordan.

H. O. Thompson, "The Excavations of Tell Siran 1972," *ADAJ* 18 (1973), pp. 5–14, figs. 1–2, pls. 1–10; J. A. Sauer, "A Ceramic Note on the Arabic 'Ostracon' from Tell Siran," *ADAJ* 18 (1973), pp. 15–16, pl. 3:2; F. Zayadine, H. O. Thompson, "The Ammonite Inscription from Tell Siran," *Berytus* 22 (1973), pp. 115–140, figs. 1–2, pls. 1–3; *id.*, "The Tell Siran Inscription," *BASOR* 212 (1973), pp. 5–11, fig. 1; F. M. Cross, "Notes on the Ammonite Inscription from Tell Siran," *BASOR* 212 (1973), pp. 12–15; H. O. Thompson, F. Zayadine, "The Works of Amminadab," *BA* 37:1 (1974), pp. 13–19, figs. 6–7; H. O. Thompson, "Tell Siran, Jordanie," *RB* 81:1 (1974), pp. 80–83.

H. Helbaek, "Grain from the Tell Siran Bronze Bottle," *ADAJ* 19 (1974), pp. 167–168; F. Zayadine, "Tell Siran," *RB* 81:1 (1974), pp. 83–85, pl. 6; C. Krahmalkov, "An Ammonite Lyric Poem," *BASOR* 223 (1976), pp. 55–57; W. H. Shea, "The Siran Inscription: Aminadab's Drinking Song," *PEQ* 110:2 (1978), pp. 107–112; L. G. Herr, *The Scripts of Ancient Northwest Semitic Seals* (1978); *id.*, "The Formal Scripts of Iron Age Transjordan," *BASOR* 238 (1980), pp. 21–34, figs. 1–4.

Sorek, Naḥal, see Yavneh Yam

Strato's Tower, see Caesarea Maritima

Subeita, see Isbeita

Summak, Khirbet

M. Avi-Yonah, "Synagogues," *EAEHL* IV (1978), pp. 1129–1138, figs.

Sûsitâ, see Hippos

Sûsiya, Khirbet

Excavated 1971–1972 by S. Gutman et al., for Hebrew University, Israel Exploration Society and Department of Antiquities and Museums.

S. Gutman, E. Netzer, Z. Yeivin, "Excavations in the Synagogues at Khirbet Susiya," *Qad.* 5:2 (1972), pp. 47–52, figs. (Hebrew); S. Gutman, "Sousiyeh Synagogue," *RB* 79:3 (1972), pp. 421–422, pl. 40; Z. Yeivin, "Inscribed Marble Fragments from the Khirbet Sûsiya Synagogue," *IEJ* 24:3–4 (1974), pp. 201–209, figs. 1–2, pls. 42–44; R. Hachlili, "The Niche and the Ark in Ancient Synagogues," *BASOR* 223 (1976), pp. 43–53, figs. 1–13; E. Kimron, "New Readings in a Hebrew Inscription from Ḥurvat Susiya," *Qad.* 9:2–3 (1976), pp. 82–83, figs. (Hebrew); S. Gutman, E. Netzer, Z. Yeivin, "Susiya, Khirbet," *EAEHL* IV (1978), pp. 1123, 1124–1128, figs.; *id.*, "Excavations in the Synagogue at Ḥorvat Susiya," *ASR* (1981), pp. 123–128, figs., pl. 2.

Suwwanet eth-Thaniya

G. M. Landes, ed., *BASOR Supplement* 21 (1975).

Swafieh, Jordan

B. Van Elderen, "The Byzantine Church at Swafieh," *ADAJ* 15 (1970), pp. 25–27, 2 pls.

Ta'anach

A. E. Glock, "A New Ta'annek Tablet," *BASOR* 204 (1971), pp. 17–30, figs. 1–5; *id.*, "Homo Faber: The Pot and the Potter at Taanach," *BASOR* 219 (1975), pp. 9–28, figs. 1–5; *id.*, "Taanach," *IDB-S* (1976), pp. 855–856, fig.; *ibid.*, *EAEHL* IV (1978), pp. 1138–1147, figs.; W. E. Rast, A. E. Glock, ed., *Taanach I: Studies in the Iron Pottery* (1978); A. Ben-Tor, *Cylinder Seals of Third Millennium Palestine BASOR Suppl.* 22 (1978), pp. 6, 7, 102, 103, 106.; N. Liphschitz, Y. Waisel, "Dendroarchaeological Investigations in Israel (Taanach)," *IEJ* 30:1–2 (1980), pp. 132–136, 3 tables, pls. 14–16.

Ṭabgha, 'Ain eṭ- 'Heptapegon

Soundings in the Church of the Multiplication of the Loaves and Fishes by R. Rosenthal, M. Hershkovitz, for the Israel Department of Antiquities and Museums, et al.

M. Avi-Yonah, "'Ain eṭ-Ṭabgha," *EAEHL* II (1976), pp. 497–501, figs.; R. Rosenthal, M. Hershkovitz, "Tabgha," *IEJ* 30:3–4 (1980), p. 207.

Tabor, Mount

B. Bagatti, "Una grotta bizantina sul Monte Tabor," *LA* 27 (1977), pp. 119–122, figs. 1–3, pls. 1–12; S. Loffreda, "Una tomba romana al Monte Tabor," *LA* 28 (1978), pp. 241–246, pl. 77.

Tamara, Qasr el-Juheniyeh

Excavated 1973–1975 by M. Gichon, D. Baatz for Tel Aviv University and Saalburg Museum, Bad Homburg.

M. Gichon, "Excavations at Thamara 1973," *Qad.* 7:3–4 (1974), pp. 114–117, figs. (Hebrew); *id.*, "Mesad Tamar (Tamara)," *RB* 82:2 (1975), pp. 275–276, pls. 28–29; *id.*, "Tamara 1975," *IEJ* 25:2–3 (1975), pp. 176–177; *id.*, "Excavations at Mezad-Tamar 1973–1974," *IEJ* 26:4 (1976), pp. 188–194, figs. 1–3, pl. 34; *id.*, *Three Years of Excavation* at Mezad Tamar (Tamara), (1976); *id.*, "Tamara," *EAEHL* IV (1978), pp. 1148–1152, figs.

Tannur, Khirbet et-

M. Lindner, ed., *Petra und das Königreich der Nabatäer* (1970); K. Schmitt-Korte, "A Contribution to the Study of Nabataean Pottery," *ADAJ* 16 (1971), pp. 47–60, figs. 1–14, 1 table; *id.*, "Die Entwicklung des Granatapfel-Motivs in der nabatäischen Keramik," *Naturhistorische Gesellschaft* (1972), pp. 40–44, figs. 1–8.

A. Negev, "A Nabataean Statuette from Jordan," *PEQ* 106:1 (1974), pp. 77–78, pls. 13–14 a; *id.*, "Nabataean Capitals in the Towns of the Negev," *IEJ* 24:3–4 (1974), pp. 153–159, pls. 27–29; P.C. Hammond, "The Capitals from 'The Temple of the Winged Lions', Petra," *BASOR* 226 (1977), pp. 47–51, figs. 1–7; R. Hachlili, "The Zodiac in Ancient Jewish Art: Representation and Significance," *BASOR* 228 (1977), pp. 61–77, figs. 1–18; N. Glueck, "Et-Tannur, Khirbet," *EAEHL* IV (1978), pp. 1152–1159, figs., P.J. Parr, "Pottery, People and Politics," *Archaeology in the Levant* (1978), pp. 202–209, fig. 1.

Tawilân

H.O. Thompson, "Iron Age Cosmetic Palettes," *ADAJ* 16 (1971), pp. 61–70, figs. 1–8; C.-M. Bennett, "Tawilan," *The Archaeological Heritage of Jordan* I (1973), p. 22; *id.*, "Edom," *IDB-S* (1976), pp. 251–252; *id.*, "Some Reflections on Neo-Assyrian Influence in Transjordan," *Archaeology in the Levant* (1978), pp. 164–171, figs. 1–4.

Tekoa

J. Escobar, "Estudio de los restos arqueológicos de Tecoa," *LA* 26 (1976), pp. 5–26, pls. 1–12.

Tel Aviv

Excavated 1976–1979 by H. and J. Kaplan for the Israel Dept. of Antiquities and Museums, Tel Aviv University.

J. Kaplan, "Sdeh Dov (Tel Aviv)," *RB* 78:3 (1971), pp. 422–423, pl. 18 b; *id.*, "The Archaeology and History of Tel Aviv-Jaffa," *BA* 35:3 (1972), pp. 66–95, figs. 2–15; *id.*, J. Kaplan, "Tel Aviv," *RB* 80:3 (1973), pp. 417–418, pl. 11 b; *id.*, "Tel Aviv," *RB* 82:2 (1975), pp. 260–263; *id.*, "A Second Samaritan Amulet from Tel Aviv," *IEJ* 25:2–3 (1975), pp. 157–159, fig. 1, pl. 15 e–f; H. and J. Kaplan, "Haaretz Museum Centre, Ramat Aviv, Tel Aviv," *IEJ* 27:1 (1977), p. 55, pl. 8 c; *id.*, "A Middle Bronze Age Tomb in Kinneret Street, Bene-Beraq, near Tel Aviv," *IEJ* 28:1–2 (1978), pp. 121–122; *id.*, "Excavations in Rishpon St., Tel Aviv," *IEJ* 28:1–2 (1978), pp. 125–126, pl. 23 d; H. Kaplan, "A Samaritan Church on the Premises of Museum Haaretz," *Qad.* 11:2–3 (1978), pp. 78–80, figs. (Hebrew).

J. Kaplan, "Tel-Aviv 1976," *RB* 85:3 (1978), p. 417, pl. 23 b; J. Kaplan, "Tel Aviv," *EAEHL* IV (1978), pp. 1159–1168, figs.; H. Kaplan, "Tel Aviv, a Burial Cave in the Qirya," *IEJ* 29:3–4 (1979), p. 241, pl. 34 c; H. Kaplan, "Tel Aviv (Kiria)," *RB* 86:3 (1979), p. 457, pl. 25.

H. Kaplan, "Tel Aviv (Rue ha-Bashan)," *RB* 86:3 (1979), pp. 457–458; *id.*, "Tel Aviv, No. 8 Bodenheimer Street," *IEJ* 29:3–4 (1979), pp. 239–241, pl. 34 a–b; J. Kaplan, "A Samaritan Amulet from Corinth," *IEJ* 30:3–4 (1980), pp. 196–198, fig. 1, pl. 21.

Tell Abu Ḥabil, see Abu Ḥabil

Tell Abu Hawam, see Abu Hawam, Tell

Tell Akko, see Acco

Tell Anafa, see Anafa, Tell

Tell Beit Mirsim, Kirath-sepher, Debir?

A. Eitan, "Tell Beit Mirsim G-F, the Middle Bronze IIA Settlement," *BASOR* 208 (1972), pp. 19–24, fig. 1; Y. Yadin, "The Tell Beit Mirsim G-F Alleged Fortifications," *BASOR* 212 (1973), pp. 23–25 fig.; W.F. Albright, "Beit Mirsim, Tell," *EAEHL* I (1975), pp. 171–178, figs.; R. Amiran, "The Lion Statue and the Libation Tray from Tell Beit Mirsim," *BASOR* 222 (1976), pp. 29–40, figs. 1–10, pls. 1–6; M. and Y. Aharoni, "The Stratification of Judahite Sites in the 8th and 7th Centuries BCE," *BASOR* 224 (1976), pp. 73–90, figs.

W.G. Dever, S. Richard, "A Reëvaluation of Tell Beit Mirsim Stratum J," *BASOR* 226 (1977), pp. 1–14, figs. 1–2, pls. 1–2; Y. Shiloh, "Elements in the Development of Town Planning in the Israelite City," *IEJ* 28:1–2 (1978), pp. 36–51, figs. 1–10, pls. 13, 14, 15 a; C.J. Davey, "Some Ancient Near Eastern Pot Bellows," *Levant* 11 (1979), pp. 101–111, figs. 1–5.

Tell Deir ʿAlla, see Deir ʿAlla

Tell ed-Duweir, see Lachish

Tell edh-Dhahab el-Gharbi

A.R.L. Gordon, "An Interim Report on the Site Survey of Tell edh-Dhahab el-Gharbi," *ASOR Newsletter* 8 (June, 1981), pp. 4–5, fig.

Tell-ej-Judeideh, see Judeideh

Tell el-ʿAjjul, see ʿAjjul, Tell el-

Tell el-Fukhar, see Acco

Tell el-Ḥammeh, see Ḥammeh, Tell el-

Tell ʿEli, see ʿEli, Tell

Tell el-Jerisheh, see Jerisheh

Tell el-Kheleifeh, see Kheleifeh

Tell el-Kudadi, Tell esh-Shuni

J. Kaplan, "Tell el-Kudadi (esh-Shuneh)," *RB* 78:3 (1971), pp. 423–424.

Tell el-Milḥ, see Malḥata, Tell

Tell er-Ras, see Gerizim, Mount

Tell er-Rumeith, see Rumeith

Tell esh-Shari'a, see Sera'. Tell

Tell esh-Sheikh Aḥmed el-'Areini, see 'Areini

Tell esh-Shuneh

H. de Contenson, "Jordan Valley," *EAEHL* III (1977), pp. 656–658. fig.

Tell es-Sa'idiyeh, see Sa'idiyeh

Tell es-Seba'

V. Fritz, "Vorbericht über die Ausgrabung des römischen Kastells auf dem Tell es-Seba'," *ZDPV* 89:1 (1973), pp. 54–65, fig. 1, pls. 1–7, plans 1–2.

Tell eṭ-Ṭaba'iq, see Rosh ha-Niqra

Tell ez-Zakariya, see Azekah

Tell Ḥesbân, see Ḥesbân

Tell Isdar, see Esdar

Tell Jemmeh, see Jemmeh

Tell Megadim, see Megadim

Tell Mevorakh, see Mevorakh

Tell Poleg, see Poleg, Tell

Tiberias

A. Ovadiah, "A Jewish Sarcophagus at Tiberias," *IEJ* 22:4 (1972), pp. 229–232, figs. 1–3, pl. 52 c; G. Foerster, "Some Menorah Reliefs from Galilee," *IEJ* 24:3–4 (1974), pp. 191–196, fig., pls. 39 b–41; B. Bar-Kochva, "Notes on the Fortresses of Josephus in Galilee," *IEJ* 24:2 (1974), pp. 108–116, fig. 1; G. Foerster, "Tiberiade," *RB* 82:1 (1975), pp. 105–109, pl. 11; M. Ben-Dov, "Fragmentary Synagogue Inscription from Tiberias," *Qad* 9:2–3 (1976), pp. 79–80, figs. (Hebrew).

R. Hachlili, "The Zodiac in Ancient Jewish Art: Representation and Significance," *BASOR* 228 (1977), pp. 61–77, figs. 1–18; G. Foerster, "The Excavations at Tiberias," *Qad.* 10:2–3 (1977), pp. 87–91, figs. (Hebrew); *id.*, "Tiberias," *EAEHL* IV (1978), pp. 1171–1177, figs.; M. Ben-Dor, "Fragmentary Inscriptions from an Ancient Synagogue at Tiberias," *ASR* (1981), pp. 157–159, figs.; T. Watkins, "Levantine Bronzes from the Collections of the Rev. William Greenwell, now in the British Museum," *Levant,* 13 (1981), pp. 119–155, figs. 1–12.

Timna'

O. Lipschitz, "Timna'." *IEJ* 22:2–3 (1972), p. 158, pl. 27; B. Rothenberg, "Timna: Inscription de Ramses III," *RB* 79:4 (1972), pp. 601–602; *id., Timna'*, (1972); C.-M. Bennett, Review of book *Timna'*, *PEQ* 105:2 (1973), pp. 174–175; R. Ventura, "An Egyptian Rock Stela in Timna'," *TA* 1:2 (1974), pp. 60–63, fig. 1, pls. 9–10; P. Watson, "Mines which Rewrite History," *ILN* (March 1975), pp. 30–40, figs.; R. Giveon, "'Lady of the Turquoise' Hathor at Serabit el-Khadim and Timna," *EI* 12 (1975), pp. 25–26 (Hebrew); B. Rothenberg, "Timna'," *EAEHL* IV (1978), pp. 1184–1203, figs.; S. Singer, "From These Hills," *BAR* 4:2 (1978), pp. 16–25, figs.

Tirat Zvi

M. Avi-Yonah, "Synagogues," *EAEHL* IV (1978), pp. 1129–1138, figs., esp. p. 1136.

Tuwail, Tell

J.C. Payne, "A Hoard of Flint Knives from the Negev," *Archaeology in the Levant* (1978), pp. 19–21, pl. 2.

'Ubeidiya

Excavated 1970–1975 by O. Bar-Yosef, E. Tchernov, for the Israel Academy of Sciences and Humanities et al.

O. Bar-Yosef, "'Ubeidiya," *IEJ* 21:2–3 (1971), pp. 170–171; O. Bar-Yosef, E. Tschernov, "'Ubeidiya," *RB* 78:4 (1971), pp. 576–581, fig. 2, pls. 24–25; O. Bar-Yosef, "'Ubeidiya," *RB* 79:3 (1972), pp. 400–401; O. Bar-Yosef, E. Tchernov, *On the Palaeo-Ecological History of the Site of "Ubeidiya* (1972); *id.*, "'Ubeidiya," *IEJ* 24:3–4 (1974), pp. 252–253.

O. Bar-Yosef, "'Ubeidiya," *RB* 82:1 (1975), pp. 71–72; *id.*, "Early Man in the Jordan Valley: The Excavations at 'Ubeidiya," *Archaeology* 28:1 (1975), pp. 30–37, figs.; M. Stekelis, O. Bar-Yosef, "'Ubeidiya," *EAEHL* IV (1978), pp. 1214–1216, figs.

Udhruh

S.T. Parker, "The 1976 Limes Arabicus Survey," *ASOR Newsletter* 5 (Feb. 1978), pp. 6–10, 1 table.

Umm el-'Amed, see 'Ammudim

Umm el-Biyarah, see Petra

Umm el-Jimal

Excavated and surveyed 1972–1977 by B. DeVries for ASOR and Jordan Dept. of Antiquities.

V.A. Clark, "New Epigraphical Material from the Harra Region of Jordan," *ADAJ* 21 (1976), pp. 113–117, figs. 1–3; J.A. Sauer, "Umm el-Jimal," *ASOR Newsletter* 3 (Nov. 1978), pp. 5–6, figs.; B. DeVries, "Research at Umm el-Jimal, Jordan, 1972–1977," *BA* 42:1 (1979), pp. 49–55, figs.

Umm Qeis, Gadara

Excavated 1974 by U. Wagner-Lux et al., for Deutsches Ev. Institut für Altertumswissenschaft des Heiligen Landes, 1974–1981 by the Jordan Dept. of Antiquities.

B. DeVries, "The North Mausoleum at Umm Qeis," *ADAJ* 18 (1973), p. 77, pls. 47–48; F. Zayadine, "A Dated Greek Inscription from Gadara-Umm Qeis," *ADAJ* 18 (1973), p. 78, pl. 49; U. Wagner Lux et al., "Bericht über die Oberflächen-forschung in Gadara (Umm Qēs) in Jordanien im Jahre 1974," *ZDPV* 94:2 (1978), pp. 135–144, pls. 11–17, 1 plan; *ibid. ADAJ* 23 (1979), pp. 31–39, 1 map, pls. 3–9; U. Wagner-Lux, "Umm Qeis 1974," *RB* 86:3 (1979), pp. 450–453, figs. 6, 7 a, 7 b; pls. 20–21, 22 a; Y. Meshorer, "A Ring from Gadara," *IEJ* 29:3–4 (1979), pp. 221–222, pl. 25. c–h; R. Usborne, "Umm Qais: In the Country of the Gadarenes," *Jordan* (Spring 1981), pp. 21–24, figs.

ʻUvda, Biqʻat

Excavated by R. Amiran et al., 1979, for the Israel Dept. of Antiquities and Museums.

R. Amiran, C. Arnon, U. Avner, "Biqʻat ʻUvda, Site 124 (8–9)," *IEJ* 29:3–4 (1979), p. 256, pl. 35 c–d.

Wâdī Dhobai, see Dhobai

Wâdī edh-Dâliyeh, see Dâliyeh

Walaida, Qubur el-

Excavated 1977 by R. Cohen for the Israel Dept. of Antiquities and Museums.

R. Cohen, "Qubur el-Walaida," *IEJ* 28:3 (1978), pp. 194–195; F.M. Cross, "Newly Found Inscriptions on Old Canaanite and Early Phoenician Scripts," *BASOR* 238 (1980), pp. 1–20, figs. 1–13.

Wardeh, Mugharet el-

Excavated 1976 by R.A. Coughenour for Western Theological Seminary, ACOR, Jordan Dept. of Antiquities.

R.A. Coughenour, "Preliminary Report on the Exploration and Excavation of Mugharet el-Wardeh and Abu Thawab," *ADAJ* 21 (1976), pp. 71–78, pls. 31–32.

Yahav

Excavated 1977 by I. Beit Arieh, R. Gophna for Tel Aviv University, Israel Dept. of Antiquities and Museums.

I. Beit Arieh, R. Gophna, "A Chalcolithic Site in the ʻArabah," *IEJ* 27:2–3 (1977), p. 163, pl. 21 a–b.

Yajuz, Khirbet

H.O. Thompson, "A Tomb at Khirbet Yajuz," *ADAJ* 17 (1972), pp. 37–45, pls. 1–11.

Yarmouth, Khirbet

A. Ben-Tor, "Tel Yarmuth," *IEJ* 21:2–3 (1971), pp. 173–174; *id.*, "The First Season of Excavations at Tell Yarmuth 1970," *Qedem* 1 (1975).

Yasser, Rujm Beni

S.T. Parker, "The Central Limes Arabicus Project: The 1980 Campaign," *ASOR Newsletter* 8 (June 1981), pp. 8–20, figs.

Yattir

F. Valla, I. Gilead, O. Bar-Yosef, "Prehistoric Survey in the Yattir Area," *IEJ* 27:4 (1977), p. 237; *id.*, "Prospection Préhistorique (Region de Yatir), 1978," *RB* 86:1 (1979), pp. 130–133, fig. 7.

Yavneh Yam

J. Kaplan, "Yavneh-Yam," *ZDPV* 91:1 (1975), pp. 1–17; Y. Rak, B. Arensburg, H. Nathan, "Evidence of Violence on Human Bones in Israel, First and Third Centuries C.E.," *PEQ* 108:1 (1976), pp. 55–58, pls. 6–7; R. Amiran, *The Israel Museum News* 12 (1977), pp. 65–69; J. Naveh, "Meṣad Ḥashavyahu," *EAEHL* III (1977), pp. 862–863, figs.; R. Gophna, "Sorek, Naḥal," *EAEHL* IV (1978), pp. 1113–1114, figs.; J. Kaplan, "Yavneh-Yam," *EAEHL* IV (1978), pp. 1216–1218, figs.

Yeruḥam

Excavated 1973 by R. Cohen for Hebrew University, Israel Exploration Society and Dept. of Antiquities and Museums.

R. Cohen, "Har Yeruḥam," *IEJ* 24:2 (1974), pp. 133–134; R. Maddin, T.S. Wheeler, "Metallurgical Study of Seven Bar Ingots," *IEJ* 26:4 (1976), pp. 170–173, tables 1–2, pl. 31; M. Kochavi, "Yeruḥam, Mount," *EAEHL* IV (1978), pp. 1219–1220, figs.

Yin'am, Tell, Tell en-Na'am

Excavated 1976–1979 by H. Liebowitz for University of Texas, Austin, Israel Dept. of Antiquities and Museums.

H. Liebowitz, "Tel Yin'am 1976," *IEJ* 27:1 (1977), pp. 53–54; *id.*, "Tell Yin'am 1976 Season," *ASOR Newsletter* 2 (Aug. 1977), pp. 9–10, figs.; *id.*, "Tel Yin'am 1977," *IEJ* 28:3 (1978), pp. 193–194, pl. 31 a–b; *id.*, "Tel Yin'am 1977," *RB* 85:3 (1978), pp. 409–410, pl. 22; *id.*, "Tel Yin'am 1978–1979," *IEJ* 29:3–4 (1979), pp. 229–230, pl. 27 a–e.

Yonim Cave

O. Bar Yosef, "Natufian Burials in the Yona Cave in Western Galilee," *Qad.* 3:1 (1970), pp. 19–21, figs. (Hebrew); O. Bar-Yosef, E. Tchernov, "The Natufian Bone Industry of ha-Yonim Cave." *IEJ* 20:3–4 (1970), pp. 141–150, 2 tables, figs. 1–2, pl. 35; O. Bar-Yosef, "Yonim Cave," *EAEHL* IV (1978), pp. 1221–1222, figs.

Yoqne'am, Tell

Excavated 1977–1979 by A. Ben-Tor for the Hebrew University and Israel Exploration Society.

A. Ben-Tor, "Yokne'am et environs, project d'étude régionale," *RB* 85:1 (1978), pp. 96–97, fig. 3; *id.*, "Tel Yokne'am 1977," *RB* 85:1 (1978), pp. 98–102, figs. 4–5, pls. 7–8; A. Ben-Tor, R. Rosenthal, "The First Season at Tel Yoqne'am 1977," *IEJ* 28:1–2 (1978), pp. 57–82, figs. 1–14, pls. 16–18; A. Ben-Tor, Y. Portugali, M. Avissar, "The Second Season of Excavations at Tel Yoqne'am 1978," *IEJ* 29:2 (1979), pp. 65–83, figs. 1–8, pls. 9–10; A. Ben-Tor, "Yoqne'am Regional Project Looks Beyond the Tell," *BAR* 6:2 (1980), pp. 30–44, figs.

Yotvata, 'Ain Ghadyan

Excavated 1974 by Z. Meshel, B. Sass, for Tel Aviv University.

Z. Meshel, B. Sass, "Yotvata," *IEJ* 24:3-4 (1974), pp. 273-274, pl. 60 a–b; E.K. Vogel, "Negev Survey of Nelson Glueck: Summary," *EI* 12 (1975), pp. 1–17, pls. 1–16, 2 maps, esp. pp. 11, 17; Z. Meshel, B. Sass, "Yotvata," *RB* 84:2 (1977), pp. 266–270, pl. 9 c.

Ẓaher, 'Arqub eẓ-

S. Mittmann, "Zwei Siegelbildscherben der frühen Bronzezeit aus dem nördlichen Ostjordanland," *ZDPV* 90:1 (1974), pp. 1–13, figs. 1–2, pls. 1–2; A. Ben-Tor, "Two Cylinder Seal Impressions from Northern Transjordan," *BASOR* 217 (1975), pp. 17–21.

Zakariya, Tell es-, see Azekah

Zarethan, see Sa'idiyeh, Tell es-

Zeraqon

S. Mittmann, "Zwei Siegelbildscherben der frühen Bronze-zeit aus dem nördlichen Ostjordanland," *ZDPV* 90:1 (1974), pp. 1–13, figs. 1–2, pls. 1–2; A. Ben-Tor, "Two Cylinder Seal Impressions from Northern Transjordan," *BASOR* 217 (1975), pp. 17–21.

Zeror, Tell

K. Ohata, *The Tel Zeror Excavation* (1974); K. Goto, "Tell Zeror," *RB* 82:4 (1975), pp. 571–573; M. Kochavi, *EAEHL* IV (1978), pp. 1223–1225, figs.; M. Kochavi, R. Gophna, "Aphek-Antipatris, Tel Poleg, Tel Zeror and Tel Burga: Four Fortified Sites of the Middle Bronze Age II A in the Sharon Plain," *ZDPV* 95:2 (1979), pp. 121–165, figs. 1–18, pls. 8–9 a; R.F. Tylecote, "From Pot Bellows to Tuyeres," *Levant* 13 (1981), pp. 107–118, figs. 1–15.

Zif, Khirbet

L.Y. Rahmani, "A Bilingual Ossuary — Inscription from Khirbet Zif," *IEJ* 22:2–3 (1972), pp. 113–116, pl. 19 a–b; Y. Yadin, "A Note on the Bilingual Ossuary-Inscription from Khirbet Zif," *IEJ* 22:4 (1972), pp. 235–236.

Ziqim

T. Noy, "Ziqim," *IEJ* 26:1 (1976), p. 49.

ADDENDA

ADAJ 24 (1980)
BASOR 239, 240 (1980)
RB 87:3, 4 (1980)

[redacted]

JOURNEY THROUGH OUR SOLAR SYSTEM

EXPLORING SATURN

By Mary Austen

KidHaven PUBLISHING

Published in 2018 by
KidHaven Publishing, an Imprint of Greenhaven Publishing, LLC
353 3rd Avenue
Suite 255
New York, NY 10010

Designer: Deanna Paternostro
Editor: Vanessa Oswald

Photo credits: Cover, back cover Vadim Sadovski/Shutterstock.com; p. 5 Tanya Zima/Shutterstock.com; pp. 6–7 abcjan/Shutterstock.com; p. 7 (inset) My Portfolio/Shutterstock.com; p. 9 Aphelleon/Shutterstock.com; p. 11 SkyPics Studio/Shutterstock.com; p. 13 Nostalgia for Infinity/Shutterstock.com; p. 15 (main) Science & Society Picture Library/Contributor/SSPL/Getty Images; p. 15 (inset) Tony Wills/Wikimedia Commons; p. 17 Johan-Swanepoel/Shutterstock.com; p. 19 (main) Comstock Images/Getty Images; p. 19 (inset) Tristan3D/Shutterstock.com; p. 21 Space Frontiers/Stringer/Archive Photos/Getty Images.

Cataloging-in-Publication Data

Names: Austen, Mary.
Title: Exploring Saturn / Mary Austen.
Description: New York : KidHaven Publishing, 2018. | Series: Journey through our solar system | Includes index.
Identifiers: ISBN 9781534522886 (pbk.) | 9781534522824 (library bound) | ISBN 9781534522541 (6 pack) | ISBN 9781534522633 (ebook)
Subjects: LCSH: Saturn (Planet)–Juvenile literature.
Classification: LCC QB671.A93 2018 | DDC 523.46–dc23
Printed in the United States of America

CPSIA compliance information: Batch #BS17KL: For further information contact Greenhaven Publishing LLC, New York, New York at 1-844-317-7404.

CONTENTS

THE PLANET OF RINGS

Saturn is the second-largest planet in our **solar system**. It's the sixth planet from the sun. Saturn is known for the rings around it.

Saturn is the farthest planet that can be seen in the night sky with the human eye.

A DAY AND A YEAR ON SATURN

Just like all the other planets, Saturn **orbits** the sun. It takes 29.5 Earth years to go around the sun once.

However, Saturn spins much more quickly than Earth. It only takes 10.5 hours to make one **rotation**.

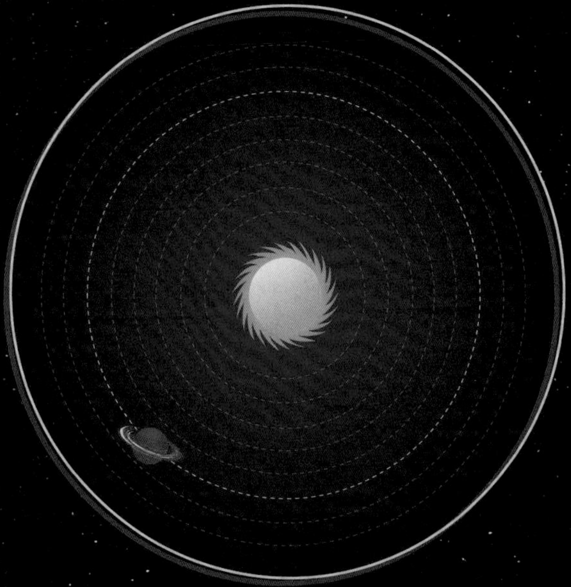

Saturn's orbit, or path, around the sun is shown here.

GIANT PLANET OF GAS

Saturn is called a gas giant. It's circled by thick clouds made up of mostly **hydrogen**. The gas giants—Jupiter, Saturn, Uranus, and Neptune—don't have solid ground.

Saturn's color comes from **ammonia** in its **atmosphere**.

THE LAYERS OF SATURN

Beneath Saturn's atmosphere is a **layer** of liquid hydrogen and **helium**. The center of the planet, known as the core, is made of hot iron and rock.

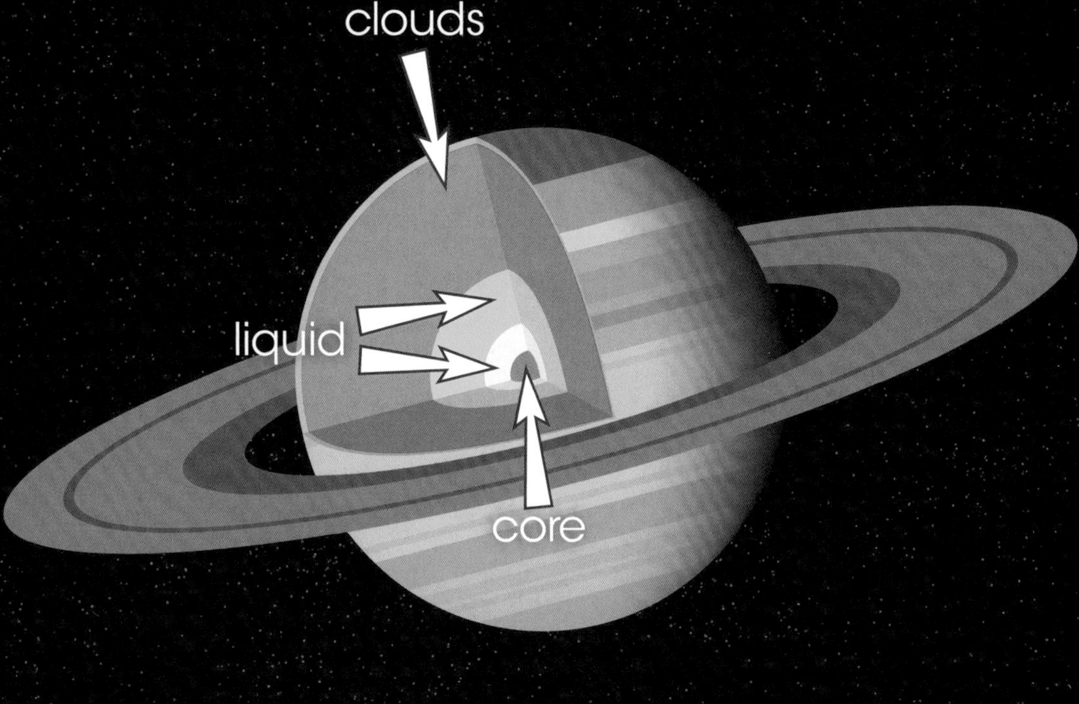

Shown here are Saturn's layers.

THE RINGS OF SATURN

Saturn has floating rings that circle the planet. These rings orbit Saturn just like Saturn orbits the sun.

Saturn has very thin rings that are thousands of miles wide.

Saturn's rings are made up of mostly ice and rocks. Scientists believe the rings were formed from **asteroids** that broke apart before reaching the planet.

Ice chunks make up Saturn's rings.

Shown here is a close-up photograph of Saturn's rings.

SATURN'S MOONS

Saturn has more than 62 moons of different sizes. The planet's smallest moon is 0.33 mile (0.5 km) wide, and its biggest moon is half the size of Earth.

Scientists believe Saturn could have many more moons that haven't been discovered yet.

Titan is Saturn's largest moon. It's the second-largest moon in the whole solar system and is made of mostly rock and ice. The only moon larger is Jupiter's moon Ganymede (GA-nih-meed).

Titan is the only moon that has clouds.

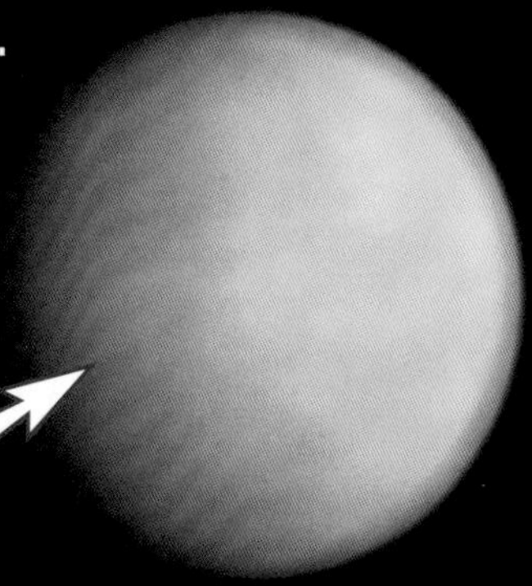

GETTING TO KNOW SATURN

Scientists have sent **probes** to study Saturn. In 1979, the *Pioneer 11* became the first probe to reach Saturn. This probe discovered the planet's outer rings. Other probes have also been sent to teach us about the ringed planet.

The *Cassini-Huygens* spacecraft has been studying Saturn since 2004. It even landed on Titan!

GLOSSARY

ammonia: A colorless gas with a strong smell.

asteroid: A large rock in space left over from the start of the solar system.

atmosphere: Gases in the air around a planet.

helium: The second lightest gas in the solar system.

hydrogen: The lightest gas in the solar system.

layer: One part of something lying over or under another.

orbit: To travel in a circle or oval around something.

probe: A vehicle that sends information about an object in space back to Earth.

rotation: The act of an object turning in a circle.

solar system: The sun and all the space objects that orbit it, including planets and their moons.

FOR MORE INFORMATION

Websites

NASA Space Place: All About Saturn
spaceplace.nasa.gov/all-about-saturn/en/
NASA provides readers with cool pictures of and information about Saturn.

National Geographic Kids: Mission to Saturn
kids.nationalgeographic.com/explore/space/mission-to-saturn/#saturn-planet.jpg
This website includes fun facts about Saturn.

Books

Bloom, J.P. *Saturn*. Minneapolis, MN: Abdo Kids, 2015.

Glaser, Chaya. *Saturn: Amazing Rings*. New York, NY: Bearport Publishing, 2015.

Radomski, Kassandra. *The Secrets of Saturn*. North Mankato, MN: Capstone Press, 2016.

Publisher's note to educators and parents: Our editors have carefully reviewed these websites to ensure that they are suitable for students. Many websites change frequently, however, and we cannot guarantee that a site's future contents will continue to meet our high standards of quality and educational value. Be advised that students should be closely supervised whenever they access the Internet.

INDEX